# ENGLISH AND THE DISCOURSES OF COLONIALISM

'This tightly argued, provocative book . . . is a poignant and urgent reminder of the need to rethink the discourse practices of ELT and to decolonize applied linguistics. A sensitive, passionate, and well-researched study that every English language teacher should read.'

Claire Kramsch, *University of California at Berkeley*

*English and the Discourses of Colonialism* opens with the British departure from Hong Kong marking the end of British colonialism. Yet Alastair Pennycook argues that this dramatic exit masks the crucial issue that the traces left by colonialism run deep.

This challenging and provocative book looks particularly at English, English language teaching, and colonialism. It reveals how the practice of colonialism permeated the cultures and discourses of both the colonial and colonized nations, the effects of which are still evident today. Rather than accepting the current popular view that English has become a neutral language of global communication, Pennycook argues that it remains a language to which colonial discourses still adhere, a language still laden with colonial meanings.

The sources drawn on are diverse: from colonial documents from India, Malaysia and Hong Kong to travel writing; from popular books on English to students' writing; from personal experiences to newspaper articles. Pennycook concludes by appealing to postcolonial writing to create a politics of opposition and dislodge the discourses of colonialism from English.

**Alastair Pennycook** teaches critical applied linguistics at the University of Melbourne. He is the author of *The Cultural Politics of English as an International Language*.

THE POLITICS OF LANGUAGE
Series editors: Tony Crowley,
University of Manchester
Talbot J. Taylor,
College of William and Mary, Williamsburg, Virginia

*'In the lives of individuals and societies, language is a factor of greater importance than any other. For the study of language to remain solely the business of a handful of specialists would be a quite unacceptable state of affairs.'*

Saussure

The Politics of Language Series covers the field of language and cultural theory and will publish radical and innovative texts in this area. In recent years the developments and advances in the study of language and cultural criticism have brought to the fore a new set of questions. The shift from purely formal, analytical approaches has created an interest in the role of language in the social, political, and ideological realms and the series will seek to address these problems with a clear and informed approach. The intention is to gain recognition for the central role of language in individual and public life.

# ENGLISH AND THE DISCOURSES OF COLONIALISM

*Alastair Pennycook*

ROUTLEDGE

London and New York

First published 1998
by Routledge
11 New Fetter Lane, London EC4P 4EE

Simultaneously published in the USA and Canada
by Routledge
29 West 35th Street, New York, NY 10001

Typeset in Bembo by
BC Typesetting, Bristol
Printed and bound in Great Britain by
T.J. International Ltd, Padstow, Cornwall

*British Library Cataloguing in Publication Data*
A catalogue record for this book is available from the British Library

*Library of Congress Cataloging in Publication Data*
English and the discourses of colonialism/Alastair Pennycook.
p. cm. – (Politics of language)
Includes bibliographical references.
1. English language – Political aspects – Commonwealth countries.
2. English language – Political aspects – Foreign countries.
3. English language – Discourse analysis. 4. Great Britain –
Colonies – Languages. 5. Communication, International.
6. Decolonization – Terminology. 7. Imperialism – Terminology.
I. Title. II. Series.
PE2751.P47 1998
306.44′9′09171241–dc21 98–11146

ISBN 0–415–17847–9 (hbk)
ISBN 0–415–17848–7 (pbk)

FOR DOMINIQUE
AND MY PARENTS

# CONTENTS

# LIST OF FIGURES

# ACKNOWLEDGEMENTS

This book is the product not only of many hours in libraries and at the computer but also of many hours in conversation, debate and argument. I thank all those who have challenged me and helped me think through and clarify my ideas. I am similarly grateful to many people who have given me feedback on talks I have given on aspects of this work over the last few years in Hong Kong, the USA, Brazil, Australia and Japan; in particular I would like to thank Walter Mignolo for the invitation to the exhilarating workshop at Duke University in May 1997, to Barry Asker for the invitation to participate in the conference in Lingnan College in Hong Kong in June 1997, and to Lynn Mario Menezes de Souza for the fascinating time in Belo Horizonte and São Paulo in July 1997. Also thanks to Ashis Nandy for a kind welcome and profound discussions at the Centre for the Study of Developing Societies in Delhi. Thanks are also due to all those who gave me further examples of the discourses I was seeking; these include my parents, Nigel Bruce, Oda Masaki, Richard Colebrook, Dominique Estival, Brian Lynch, Tse Lai Kun and Colin Barron. I owe a great debt of thanks to librarians who have given me assistance in London, Toronto, Singapore, Kuala Lumpur, Hong Kong, New Delhi and Melbourne. And many thanks to Tony Crowley, Louisa Semleyen, Miranda Filbee and others at Routledge, who had the vision to see that there was indeed a book in all this, and the energy to make it happen. And to Dominique, thanks for everything.

Part of this research was supported by a Special Initiative Grant from the University of Melbourne, for which I am duly grateful. Final production costs were also assisted by a Faculty of Arts publication subsidy grant.

Some parts of Chapter 4 were published previously in Chapter 3 of *The Cultural Politics of English as an International Language*. They are gratefully reprinted by permission of Addison Wesley Longman Ltd.

An earlier version of Chapter 4 was published as 'Language policy as cultural politics: the double-edged sword of language education in colonial Malaya and Hong Kong', *Discourse* 17 (2), 133–52. Reprinted by kind permission of Carfax Publishing Limited, Abingdon, Oxfordshire, UK.

Thanks to the Baillieu Library, University of Melbourne, for permission to copy from books held in their special collection. To Blackwell Publishers for permission to reproduce a figure from R. Kaplan (1966) 'Cultural thought patterns in intercultural education', *Language Learning* 16, 1–20. The Foreign and Commonwealth Office Library Photograph Collection for permission to reproduce figure 4 'Group photograph of British and Chinese Commissioners'. And finally to the Mary Evans Picture Library for supplying figure 5 'Missionaries at work in Southern Africa'.

# 1

# ENGLISH AND THE CULTURAL CONSTRUCTS OF COLONIALISM

> Why is it that the colonial paradigm persists, and even acquires an urgent, *contemporary* validity? . . . cultural, racial, and moral differences established by colonialism continue to have broad ramifications for the way in which marginal, subordinated races, cultures, economic groups, and sexualities are defined and figured as 'others' in relation to dominant privileged categories
>
> (Singh, 1996, p. 5)

> What is striking . . . is the persistence of primitivist constructions of Aboriginality in a liberal culture that likes to think that its colonial and racist roots have been rejected
>
> (Thomas, 1994, p. 30)

> Use a language to conceive, organize, and justify Belsen; use it to make out specifications for gas ovens; use it to dehumanize man during twelve years of calculated bestiality. Something will happen to it. . . . Something will happen to the words. Something of the lies and sadism will settle in the marrow of the language.
>
> (Steiner, 1959/1984, p. 213)

It is a little after midnight. The night of June 30/July 1, 1997. It has been a long, steamy evening, with fireworks dampened by rain, and crowds of people in the streets. I lean on the weathered, varnished wooden rail of the Star Ferry as it plows back across Hong Kong Harbour. Over the dark, choppy water, beyond a ring of protective boats, the *Britannia* is pulling slowly away from the quay. On board, Prince Charles and Governor Patten, signalling this symbolic end to colonialism in Hong Kong. The Royal Yacht swings round and moves quietly past the brightly lit Convention Centre, full still of many of the world's dignitaries, where soldiers had marched back and forth, flags had been hoisted and lowered, speeches made. The Handover. The Handback. A great piece of political theatre. I lean my chin on the backs of my hands on the rail of the Star Ferry and watch the *Britannia* edging past the Convention Centre. The end of British colonialism.

I am here in Hong Kong to watch this. I am also here in Hong Kong to argue that in many ways it doesn't make a whole lot of difference. There is a conference here, a conference to talk about the future, about building bridges, about language and education in the new Hong Kong. And I am here to argue that many things won't be changing. My argument is not one that suggests that the recolonization of Hong Kong by the Chinese is as bad as or worse than the British colonial presence (though there are indeed a lot of interesting arguments to be made about such matters). Nor am I arguing that it doesn't matter that the British colonial administration sailed off at sunset (or a little afterwards) in the Royal Yacht. It's good that they've finally gone. But my interest is more in the point that this mighty symbol of the governor sailing away masks the crucial issue that the traces left by colonialism run deep. And these traces, these discourses, are not just to do with Hong Kong, or with other former colonies, but have emanated from these colonial contexts to inhabit large domains of Western thought and culture.

Hong Kong is often described as a vast construction site, as towering glass buildings push up into the air from tiny plots of land, and as new building sites are reclaimed from the sea. Yet my interest is in Hong Kong as a construction site of a different sort, as a site of colonial constructions, as a site that has been producing the cultural constructs of colonialism into the late end of the twentieth century. When I talk of the cultural constructs of colonialism, I am drawing attention to the need to see colonialism not merely as a site of colonial imposition, not merely as a context in which British or other colonial nations' cultures were thrust upon colonized populations, but also as a site of production. The practice of colonialism produced ways of thinking, saying and doing that permeated back into the cultures and discourses of the colonial nations. And, as I shall try to show, these cultural constructs of colonialism have lasting effects even today.

Rather than trying to map out this vast domain of colonial and post-colonial history, however, this book looks particularly at English, English language teaching, and colonialism. It attempts to show how the English language teaching enterprise was important not so much because it led to the current massive spread of English around the world but because on the one hand it was at the heart of colonialism and on the other because it is deeply interwoven with the discourses of colonialism. This book, then, seeks to locate English language teaching and policy within the broader context of colonialism, to show how language policies and practices developed in different colonial contexts, and to demonstrate how the discourses of colonialism still adhere to English. In the remaining parts of this chapter, I shall sketch out the arguments and issues underlying the position I am taking here.

## Why English?

There are a number of reasons why I have chosen to deal with English here. In a controversial essay from his 1959 book *Language and Silence,* George Steiner (1984) argues that Germany's remarkable postwar development is a 'hollow miracle', for although Germany has advanced to a position of great material wealth and prosperity, the German language itself is dead. 'The German language,' Steiner (1984, p. 210) suggests, 'was not innocent of the horrors of Nazism', since it was in German that many of the savageries of Nazism found expression. A particular feature of this era, Steiner argues, was the immense amount of documentation of Nazi atrocities:

> It was one of the peculiar horrors of the Nazi era that all that happened was recorded, catalogued, chronicled, set down; that words were committed to saying things that no human mouth should ever have said and no paper made by man should ever have been inscribed with.
>
> (p. 211)

Thus, despite the resilience and flexibility of languages, there must inevitably come a time when they break:

> Use a language to conceive, organize, and justify Belsen; use it to make out specifications for gas ovens; use it to dehumanize man during twelve years of calculated bestiality. Something will happen to it. . . . Something will happen to the words. Something of the lies and sadism will settle in the marrow of the language.
>
> (p. 213)

Steiner's argument here is an uncomfortable one. It also carries many assumptions that are questionable. To call a language dead, to justify this statement – as Steiner does – in terms of the supposed paucity of 'good literature' in German, to assume that certain uses of German have rendered all its uses corrupt, all these seem problematic. And what, we might want to ask, does it actually mean to say that 'something of the lies and sadism will *settle in the marrow of the language*'? Where, ultimately, does this 'marrow' exist? And if German is indeed dead, there must be a lot of other languages with at least one foot in the grave; for example, English, Japanese, Russian, Spanish, Chinese, French, Serbian, Hutu, Afrikaans, amongst many others. And yet, on another level, I think Steiner is making an important point here. Could it not be the case that it is easier to articulate certain ideas in certain languages? And is it not even more plausible that there must be some long term effect of such articulations? If it seems perhaps rather extreme to suggest that there may have been something about English that made it a useful language of colonialism, it would nevertheless make sense to suggest that the long term conjunction between English and colonial discourses has produced a range of linguistic-discursive connections between English and colonialism. Although there are problems with any proposition that suggests that German is either dead or inherently fascistic, and thus with the proposition that English is either dead or inherently colonial, I do want to suggest that these connections run deep, that the long history of colonialism has established important connections to English. Such connections do not lie so much in 'the marrow' of English but in the intimate relations between the language and the discourses of colonialism.

### English and racial definitions

The first cricket team from Australia to tour England – in 1868 – was an Aboriginal side. The announcement of their arrival in Britain, in *Sporting Life*, 16 May 1868, advised its readers that it 'must not be inferred that they are savages; on the contrary, the managers of the speculation make no pretence to anything other than purity of race and origin. They are perfectly civilised, having been brought up in the bush to agricultural pursuits as assistants to Europeans, and the only language of which they have a perfect knowledge is English' (in Mulvaney and Harcourt, 1988, Figure B). How is it that this language, English, can so easily confer civilization on these Aboriginal cricketers, while at the same time it is this very language that is constructing these Indigenous Australians racially? If this seems an odd question, I also want to suggest that it is a crucial one, one that presents a fundamental dilemma for many learners of English. English is both the language that will apparently bestow civilization, knowledge and wealth on people and at the same time is the language in which they are racially defined.

Looking at how Torres Strait Islander cultures have been continually defined as 'different, exotic, traditional, etc.', Martin Nakata (1995) argues for the importance of having access to the language and knowledge that has defined him and his family:

> Whether my girls perceive themselves primarily as Torres Strait Islanders or are perceived by others as such, one thing I do know: they will always, without question, be perceived in Australia as *girls of colour*, and to contend with this I feel as my father, grandfather and great-grandfather did, that what they need most is an understanding of the political nature of their position – and that this requires both the language and the knowledge of how that positioning is effected in the mainstream world.
>
> (Nakata, 1995, p. 73)

And this is why, Nakata argues, it is crucial not for his daughters to have courses in Torres Strait Creole maintenance, but to be good at English, for this is the language in which they are racially defined. As Mudrooroo (1995) suggests, 'The construction of the Indigenous person in Australia is in the main a matter of discourse, of language, and if we are to gain a glimpse of the reality existing as a trace within the language we must seek to deconstruct it' (p. 9). Thus, for a number of Australian Indigenous writers the significance of English in their lives is that it is the language in which they are 'racially defined'.

Such an argument raises a number of highly important concerns, both theoretical and political. If we look beyond the position that this is merely a coincidental historical conjunction, we are left with the question as to whether there is in fact something about English itself that continues to construct racial definitions. Thus, a central interest here is to explore across a number of different contexts how we can examine what this question could mean, how we can deal with Shapiro's claim that 'the Other is located most fundamentally in language, the medium for representing selves and others' (1989, p. 28). Rather than seeking the relationship between definitions of the Other and English in the grammar or lexicon of English itself, I am trying to locate ways in which certain discourses *adhere to English*. Thus, such positionings occur through the history of the ways in which certain discourses become linked to English.

This is, then, an exploration of ways in which we can come to terms with the challenge of considering how it is that certain meanings in a sense become attached to a language, what it means to suggest that a language carries particular meanings with it. These questions arise from a number of different interests around English in different contexts, including the politics of language in Australia and Hong Kong today, colonial documents in Malaya and Hong Kong, travel writing on China, and textbooks for teaching English as a second language. In a sense, this book is an attempt to flesh out arguments such as those made by Bakhtin that every utterance comes laden with the history of past utterances, that the history of the word is always present, that 'Our speech, that is all our utterances,' are 'filled with others' words' (1986, p. 89).

Of course, it has not been uncommon to make such claims about language. Take for example Fanon's well-known remark: 'To speak means to be in a position to use a certain syntax, to grasp the morphology of this or that language, but it means above all to assume a culture, to support the weight of a civilization' (1967, pp. 17–18). Or Ndebele discussing English in South Africa: 'The problems of society will also be the problems of the predominant language of that society. It is the carrier of its perceptions, its attitudes, and its goals, for through it, the speakers absorb entrenched attitudes. The guilt of English must then be recognized and appreciated before its continued use can be advocated' (1987, p. 25). Or Chris Searle on English in the world:

> Let us be clear that the English language has been a monumental force and institution of oppression and rabid exploitation throughout 400 years of imperialist history. It attacked the black person with its racist images and imperialist message, it battered the worker who toiled as its words expressed the parameters of his misery and the subjection of entire peoples in all the continents of the world. It was made to scorn the languages it sought to replace, and told the colonised peoples that mimicry of its primacy among languages was a necessary badge of their social mobility as well as their continued humiliation and subjection. Thus, when we talk of 'mastery' of the Standard language, we must be conscious of the terrible irony of the word, that the English language itself was the language of the master, the carrier of his arrogance and brutality.
>
> (1983, p. 68)

An initial question, therefore, has been how, and where, to explore the possibilities of these connections. In her study of the continuity of discourses of race and gender across a number of texts that deal in different ways with the murders committed in 1900 by Jimmy Governor, a 'half-caste aboriginal,' Threadgold (1997) shows how these

> identity- and reality-constructing discourses and genres, dialogism and debate, are constantly remade, rewritten and recontextualised by differently positioned writers and readers across a range of genres produced in a diversity of institutional sites and in relation to complex networks of knowledges and reading and writing practices.
>
> (p. 136)

What Threadgold is able to demonstrate in her close readings of these texts – newspaper reports from 1900, an expository journalistic commentary 50 years later, and a novel another twenty years later – is how these texts have an intertextual coherence. 'It is the resilience,' she suggests, 'of these patterns of racist thought and behaviour, and their complex intersections with an institutionalized sexism, that the retellings and reactivations of the Governor stories across almost a century indicate most clearly' (p. 147).

Threadgold shows, therefore, how meanings stay remarkably consistent across disparate texts, even those that aim to take on and criticize each other. Indeed, it is that very process of 'taking on' that produces the intertextual consistencies and continues to reproduce everyday discourses of gender and race. The parallels with my own interests here are clear, though my focus will be not only on how a discursive field is mapped out in a particular

6

domain – how, for example, particular meanings remain particularly available over a period of time – but also on how such discursive fields become linked to a particular language. I am not suggesting, however, that such continuity occurs in immutable ways. In Thomas' mapping of colonial discourse, for example, he shows how the earlier discourses on primitivism re-emerge in a postcolonial space as 'constructions of the exotic and the primitive that are superficially sympathetic or progressive but in many ways resonant of traditional evocations of others' (1994, pp. 170–1).

Thomas goes on to argue that

> Although competing colonizing visions at particular times often shared a good deal, as the racist discourses of one epoch superficially resembled those of others, these projects are best understood as strategic reformulations and revaluations of prior discourses, determined by their historical, political and cultural contexts, rather than by allegedly eternal properties of self-other relations, or by any other generalized discursive logic.
>
> (p. 171)

Thus, although primitivism has much in common with earlier constructions of the primitive, it must also be understood in its current context relative to other contemporary discourses, such as New Age, environmentalism, multiculturalism, identity politics, and so on. Similarly, I am arguing that there is both continuity and change in the discourses around English. Although one can trace similar patterns, domains and strategies over time, it is also clear that such discourses change in themselves, in relationship to language, and in relationship to other discourses. Contemporary discourses of Self and Other in relation to English, therefore, have historical continuity with colonialism but also sit in ever-changing relationships with other discourses.

### The adherence of discourse

There are two levels of connectedness that I intend to look at here. The first has to do with the history of use. This process – the continued use of certain lexico-grammatical realizations of particular discourses and the continued recalling of certain discourses by the use of particular items – I am suggesting, is not just a matter of a coincidental, contemporary or even long-term historical conjunction but rather becomes a reciprocal relationship of mutual support. In a similar way to Escher's picture of two hands drawing each other, discourses organize and give meaning to texts; they also become institutionalized ways of mapping out knowledge. As this happens, particular words, phrases, texts become common realizations of particular discourses; and their use calls forth those discourses. While I am not arguing that this produces an absolute fixity of meaning, or precludes change and resistance,

I am suggesting that, with powerful discursive fields, there is often a remarkable continuity and resilience to this relationship.

The second aspect to this relationship has not only to do with how discourses may become tied to a language but also how *particular* discourses that are themselves to do with language may in turn set up particular language-discourse relationships. What I am interested in here is not only how certain discourses adhere to English but also how certain discourses about English adhere to English. In this particular case, I would suggest, then, that there is a double reciprocation: on the one hand, as I have already argued, discourses become in a sense entwined with language, each mutually reproducing the other; on the other, these discourses support the role of English as the bearer of this discursive weight. By this I mean that these discourses construct English as a language already in a particular relationship to certain discourses.

Significantly, too, as I want to argue, discourses about English sit in a reciprocal relationship with other discourses, particularly the discursive field that constructs English in relation to other languages and cultures. I am particularly interested in what I call discourses of Self and Other, discourses linked to English that construct English and learners of English in particular ways. This leads me on to another key point, the production of these discourses. One of the problems in moving from a Marxist-based materialism, which locates the production of ideologies in the superstructural reflection of infrastructural social and economic relations, to a Foucauldian notion of discourse is that the production of such discourses is hard to locate: they appear to exist in the air without a material location. What I am interested in showing, by contrast, is how these discourses of Self and Other are part of what I have been calling the cultural constructs of colonialism. This leads on to my next question: Why colonialism?

## Why colonialism?

As I suggested above, it is important to locate the production of discourse in historical and cultural contexts. But why choose colonialism as a particular set of historical and cultural formations? There are at the very least three strong reasons for making this connection. First, because English has clearly been interwoven with British colonialism throughout colonial and post-colonial history. Thus, if I am seeking histories of connectedness, this may be a fruitful site for exploration. Second, as many writers have argued, colonialism was a significant site of cultural production: it was indeed in this context that many constructions of Self and Other were produced. And third, colonialism remains, despite the increased focus on colonial histories in recent years, a location of discourses, cultures and histories that merits constant further investigation.

### *Colonial histories in English*

Turning first to the interweaving of English and colonialism, it is clear both that English language teaching was a crucial part of the colonial enterprise, and that English has been a major language in which colonialism has been written. I shall be exploring these issues in considerable depth in future chapters – indeed I shall even be arguing that English is a product of colonialism – so here it may suffice to give a brief example of colonial interweaving. Looking, for example at histories of colonialism, it is interesting to see how certain texts in English are interconnected with the colonial project. Take, for example, the following introduction to Indigenous Australians in W.H. Lang's (no date) *Australia* in the *Romance of Empire* series. Discussing the 'natives of Tasmania', he explains that 'they are now all dead; the white man has only been there for a little over a hundred years, but he has eaten them out, even as the brown Norway rat has eaten out the old English black rat' (p. 9). As recent histories of Tasmania have argued (e.g. McGrath, 1995b; Maykutenner, 1995), such histories both ignore the planned genocide of Aboriginal Tasmanians, and simultaneously deny Aboriginality to the Pallawah who did survive. I am arguing that such histories are also part of the process by which discourses adhere to English.

While it is now far less possible to write history in the manner of the former great colonial historians – making such bold statements as the first sentence in Manning Clark's (1962) history of Australia that 'Civilisation did not begin in Australia until the last quarter of the eighteenth century' (p. 3) – it is important to see how such histories are still linked with English. An interesting example of this can be found in A.G. Eyre's *An Outline History of England*, a book published in 1971 in a Longman series of books giving background information about Britain in simplified English. Thus, the connections between colonial history, English and English language teaching become increasingly apparent here. According to Eyre, there were two types of colonizers: On the one hand, there were the settlers of North America, who 'did not have to fight for their lands; the existing population was so small and unsettled that there was room for all' (p. 147). 'British settlers in Canada, Australia and New Zealand,' we are told, 'were true colonists who went to make new homes in empty lands. . . . They settled down to farm their new lands in peace, as no man's rival' (p. 150).

On the other hand, there were the colonists in India and Africa, whose story goes like this: 'The traders were welcomed by the coastal peoples, they set up trading stations, and they made friendly agreements with local rulers. But sooner or later they and their hosts were attacked by jealous inland peoples. To protect themselves, they employed armed forces of local men under British officers.' (p. 150). Meanwhile, however, other European powers were doing the same and even taking possession of land, a practice resisted by the British: 'French rivalry led to the gradual extension of British control over the whole of India, which had been left in confusion by the breakdown of the Mogul Empire' (p. 151). Having thus explained how Britain acquired its colonies, Eyre goes on to explain the benefits to Indians: 'English was taken as the official language of education, which opened to Indians the literature and the universities of Europe' (p. 151). Despite these benefits, Indians were unable to take advantage of them because 'the extreme poverty and the deep-rooted customs of India's ever-increasing population made social progress as slow and difficult as it still is today' (p. 151).

This text, then, puts many of the standard tropes of colonial discourse into play: peaceful farmers moved into empty lands with no rivals; other colonies were formed when peaceful traders were forced to protect themselves; colonialism brought great benefits to the colonized peoples; but because of primitive customs they have not been able to benefit from these opportunities. As Frantz Fanon described this sort of history:

> The settler makes history; his life is an epoch, an Odyssey. He is the absolute beginning: 'This land was created by us'; he is the unceasing cause: 'If we leave, all is lost, and the country will go back to the Middle Ages.' Over against him torpid creatures, wasted by fevers, obsessed by ancestral customs, form an almost inorganic background for the innovating dynamism of colonial mercantilism. . . . Thus the history which he writes is not the history of the country which he plunders but the history of his own nation in regard to all that she skims off, all that she violates and starves.
>
> (1963, p. 40)

As we shall see, this construction of *terra nullius* – the legally endorsed premise of British occupation of Australia and other countries (McGrath, 1995a) – and indeed its extension into a notion of *persona nullius* has remained a central construction of colonialism interwoven with English.

### Constructions of Self and Other: Crusoe's footsteps and Crusoe's footprint

I have already suggested that one of my interests here is in the ways constructions of Self and Other occur in relationship to English. Colonialism, I am also suggesting, is probably the context without equal of such constructions. At the end of my book *The Cultural Politics of English as an International Language* (1994b), I pointed to two different interpretations of Daniel Defoe's *The Life and Adventures of Robinson Crusoe* (1910). I did not realize at the time, however, the size of the can of worms I had opened up. In some ways this book takes up where that last chapter left off. The issue that I pointed to there was that although Phillipson's (1992) discussion of Robinson Crusoe's English lessons to Friday as one of the earliest instances of English linguistic imperialism was a significant point, it missed another side of colonial relations.

Phillipson argues that Crusoe's lessons to Friday, in which he made it his business to 'teach him everything that was proper to make him useful, handy and helpful' (1719/1910, p. 195) is perhaps the *locus classicus* of the start of English linguistic imperialism, a moment emblematic of the origins of the British Council and the constant attempts to spread English around the globe. He goes on to point out that when simplified readers were first produced by a British publisher to further the expansion of English, the first title published was *Robinson Crusoe* (Longman New Method Series, 1926). Indeed, it is interesting to observe the connections between the simplified version of *Robinson Crusoe* and the simplified Longman history discussed above. Phillipson's main point here is that Crusoe's relationship with Friday reflects the 'racial structure of western society at the heyday of slavery' (p. 109) and that Crusoe's assumption of mastery over Friday and his immediate start on the project of teaching Friday English (rather than, for example, learning Friday's language), are iconic moments in the long history of the global spread of English. This is a significant observation and it is perhaps always worth asking ourselves as English teachers to what extent we are following in Crusoe's footsteps (see figure 1).

Nevertheless, there is an alternative and equally important interpretation to be made of the relationship between Crusoe and Friday. Whereas Phillipson sees Crusoe as the epitome of imperialist mastery, a key figure in the European attempt to gain political and economic mastery over vast areas of the world, Brantlinger (1990), by contrast, focuses on Crusoe as the epitome of the 'irrational' mastery over and construction of the Other. For Brantlinger, the crucial moment in this story is the discovery in the sand of the footprint (see figure 2). As he points out, from that moment on, Crusoe is plagued by wild imaginings of 'savages': Crusoe is a man 'perfectly confused and out of myself' (Defoe, 1719/1910, p. 143); '. . . nor is it possible to describe how many various shapes affrighted imagination represented things to me in, how many wild ideas were found every moment in my fancy, and what strange unaccountable whimsies came into my thoughts by the way' (p. 143). From this moment on, his cave is renamed his castle, and he lives in perpetual fear of the arrival of the cannibals, a fear that grows ever greater as his wild imaginings increase: 'The further I was from the occasion of my fright, the greater my apprehensions were' (pp. 143–4).

In the introduction to the 1910 edition, A.C. Liddell argues that:

> we enjoy the stolid, business-like way in which Crusoe sets to work to make, and succeeds in making, the best of a very bad job, and as Britons we like to think of him as typical of the Britons who, before his time and since, have by pluck and perseverance planted colonies all the world over, and turned howling wildernesses into regions of prosperity and plenty.
>
> (Liddell, 1910, p. xi)

11

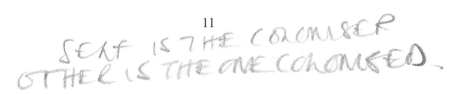

*Figure 1* Crusoe instructing Friday

Here we can see, on the one hand, the stress on Crusoe as the model for the rational and dedicated way in which the British created their empire. But this statement, on the other hand, rings not only with the uncomfortable celebration of colonialism, but also with the strange production of the fictional Other, in this case the 'howling wildernesses' into which the British moved (and compare the history text discussed on pp. 9–10).

*Figure 2* A footprint in the sand

While it is possible, therefore, to dwell on the theme of Crusoe as the model of rational economic mastery and imperialism, he can also be seen as the model of madness, as the delirious constructor of the fictional Other. When Crusoe first comes across a site where the cannibals had visited the island, he is horrified to find:

> the shore spread with skulls, hands, feet, and other bones of human bodies; and particularly, I observed a place where there had been a fire made, and a circle dug in the earth, like a cockpit, where it is supposed the savage wretches had sat down to their inhuman feastings upon the bodies of their fellow creatures.
>
> (pp. 152–3)

The effect of this 'pitch of inhuman, hellish, brutality' is first to make him sick and second to give God thanks that he had 'cast my first lot in a part of the world where I was distinguished from such dreadful creatures as these' (p. 153). And yet, Crusoe's life, Defoe's writing and the European imagination keep returning to these savage rituals. The horror of the cannibalistic rituals has a profound effect on Crusoe, who 'kept close within my own circle for almost two years after this' (p. 154). A few years (and fourteen pages) later, however, they are back and Crusoe watches them through his 'perspective glass' as they sit around a fire 'not to warm them, for they had no need of that, the weather being extreme hot, but, as I supposed, to dress some of their barbarous diet of human flesh . . .' (p. 168). When they have left, Crusoe cannot resist visiting the site of their feast, where he gazes at the 'marks of horror which the dismal work they had been about had left behind it, viz. the blood, the bones, and part of the flesh of human bodies, eaten and devoured by those wretches with merriment and sport.' (p. 169) A year and three months later, they are back again: 'The place was covered with human bones, the ground dyed with their blood, great pieces of flesh left here and there, half-eaten, mangled, and scorched; . . . I saw three skulls, five hands, and the bones of three or four legs and feet, and abundance of other parts of the bodies' (pp. 192–3). And so on.

As Hulme (1986) comments, this 'paradigmatic manifestation of cannibalism finally allows Crusoe to clearly distinguish himself from others' (p. 198). After this extensive revelling in the European-imagined cannibalism of the primitive Other, almost any act by Crusoe to oppose such barbarisms may seem justifiable (by page 221 he is presenting a list of savages killed rather like a cricket score-card: '3 killed at our first shot from the tree, 2 killed at the next shot . . . 21 in all') and European culture will condone any action in the name of colonialism. It is in this context, as Crusoe passes sleepless nights wondering whether to attack the next party of savages, that he has a dream, almost a religious revelation, in which a 'savage' escapes from his captors and pleads to Crusoe for help. Thereafter, Crusoe resolves 'to get a savage into my possession' (p. 183). His dream turns out to be prophetic and eventually he is able to start on his dual project of civilizing and teaching English: 'In a little time I began to speak to him, and teach him to speak to me; and, first, I made him know his name should be Friday, which was the day I saved his life. . . . I likewise taught him to say master, and then let him know that was to be my name' (p. 192). As Fulton (1994) suggests, it is in the dialogues between Crusoe and Friday that we can observe the process of the construction of Self and Other:

> *Master:* Well, Friday, and what does your nation do with the men they take? Do they carry them away and eat them, as these did?
> *Friday:* Yes, my nation eat mans up too; eat all up.
>
> (p. 199)

And in such dialogues, we can start to see the relationship not only between Self and Other as constructed by colonialism but also between these and English. Not only does Friday not get to speak in his own language, but he has been given very particular, colonizing English words to express his cultural background.

According to Brantlinger, 'What Crusoe cannot master – or get to call him "master" – he sees only as savagery and desert island' (1990, p. 2). This is not, of course, new to Defoe, for the long tradition of creating these often cannibalistic, always primitive and savage Others can be traced in European imagination from Columbus and Caliban to Kipling and Conrad (see Tatlow, 1993; Ngũgĩ, 1993). The lesson Brantlinger draws from this is that while Defoe's intended moral lesson was presumably one of mastery and self-mastery, 'it seems just as possible to see in Crusoe's mastery – of the island, of the cannibals, of Friday, of fate – a kind of madness, the antithesis of self-mastery' (p. 3). And yet, this almost delirious and fantastical construction of the native Other needs to be seen, I believe, neither as irrational madness nor as rational mastery. It is clearly not merely the random ramblings of European imaginations but neither is it useful to explain it only in terms of a rational attempt to justify the colonial project. Rather, I want to take this up in terms of the *cultural constructions of colonialism,* the ways in which colonialism was helped by and in turn produced images of both the Self and Other. This, then, is the other side of the colonial coin, not the Anglicist imposition of English for economic and political gain, but the Orientalist construction of the inarticulate Other. As Fulton (1994) puts it, 'We live with the results of what colonial regimes have made of others; in listening to the deployment of dialogue in texts like this one, by interpreting the resistance imputed to figures like Friday and noticing the turns taken away from them, we can recognise what colonial enterprise had to repress of its own culture as a condition of its construction of others' (p. 19).

A crucial dimension of how I intend to deal with colonialism, therefore, concerns an understanding of colonialism in *cultural* rather than political or economic terms. Although the economic exploitation and political rule of colonialism should of course never be downplayed since they have had very real material effects on colonized people, the cultural effects of colonialism need to be given equal weight, not as mere rationalizations or products of social and economic relations but rather as a significant site of colonialism in their own right. As Thomas (1994) puts it:

> colonialism is not best understood primarily as a political or economic relationship that is legitimized or justified through ideologies of racism or progress. Rather, colonialism has always, equally importantly and deeply, been a cultural process; its discoveries and trespasses are imagined and energized through signs, metaphors and narratives; even what would seem its purest moments of profit and violence have been mediated and enframed by structures of meaning. Colonial cultures are not simply ideologies that mask, mystify or rationalize forms of oppression that are external to them; they are also expressive and constitutive of colonial relationships in themselves.
>
> (p. 2)

It is important to understand here that I am not merely switching the focus from economic exploitation to cultural imposition. Rather than looking at cultural imperialism, at how European culture was *imposed* on local people, I am interested in how colonialism *produced* European culture, in the cultural legacies of colonialism. The point here is that if on the one hand we need to understand how, as language teachers, we walk in Crusoe's footsteps, how European languages and cultures have been forced upon other people, we need, on the other hand, to consider how that footprint in the sand, the threatening mark of the colonized Other, has left a long cultural imprint through the discourses of colonialism.

### Colonialism and postcolonialism

If the above arguments do not in themselves adequately justify a focus on English and colonialism, I think it is also worth considering the extent to which an exploration of English and English language teaching sheds light on colonialism itself. Colonialism has emerged recently as an important refocus of study. There appear to be a number of reasons for this, including the historical focus of writers such as Michel Foucault in his work on madness, prisons and sexuality, influencing in turn the work of Said (1978) and many others. Probably most significant has been the emergence of postcolonialism as a term used far beyond its temporal reference (after colonialism). Like poststructuralism and postmodernism, it calls for a major rethinking of pre-given categories and histories, a major calling-into-question of assumed givens and fixed structures. Unlike the other 'posts', however, it has also brought with it a stronger sense of the political, a greater emphasis on social and cultural change. With this has come a redressing of what it is 'post', that is, colonialism. As postcolonial writers and academics have sought to rewrite histories against the grain of the colonial histories discussed above, the practices and discourses of colonialism have emerged as a central focus of interest.

Recent years have therefore seen a wide range of work focusing on colonialism. There is, to mention but a few relevant books, work such as Blaut (1993) that looks at the connections between colonialism and geography; Thomas (1994), Pratt (1992) and Spurr (1993), which explore relationships between anthropology, travel-writing, journalism, government and colonialism; books that look at the ideologies and knowledges produced by colonialism, such as Metcalf (1995) or Cohn (1996) or Nandy's (1983) study of the psychology of colonialism; reworkings of colonial history, such as McGrath's (1995c) edited book; work on colonialism and translation, such as Niranjana (1992); and a vast quantity of work related to English studies, such as Suleri (1992), Said (1993), Spivak (1987), and a number of collections such as Williams and Chrisman (1994).

Despite all this work, colonialism still warrants revisiting many more times in order both to better understand the colonial past and to see how it echoes into the present. The scale and brutality of the Holocaust, and the determination of Jewish people never to allow the world to forget what was done to them, have kept alive the need to remember, to mourn and to learn from the Holocaust. Meanwhile, despite pressure from China, South Korea and other East Asian countries, Japan is less often and less openly called on to remember the massacres in China and elsewhere. And despite the shouts from the former colonies on the margins of international powers, the European nations are rarely held accountable for the colonial histories they brought to the world. Thus, while the Holocaust needs to be understood for the uniqueness of the single-minded attempt to exterminate a people, the brutality of colonialism needs to be seen as a history that has not been sufficiently acknowledged in the world because of its extra-European context.

Discussing the effects of the opium trade on China, for example, Yee (1992) points out that:

> While Hitler's mad genocide lasted less than a decade and murdered six or more million men, women and children, the British imperial opium system in Asia began in Bengal in 1757, with a solid market going in China in the 1780s, until World War II, the better part of two centuries, and killed an incalculable number but surely in the hundreds of millions.[1]

Thus, he argues, the British imperial system 'must be held accountable. The leader in imperialism and opiate profits, it is responsible for the hundreds of millions that died and suffered as well as the societal damage caused by the opium system that was established and intertwined into China and throughout Asia' (p. 43). To understand European culpability not just for the Holocaust but also for the devastation that was imperialism and colonialism is, then, a further reason to deal with colonialism. And the study of English and English language teaching in this context can shed important light on the ideologies and practices of colonialism.

A final important reason for dealing with colonial history is that colonialism should not be seen merely as an historical period but rather, as I have been suggesting, should be understood in terms of its legacies to European thought and culture. Indeed, the connection between Nazism and colonialism has another side to it. Césaire (1972) argues that Europeans are all complicit with Nazism since 'before they were its victims, they were its accomplices'. Europeans tolerated Nazism 'before it was inflicted on them, . . . they absolved it, shut their eyes to it, legitimized it, because, until then, it had been applied only to non-European peoples' (p. 14). That is to say, Nazism was nothing less than the barbarity of colonialism brought back to its European home. But it is not just the barbarity of European fascism that is closely tied to colonialism, for the development of modern European and North American science, philosophy, anthropology, history, thought and culture are crucially tied up with colonialism. Not only did they occur at the same time, but they had profound effects on each other. As Young puts it:

> European thought since the Renaissance would be as unthinkable without the impact of colonialism as the history of the world since the Renaissance would be inconceivable without the effects of Europeanization. So it is not an issue of removing colonial thinking from European thought, of purging it, like today's dream of 'stamping out' racism. It is rather a question of repositioning European systems of knowledge so as to demonstrate the long history of their operation as the effect of their colonial other, a reversal encapsulated in Fanon's observation: 'Europe is literally the creation of the Third World.'
>
> (1990, p. 118)

Following Fanon's and Sartre's critique of the complicity of Western humanism with colonialism, Young argues that humanism itself, that much vaunted corner-stone of the European Enlightenment, was deeply complicit with colonialism: the development of such ideas as 'human nature', 'humanity', and universal qualities of the human mind occurred at the same time as the violent spread of colonial activity. The study of colonialism, then, becomes far more than the study of an historical era; rather, it opens up a wide range of questions concerning the development of current aspects of European and North American thought and culture.

## English language teaching and colonialism

I have been arguing for the importance of understanding English in its colonial context. I intend to look at this in the particular context of English language teaching (ELT). It seems to me, having been involved for many years with teaching English as a so-called second or foreign language, that there are deep and indissoluble links between the practices, theories and contexts of ELT and the history of colonialism. Such connections, I want to suggest, run far deeper than drawing parallels between the current global expansion of English and the colonial expansion that preceded it. Rather, I want to argue that ELT theories and practices that emanate from the former colonial powers still carry the traces of those colonial histories both because of the long history of direct connections between ELT and colonialism and because such theories and practices derive from broader European cultures and ideologies that themselves are products of colonialism. In a sense, then, ELT is a product of colonialism not just because it is colonialism that produced the initial conditions for the global spread of English but because it was colonialism that produced many of the ways of thinking and behaving that are still part of Western cultures. European/Western culture not only produced colonialism but was also produced by it; ELT not only rode on the back of colonialism to the distant corners of the Empire but was also in turn produced by that voyage.

Colonialism and postcolonial struggles have been central to world history over the last two centuries. They have produced and reduced nations, massacred populations, dispossessed people of their land, culture, language and history, shifted vast numbers of people from one place to another. And they are also the ground on which European/Western images of the Self and Other have been constructed, the place where constructions of Superiority and Inferiority were produced. Within this context, ELT needs to be seen not only as a tool in service of Empire but also as a product of Empire. The history of the ties between ELT and colonialism has produced images of the Self and Other, understandings of English and of other languages and cultures that still play a major role in how English language teaching is constructed and practised: from the native speaker/non-native speaker dichotomy to the images constructed around English as a global language and the assumptions about learners' cultures, much of ELT echoes with the cultural constructions of colonialism. And sadly, there seems to be a loud absence about such connections in applied linguistics and TESOL, showing, I think, the strange isolation of much thinking in applied linguistics from academic and political work going on outside it.

Under various signs such as postmodernism and postcolonialism, a great deal of recent work has come to question the assumed universalisms of Western thought and to ask how they have been produced and what other possibilities they have denied in the process. While we might wish to be sceptical about the frenetic production of postmodern academic work, I think we would do well to consider the significance of Young's (1990) observation that postmodernism can be understood as a Western cultural crisis in face of the realization that it is no longer the unquestioned centre of the world. Studies of colonialism and postcolonialism have increased massively over the last few years as profound questions have been raised about the nature of power and knowledge in the world. With the emergence of a growing voice from the former colonies – both those people such as Australian and North American Indigenous people who remain marginalized within their own countries and those people whose colonial past has left them marginalized internationally – the study of the continuing effects of colonialism and the postcolonial strategies to resist such effects has become a major focus of work in many disciplines. Its virtual absence from applied linguistics and TESOL becomes even stranger when one considers the centrality of English language teaching to the colonial project.

First, English language teaching (ELT) was always a highly significant part of colonial policy. Where the empire spread, so too did English. A study of English language teaching and colonialism, therefore, can add important dimensions to the understanding of how colonialism operated. Policies about providing or withholding an education in English were not simple questions to do with the 'medium of instruction' (to name the reductive framework in which much discussion of such issues occurs today) but rather were concerned with different views of how best to run a colony. To some, provision of limited English was a pragmatic policy to facilitate colonial rule; to others provision of English was an essential part of the messianic spread of British language and culture. To some, provision of vernacular education was a colonial obligation; to others it was a crucial tool in the development of a workforce able to participate in colonial capitalism; to others it was an important means to maintain the status quo. A study of policies around English language education, therefore, can give important insights into the more general operation of colonialism. Such an understanding also has considerable significance for understanding current language policies.

Second, since the growth of empire also implied a massive growth in English language teaching, the period of colonialism is a highly significant one for the study of the development of ELT. When he arrives at the end of the eighteenth century in his history of English language teaching, Howatt (1984) discusses John Miller's *The Tutor, or a New English & Bengali Work, Well Adapted to Teach the Natives English*, published in Serampore in Bengal in 1797, suggesting that it may be the first textbook produced for teaching English in the Empire. Howatt argues that the history of ELT forks into two streams at this point, one following the path of imperial expansion and the role of English in the Empire, and the other following the development of teaching methodology within Europe. Acknowledging that the former is a 'vast subject that requires a separate series of studies in its own right,' Howatt opts for the latter, which 'is more limited in scope and is primarily concerned with the response of language teaching methodology to educational and social change in nineteenth century Europe' (p. 71). Howatt's decision is an understandable one, a necessary attempt to limit the scope of his project, but it must also be seen in terms of the histories it avoids and the histories it takes up. While this book will also not attempt to map out this 'vast subject' in detail – this is not intended to be a history of language teaching – it will argue that the development of ELT cannot be adequately accounted for without understanding its colonial background.

Third, not only would a history of ELT be incomplete without acknowledging the developments within the Empire, but it would also fail to acknowledge that developments occurred first in the colonies and were then brought to Britain. In his exploration of the development of psychometric testing in ELT, for example, Spolsky (1995) refers to Macaulay's (1835) argument that examinations 'could offer a solution to the problems of governing India' (1995, p. 7). Spolsky goes on to point out that written examinations 'were first used in the middle of the nineteenth century as a means of selecting candidates for the upper grades in the Indian Civil Service, and later adopted for admission to the Home Civil Service and other professions' (p. 10). Such observations point to the conclusion that examinations were first developed in relationship to the governance of Britain's colonies and only then introduced into Britain once they had been proved effective. This matches Viswanathan's (1989) demonstration of how the English literary canon was first developed in India as a means to continue to teach British culture and only then imported into Britain. Similarly, it can be argued that the theories and practices of ELT were not so much products of Britain that were exported to the Empire but rather were products of the Empire that were imported to Britain. The significance of this is that to understand the development of aspects of ELT, we have to understand the colonial contexts in which they grew up.

A fourth dimension of these relationships can be found in another rare reference to connections between ELT and colonialism. In their discussion of the racism that underlies apparent cross-cultural miscommunication in interactions between South Asians and Anglo-Celtic British, Jupp, Roberts and Cook-Gumperz (1982) argue that:

> The original social and economic backgrounds of this group of people are diverse and include widely different educational levels, expectations of life in Britain, experience of British institutions, as well as differences in the degree of fluency in English. However,

one common factor is Britain's former colonial relationship with their countries of origin. This has provided a significant historical dimension to expectations and stereotypes both amongst the white British and amongst the immigrants themselves whatever their particular backgrounds.

(p. 233)

This comment raises the issue that with the dissolution of Empire and the increase of immigration into the English-dominant nations, the racism that underlay so much of colonialism was brought back home with it. This argument parallels the larger point made by Fanon (1963) and Young (1990) that the rise of European fascism was merely the result of colonialism's return to Europe. If it is indeed the case that a great deal of contemporary European and North American thought has its origins in the colonial relationship, this must surely apply even more so to those domains of thought, such as ELT theories, whose connections to colonialism have been especially close. What I want to suggest, then, is that some of the central ideologies of current English Language Teaching have their origins in the cultural constructions of colonialism. The colonial construction of Self and Other, of the 'TE' and 'SOL' of TESOL remain in many domains of ELT.

Fifth, I also want to make a case for understanding that the primary influences on ELT, on what happens in classrooms, what research agendas get taken up, how decisions get made for developing school curricula, and so forth, may be just as much the domains of popular culture as the domains of applied linguistic theory. That is to say, I think we may often make the error of assuming that practices and theories of ELT are governed by the rational actions of applied linguists. Instead, I am suggesting that much of what we do as language teachers, teacher educators, parents, applied linguists and so on may be directed by popular discourses on language and education that do not seem − at least on the surface − to be so current within the rarefied thinking of applied linguistics. Importantly, furthermore, these popular discourses circulate as part of European or Anglo-American culture and have their origins in the same colonial context as ELT. Connections between ELT and colonialism, therefore, can be found in the relationship between ELT and the popular discourses on English and other cultures which circulate in the same contexts.

Finally, I hope that this attempt to map out connections between ELT and colonialism will at least start to redress the strange imbalance that seems to exist here, the massive absence of discussions of ELT and colonialism. The two main histories of language teaching − Kelly's (1969) of language teaching in general and Howatt's (1984) of ELT − remain 'scrupulously ethnocentric',[2] studying the origins and developments of language teaching practices and theories as if Europe were an island unto itself. They are also concerned principally with the development of teaching methods and thus do not turn their attention to broader cultural or political concerns. There are a few passing references to colonialism in work on 'world Englishes': Platt, Weber and Ho (1984), for example, on their way to suggesting that English in multilingual countries 'can be considered a neutral language of communication' (p. 14), locate this argument in an historical context in which 'the end of the colonial era has not seen a reversal of the spread of English' as Britain's former colonies have since 'realized the importance of English . . .' (p. 1). Kachru (1986) devotes a bit more space to a discussion of colonialism but again with the objective of showing how the 'legacy of colonial Englishes has resulted in the existence of several transplanted varieties of English having distinct linguistic ecologies – their own contexts of function and usage' (p. 1). One exception to this reluctance to deal with colonialism is Phillipson (1992), who devotes a whole chapter to what he calls the 'colonial linguistic inheritance', arguing that colonial linguistic ideology laid a foundation for 'the maintenance of structural and cultural inequalities between English and other languages in the post-colonial age' (p. 123). Although my approach to some of these questions differs from Phillipson's (see Pennycook, 1994b), this point – that colonialism should not be seen as a forgotten era in the past but rather as the context in which current ideas were framed – comes closest to the arguments I am trying to make here. But Phillipson remains one of the few writers on ELT who have seen the significance of these connections.

The strangeness of this absence needs to be set against the vast amount of work in colonial and postcolonial studies outside applied linguistics and TESOL in areas such as geography, history and anthropology (mentioned on p. 17), and the growing volume of work in related areas, such as translation and literary studies. Significant here is work such as Viswanathan's (1989) *Masks of conquest: Literary study and British rule in India,* which makes the important point that the English literary canon was developed in India in order to facilitate colonial governance and then imported to Britain, while work in Rajan's (1993c) edited book *The lie of the land: English literary studies in India* points to themes to which I shall return, such as the complicity of Orientalism in colonial rule (Rajan, 1993b), the role of the British council in promoting colonial culture (Rajan, 1993a), the development of postcolonial pedagogy (Niranjana, 1993, Spivak, 1993), and more. This work, however, although clearly related to the themes of my book, remains only partially relevant because of its emphasis on English literature. My interest, then, is to try to draw some connections, perhaps in rather preliminary fashion, between a massive body of work on colonialism and postcolonialism and ELT past and present. I want to suggest, too, that this project is not merely one of linking work in applied linguistics to a currently trendy area of research but rather, as with much of the better work within the broad field of colonial and postcolonial studies, trying to reread current cultural relationships in light of a different understanding of global politics.

## Personal histories, colonialism and English

There are a number of ways in which I am personally located within this project, though I want to use these personal relations as a means to explore broader issues. As I argued above, it seems to me that the connections between ELT and colonialism are unmistakable. My current position as a teacher in Australia cannot be removed from Australia's colonial past and the continuing colonial relationship with Aboriginal people. My own involvement in ELT over many years brings up more immediate connections to colonialism, most obviously and literally in my time teaching English in Hong Kong. This period gave me a number of insights into and angers about colonialism. To put it very briefly, three principal issues emerged. First, that it is important to understand colonialism not only in terms of its macro-political structures but also in terms of the cultural politics of everyday life. While it is important, therefore, to understand the role and effects of a colonial government, of the presence of an appointed Governor to run Hong Kong, of the large-scale economic implications of colonial business, it is equally important to explore how the cultures of colonialism manifest themselves in the micropolitics of daily life. Often, if you raise questions of colonialism among 'expatriates'[3] in Hong Kong, you are met by remarks that Hong Kong people do not seem so oppressed or downtrodden. Apart from the absence of democracy and the presence of a colonial administration, it is suggested, there does not seem to be anything very colonial about Hong Kong. My argument is that stereotypes of colonialism as only the brutal oppression and economic exploitation of a people draw attention away from the constant cultural and micropolitical operation of colonialism.

Second, it became clear to me that colonialism was both more complex and more simple than it was commonly taken to be. There is of course an obvious contradiction in such a statement, but I think it is important to continue to work with this ambivalence. My point is that on the one hand, as I looked at colonialism in Hong Kong's history and present, I was struck by how complex its operation often was. This is of particular significance historically, since we often appear to operate with simple stereotypes of colonialism, images of pith-helmeted Brits marching around in the noon-day sun. As I shall argue particularly in Chapter 3 with respect to discussions of Macaulay and his famous Minute, this tendency to work with simplistic stereotypes has led to limited understandings both of colonialism and of its relationship to the present. On the other hand, however, I was also struck in Hong Kong by the simple crassness of colonialism, by its very basic racisms. These two themes – the need to complexify and the need to understand the basic nature of colonial dichotomizing – resurface in this book in the discussion of colonial language policies and images of Self and Other. This juxtaposition of the simple and the complex is a key issue to which I shall return in the next section and in later chapters.

A third issue was the common demand that I should, along with a critical view of colonialism, also be looking at the 'benefits' of colonialism. This question, I must say, frustrates me. It is problematic because of the view of colonialism that it puts into play through a liberal apoliticism that seeks to see 'both sides' of things, to present a 'balanced' view. My point is not so much that positive effects cannot be found in colonialism (for some people, some of the time) but rather that, first, there is still a pressing need to write against the massive history that has extolled the benefits of colonialism for so long, and, second, this history cannot be reduced to some even-handed balance sheet in which some things were lost and others gained. As Holland (1977) suggests:

> Too often Europeans emphasize the advantages of colonialism, asserting how much the British did to 'civilise' and modernise Africa and Australia. The truth is that the major effect of colonialism was to destroy African and Australian society and halt its natural progress by excluding the native people from any say in making the decisions that controlled their lives.
>
> (p. 190)

Having myself watched – and in some senses participated in – the micro-politics of colonialism, the constant dismissals, inequalities, putdowns, racisms of everyday life in Hong Kong, I see no good reason to go looking for the 'good' in colonialism. Thus, I cannot see any good moral or political reasons to attempt some 'balanced' overview of colonialism. This is not to say that I intend to paint some simplistically negative view of colonialism; rather, my interest is in exploring its complexities. But this does not mean, either, that I wish to present colonialism as a process of give and take or intercultural communication. In any case, such arguments over the benefits or harms of colonialism miss the point of my project here. I am not trying to give an overview of colonialism, a linear history of the relationship between ELT and colonialism, but rather to trace the cultural effects of colonialism on current practices.

It is not so much that colonialism produces unique behaviours, words and ideas but rather it makes a set of practices and discursive frames more available, more acceptable. The processes of colonialism in Hong Kong can be seen for example in the housing and other benefits that expatriates receive while their (our) local colleagues do not, benefits which even the normally staid *South China Morning Post* referred to as 'racially based discrimination as practised by the tertiary institutions' that is 'offensive and unacceptable and indicative of a colonial mentality that even the administration might disavow' ('System needs review', editorial, November 1, 1994, p. 18). But they can also be seen on a much smaller scale: in the way an expatriate language teacher at a restaurant deals angrily and dismissively with a waiter because of his 'dreadful English'; in the way the old drinkers at the Hong Kong University Senior Common Room bar speak to the local bar staff; in the ease with which a British professor of philosophy can explain why he has no Chinese members of staff: 'There's no such thing as Chinese philosophy'; in the all-British dinner parties where the discussion vacillates between the memories of other colonial outposts and how well they treat their maids; in the English teachers who pick up the paper and turn immediately to check the share prices; in the Filipino maids walking the dogs; in the dominance of expatriates in senior jobs; in the refusal to learn Cantonese because 'it's an ugly language' or 'I would never have a chance to use it' or 'in the sort of restaurants I go to, they speak English'; in the use of colonial Englishes. I shall return at other points in this book to the interaction of the personal and the colonial.

## Discourse, history and the present

I have tried in this introductory chapter to raise in fairly informal fashion some of the key issues I wish to deal with in this book. Before moving to an outline of the book itself, it may be helpful to raise some theoretical and methodological concerns. The first has to do with history and the present, the second is concerned with the notion of simplicity and complexity discussed above. Both have to do with this book as an exercise in discourse analysis. As I have suggested already, although I shall be looking quite extensively at historical documents, this book is not intended to be a history of ELT and colonialism in any traditional sense. Dean (1994) points to three forms of historical theory: the first he calls *progressivist,* an approach to history which 'proposes a model of social progress through the teleology of reason, technology, production, and so on' (p. 3). This version sees history as a recounting of the upward march towards a better world.

The second approach Dean describes as *critical,* by which he means work based on Western Marxist views of progress and emancipation. This 'critical modernism' 'offers a critique of modernist narratives in terms of the one-sided, pathological, advance of technocratic or instrumental reason they celebrate, in order to offer an alternative, higher version of rationality' (p. 3). This, then, is the classic version of rationalist critical theory which offers enlightenment and emancipation by revealing structures of oppression. The third version Dean calls a *problematizing* one which 'establishes an analysis of the trajectory of the historical forms of truth and knowledge without origin or end' (p. 4). This view 'remains critical as it is unwilling to accept the taken-for-granted components of our reality and the 'official' accounts of how they came to be the way they are' (p. 4). This form of history, then, which Dean, following Foucault, calls *critical and effective history,* disavows the beliefs in transparent language, historical progress, enlightenment, or emancipation, constantly seeking to question the discursive construction of reality, both in the past and the present. Dean suggests that it may be termed *post-*

*modern*, if by that term we mean 'the restive problematisation of the given' (p. 4).

This line of thinking draws explicitly on Foucault's view of history. At the beginning of *Discipline and Punish*, Foucault's (1979) broad-reaching study of prisons, punishment and institutions such as education, he asks why he is engaging in such a history: 'Simply because I am interested in the past? No, if one means by that writing a history of the past in terms of the present. Yes, if one means by that writing a history of the present' (1979, p. 31). Following this notion of the 'history of the present', this book is not, therefore, a linear history of the development of certain ideas over time, and certainly not a story of progression from bad past to better present; rather, it is an attempt to understand historical periods and events in their own terms and then to trace, *genealogically*, how ideas, concepts and beliefs have both shifted and continued into the present (see Foucault, 1980, 1984a, 1984b). Following Dean's (1994) argument that Foucault's two approaches to historical questions, *archaeology* and *genealogy*, are often unhelpfully seen as representing radically different periods of his thought (see, for example, Dreyfus and Rabinow, 1983), I want to acknowledge the possibility of using both. In this view, while genealogy becomes the 'history of the present' 'because it is able to undertake an analysis of those objects given as necessary components of our reality', it can only do so because 'archaeology provides the point of attack on discourse' (p. 33). Archaeology, then, remains as the systematic and analytical description of particular discourses, while genealogy becomes the 'history of the present' whereby the struggles over 'subjugated knowledges' (Foucault, 1980) are traced into the present.

Historically, then, my aim is not to try to give an overview of an historical period of English or English language teaching, or to attempt to demonstrate some linear unfolding of English, language policies and teaching practices, but rather to illuminate understandings of English and its teaching in light of colonial precedents. I hope to try to understand historical aspects of colonialism and ELT in their own terms, according to their own rationalities, and then to trace the continuance of these rationalities into the present day. This is not, then, an exercise in 'retrospective vindictiveness' (Said, 1993, p.xxiv) but an attempt to map out the discourses of colonialism as they relate to English and then to trace these genealogically into the present. One of the key themes of this book will be the continuity of the cultural constructs of colonialism. Importantly, too, this means that this book is not an exercise merely in historical analysis, nor an attempt to investigate empirically the effects of colonialism. Rather it is a form of discourse analysis, an attempt to map out cultural and discursive frames that influence our lives.

As I have said, this is not intended to be a history of colonialism and ELT. And neither will it presume to write a history for the colonized, to suggest that I can speak on their behalf. Thus, this is not a history of the effects of white oppression on colonized people. Such histories I prefer to leave to colonized peoples. As Thomas (1994) explains his work:

> My aim . . . is not to 'sympathize with' Aborigines, as though they should be grateful recipients of such intellectual charity; still less is it to write colonialism from the other side, on their behalf, as it were; that has been done often enough. My departure point is not the 'problems' or 'experiences' of blacks, but the problematic way in which contemporary white culture deals with Aboriginality.
>
> (p. 28)

Similarly, my concern here is with the problematic ways in which contemporary white culture, and contemporary cultures of ELT deal with cultural Others.

What I am trying to get at is the effects on the colonizers of colonial practices. This move is not, of course, to ignore or downplay the effects of colonialism on the colonized but rather on the one hand to avoid the often patronising attempts to speak on behalf of other people, to claim to interpret others' lives for them, and on the other, to deal with the cultural and political contexts of which I am a part, a self-reflexive move to try to explore the ways colonialism has constructed Western ways of being. This allows me to explore the complicities of my position and invite others to do so too. There is a parallel here between this postcolonial space and the space opened up by feminist critiques of culture and knowledge: it is important not only that women continue their explorations into the deeply gendered nature of our worlds but also that men come to explore how we have been constructed by masculinity and patriarchy, how we come to be complicit in engendering difference.

What I shall be doing predominantly is looking at the effects of colonialism on Europeans, at the way Self and Other have been constructed through the discourses of colonialism. Young (1990) suggests that postmodernism is not so much a crisis of 'late capitalism' as it is a European cultural crisis, a realization that its central constructs – 'Man', the 'West', 'Humanity' and so on – can no longer hold, an acknowledgment that European History and Culture can no longer assume 'their unquestioned place at the centre of the world' (p. 20). It is into this postmodern and postcolonial space that I hope to write, challenging both conservative and critical discourses that have been themselves complicit with the colonial project. I hope to be able to explore how English language teaching has been bound up with colonialism and that the discourses of colonialism still echo through its theories and practices. I want to respond to Memmi's (1965) challenge that if I can play any role in helping reduce the pernicious effects of colonialism, then, as a European, I must first seek out and question the colonizer within myself. This is not, of course, to suggest that what I have to say here is of no interest to people of non-European/American background; rather, this is a question of not trying to read effects on others of processes I am trying to understand myself.[4]

### Simple pasts and complex presents

Finally I want to address a key strategy in what I am trying to do. As I suggested above, I was struck in Hong Kong by the complexity of colonial discourses and yet at the same time the possible simplicity of colonial constructs. As I shall argue in greater depth in Chapters 3 and 4, this juxtaposition is a crucial one for what I am trying to do here. A common conception of history seems to posit a simple past in comparison with a complex present. While this may seem an obvious product of available knowledge and lived contexts, it is also, I want to argue, a strategy that allows for a problematic distancing from the past. There is, once again, a parallel to be drawn here between this understanding of colonialism and an understanding of the Holocaust. One of the problems here has been the tendency to view the Holocaust as the product of Hitlerian or more generally Nazi extremism rather than equally the product of the everyday actions of ordinary people. Thus, in this view, we live in a more complex and less anti-Semitic present than the racist eras before us. Such a view denies the roles and complicities of liberalism and ordinariness in the Holocaust, while distancing the present from clear connections.

Similarly, there is a tendency to view colonial history as a simple tale of old-fashioned bigotries which are very different from the complex liberalisms of the present. I want to suggest here that it is important not only to question the racist stereotypes of the colonized but also to question the images of the colonizer. While the attitudes toward the archetypal colonial – those moustachioed men in their pith helmets – have shifted significantly, the stereotype itself has altered little. Thus, although anti-colonial and post-colonial writing has started to redress the nature of the images of the colonized and the nature of colonial histories, the rather limited stereotype of the colonizer often remains intact. I want to suggest that it is also important to draw a more complex vision of the colonizers because this image also serves to distance ourselves from the colonial era. By seeing the complexity of colonial relations, we are also more able to see how colonialism is more closely linked to the complexities of current relationships.

The tendency to distance ourselves from the past leads to two problems: on the one hand, there is an inability to see that colonial contexts were in themselves complex domains of competing discourses and that liberal doctrines were as much an aspect of colonialism as illiberal ones. On the other hand, there is the concomitant inability to see that discourses of the present may have direct lineages to the colonial past. It is my contention, therefore, that we need to see how the complexities of the present may be mirrored in the complexities of the past, and thus how current understandings of language and language teaching may mirror earlier understandings; and we need to see how the simplicities of the past are mirrored by simplicities of the present, and thus how, for example, constructions of Self and Other continue into the present. My strategy to combat these images of past and present, therefore, has been to develop on the one hand an understanding of colonial complexity in order to mirror the present, and an understanding of present simplicity in order to mirror the past.

## Outline

In the rest of this book I shall try to pull together the themes that I have raised here. In the next chapter I shall discuss the background to colonialism. As the discussion so far has already suggested, my interest here will be not so much in some meticulous linear history of the material aspects of colonialism but rather in the cultural constructs that produced and were produced by this exploitation, on the one hand the construction of the colonial Other, the discourses that have named and derogated native peoples in different colonies, and on the other hand the construction of the Self, those colonial discourses that named and prioritized the European colonizers. Thus, after discussing various important concepts and distinctions for the understanding of colonialism, I shall chart out how colonialism produced a series of dichotomous constructs – the cultured and the natural, the industrious and the indolent, the clean and the dirty, the adult and the child, the male and the female – for colonized people (the second item in each pair) and colonizers. These constructions of Self and Other have then continued to produce images of Us and Them, of Our language and culture and Theirs. These two themes will then be taken up separately in Chapters 5 and 6.

Chapter 3 looks at the construction of education policy in India. A central point here will be to argue against the common understanding of the dominance of Macaulay's Anglicism and to show, by contrast, that colonial language policy was a complex site of cultural construction. This chapter will look at how, amid the often competing demands of colonial governance, various colonial language policies emerged that both reflected and produced colonial discourses: the liberal discourse of the civilizing mission and the moral obligation to bring enlightenment to backward peoples; the need to provide a productive and docile workforce who would also become consumers within colonial capitalism; the various Orientalist positions, including an exoticisation and glorification of a distant Indian past and a belief that vernacular languages were the most efficient way to spread European knowledge in India; and the Anglicist insistence that English should be the language of education. Such discourses, it is suggested, had important effects in terms of the production of the cultural constructs of colonialism. While the proper role for English was being debated, constructions of Self and Other were constantly produced, and as the debates wore on, such constructions came increasingly to adhere to English.

Chapter 4 turns to look at educational policy in Hong Kong as a cultural construction of colonialism emerging in very clear response to material circumstances. This chapter traces how certain discourses of language education were constructed and reconstructed with particular implications – both material and discursive – down to the post-colonial present in Hong Kong. As I try to show, we need to understand how Anglicist and Orientalist discourses, images of Self and Other, views on Chinese education or the need for muscular morality, intersect, that policies favouring English and policies favouring Chinese frequently emerged from different approaches to using education for colonial purposes. Thus, this chapter explores what I call the 'double-edged sword of language education', the quandary that provision of both education in the first language and education in English were equally part of colonial rule.

Chapter 5 focuses on one particular aspect of this colonial production of images: the construction of English. This chapter, then, develops the arguments of this book further by looking at the colonial origins and the colonial continuity of images of the Self, the colonizers and their language and culture. I examine various discourses on English, pointing to some remarkable similarities between the rhetoric of nineteenth century writers on the English language and current writing on the global spread of English. These Anglicist discourses of the colonizers show how constructs of European and more particularly English superiority play an important role in how English is understood as a language and how the native speaker in particular is portrayed. This chapter also argues for the importance of seeing the predominant use of English in ELT classes not so much as a methodological issue but as a product of colonialism.

Chapter 6 addresses the other side of this relationship: returning to the theme of the construction of the Other, it focuses particularly on how images of Chinese culture have been produced through the discourses of colonialism. It shows how Orientalist discourses on China have evolved and yet also remained strangely consistent from the fifteenth to the twentieth century. Through an analysis of a range of different texts, but with a particular focus on travel writing, this chapter argues that it is in such popular cultural constructs that part of the construction of the instructed Other may be found. It then looks at how such images of China have particular implications for how Chinese learners are understood as language learners. Finally, it discusses how these observations relate to constructions of other language learners.

Finally, Chapter 7 returns to the question of possible resistance to such adherent discourses. Arguing that such resistance and change is hard work, that the adherence of these discourses to English, and their constant reinvocation in many contexts from travel writing to English language teaching, make attempts to change this relationship between language and discourse an uphill task, this chapter looks at current issues in education in Hong Kong, students' writing on their relationship to English, and some of the challenges, limitations and possibilities for change posed by the view of English and the discourses of colonialism that I have developed here. It concludes on a pessi-mistic note in light of recent resurgences of colonial discourses in Australia.

# 2

# THE CULTURAL CONSTRUCTS
# OF COLONIALISM

A relentless reciprocity binds the colonizer to the colonized.

(Sartre, 1957 p. xxviii)

Colonization works to *decivilize* the colonizer, to *brutalize* him in the true sense of the word, to degrade him, to awaken him to buried instincts, to covetousness, violence, race hatred, and moral relativism.

(Césaire, 1972, p. 13)

Europe undertook the leadership of the world with ardour, cynicism and violence. . . . That same Europe where they were never done talking of Man, and where they never stopped proclaiming that they were only anxious for the welfare of Man: today we know with what sufferings humanity has paid for every one of their triumphs of the mind.

(Fanon, 1963, p. 251)

The Native, the Indigenous person, the Aboriginal, is, I believe, as much a construction of the Master text of the European as is the Master himself.

(Mudrooroo, 1995, p. 8)

As I suggested in the previous chapter, a central focus of this book is how colonialism produced cultural forms, how it was a site of cultural production rather than just a site of cultural imperialism (see Viswanathan, 1989; Young, 1990). These cultural products of colonialism, I argued, are the discourses that map out relationships of Self and Other. And these discourses of Self and Other have a particular relationship to English because of their interwoven histories and because of the particular relationships they articulate around English. Discourses of the Other adhere to English both because of the history of co-articulations and because of the relationship between English and the discourses of the Self (discourses about English) and between the discourses of the Self and the discourses of the Other.

This chapter seeks to map out the background to the idea of the cultural constructs of colonialism. The focus of this chapter, therefore, is not on colonial exploitation in material terms but rather on the cultural conditions that produced and were produced by this context of exploitation. These cultural constructions may be seen as a series of dichotomous pairs, such as adult and child or industrious and indolent, dividing colonizers from the colonized. As constructions of Self and Other, these dichotomous images have continued to reproduce images of Us and Them, of colonizing languages and cultures and colonized languages and cultures. And, perhaps most importantly, these constructs have left their colonial origins behind and continue to reproduce in a discursive field linked to many institutions and domains. Before exploring these constructs, however, I shall turn first of all to a discussion of various key issues around colonialism in order to explain more clearly what I am trying to deal with here and how my view of colonialism fits in with imperialism, neo-colonialism, and postcolonialism.

## Colonialism, imperialism and culture

At one level the concept of colonialism is fairly unproblematic, referring to the settlement of territory in one region or country by people from outside that area, with control over the new territory generally remaining in the hands of the country from which the colonizers have come. Imperialism, generally speaking, can then be seen as the larger organization of colonies into one economic, military or political system controlled by the imperial power. Even at this level, however, various difficulties emerge. Imperialism, as Raymond Williams (1983) points out, is ambiguous as to whether it refers primarily to an economic or a political system. If it is the latter, then the political independence of colonies signifies the end of colonialism and ultimately the end of imperialism. If, however, as many have argued, it is understood primarily in economic terms, political independence may not signal any particular change in the economic imperialism to which a country may be subjected. It is in this sense that the terms 'neo-imperialism' and 'neo-colonialism' have come into common usage, though there is also a possible confusion here since it would generally seem to be 'neo-imperialism' which is being referred to in the more common term 'neo-colonialism'.

Thornton (1965) suggests that 'colonialism is only imperialism seen from below' (p. 6). Colonialism in this view, therefore, is not so much a status as it is a state of mind, the 'context of existence' for those who are subject to rather than agents of international power. 'Imperialism', he suggests, was used to dignify Crusoe's relationship to Friday; 'colonialism' was Friday's awareness of his subjugation. On the one hand, such a position opens up a fruitful avenue of thought, namely that colonialism is not a secondary aspect of imperialism but rather the lived experiences of those that experience imperialism. On the other hand, this seems to suggest rather problematically that colonialism is only experienced by the colonized and imperialism by the colonizers. I shall be arguing that colonialism is also a lived experience of the colonizers, one that has very broad implications.

Said (1993) adopts a fairly standard position on the relationship between colonialism and imperialism: 'As I shall be using the term, "imperialism" means the practice, the theory, and the attitudes of a dominating metropolitan centre ruling a distant territory; "colonialism", which is almost always a consequence of imperialism, is the implanting of settlements on distant territory' (p. 8). It is evident from Said's comments, however, that imperialism must also be seen in terms of practices, theories and attitudes as well as material exploitation and control. I shall argue, furthermore, that rather than this diffusionist model of Said's, whereby imperialism is the superordinate category and colonialism merely the site of its implementation, colonialism needs to be seen as a primary site of cultural production whose products have flowed back through the imperial system.

### Material or cultural colonialism

First of all, then, there is a long tradition of critical commentary that has sought to show the fundamental inequities of colonial exploitation as one aspect of imperialism. A classic early example of this line of criticism is Hobson's (1902) book on imperialism.[1] Through extensive analysis of imperial economics, he argues that imperialism has been 'bad business for the nation' but 'good business for certain classes and certain trades within the nation' (p. 51). He goes on to criticize the hypocritical claims that imperialism promotes self-government: this 'theory that Britons are a race endowed, like the Romans, with a genius for government, that our colonial and imperial policy is animated by a resolve to spread throughout the world the arts of free self-government which we enjoy at home' is 'quite the largest misstatement of the facts of our colonial and imperial policy that is possible'. 'Upon the vast majority of the populations throughout our Empire,' he continues, 'we have bestowed no real powers of self-government, nor have we any serious intention of doing so, or any serious belief that it is possible for us to do so' (p. 120).

He then takes to task the tendency to claim that imperialism is in the name of a moral mission. The principal emphasis of this criticism is on the way that 'a natural history law', namely the natural struggle between the races, is turned into 'a moral enthusiasm', and thus a doctrine 'emerging from natural history' 'soon takes on a large complexity of ethical and religious finery, and we are wafted into an elevated atmosphere of "imperial Christianity", a "mission of civilization", in which we are to teach "the arts of good government" and "the dignity of labour"' (p. 166). Hobson's critique moves on to look at how the economic and political motivations for imperialism become submerged beneath moral and sentimental excuses. Why, he asks, 'does

Imperialism escape general recognition for the narrow, sordid thing it is?'
(p. 207). He sees similar problems in the growing imperial presence in China
and concludes that 'For Europe to rule Asia by force for purposes of gain,
and to justify that rule by the pretence that she is civilizing Asia and raising
her to a higher level of spiritual life, will be adjudged by history, perhaps, to
be the crowning wrong and folly of Imperialism' (p. 346).

He also turns to look at the iniquitous realities of the treatment of 'lower
races'. Where white settlers find local people in possession of land rich in
resources, they are subject to a 'double temptation':

> They want possession of the land and control of a cheap native
> supply of labour to work it under their control and gain. If the
> 'natives' are of too low an order or too untamable to be trained for
> effective labour they must be expelled or exterminated, as in the
> case of the 'lower nomads' the Bushmen of Australia and South
> Africa, the Negritos, Bororos, Veddhas, &c, and even the Indians of
> North America. War, murder, strong drink, syphilis and other
> civilised diseases are chief instruments of a destruction commonly
> couched under the euphemism 'contact with superior civilisation'.
>
> (pp. 271–2)

He thus questions both the practices by which European nations seek to
implant their alien institutions into their colonies and the way in which they
refuse to acknowledge the deep-seated hypocrisies that underlie these
practices:

> What actually confronts us everywhere in modern history is selfish,
> materialistic, short-sighted, national competition, varied by occa-
> sional collusion. When any common international policy is adopted
> for dealing with the lower races it has partaken of the nature, not of
> a moral trust, but of a business 'deal'.
>
> (p. 254)

It is not the intention of this book, however, to conduct a critique in this
style. I have quoted at length from Hobson here to illustrate the significance
and the long history of such critique. But, as can also be seen from Hobson's
discussion, his critique of imperialism leaves unquestioned the notion of a
natural struggle between races or existence of 'lower races': he is critical
about their treatment but does not question their existence. As I have been
suggesting, the primary focus of my analysis is not the economic or political
domains. From this more materialist point of view, whatever one's focus of
analysis – colonial history, art history, literary studies – this will always be
related back to issues of colonial and imperial exploitation. Chrisman and
Williams (1994), for example, argue that the connection between politics

and economics made possible by Marxist thought gives the clearest way of understanding the relationship between colonialism and imperialism:

> In this view, colonialism, the conquest and direct control of other people's land, is a particular phase in the history of imperialism, which is now best understood as the globalisation of the capitalist mode of production, its penetration of previously non-capitalist regions of the world, and destruction of pre- or non-capitalist forms of social organization.
>
> (p. 2)

While acknowledging the importance of these arguments, there are a number of implications of this statement that I want to resist. First, it suggests that colonialism is necessarily subordinate to imperialism, a stage in the larger history of imperial expansion; second, it locates the central problematic in the global spread of a capitalist mode of production; and third, by doing so, it relegates non-economic questions to the background.

I do not intend to argue systematically against such assumptions, but rather to explain the position on colonialism that I wish to take up here. Importantly, there are a number of different ways of viewing colonialism. In the introduction to his book on the psychological structures and cultural forces of colonialism in India, Nandy (1983) points out that he uses the term in three different senses: from one point of view, colonialism started in India in 1757 (with the Indian defeat at the battle of Plassey) and ended in 1947 (when India gained its independence); from a different perspective, colonialism began in the late 1820s, with the development of colonial theories of culture, and ended in the 1930s, when Ghandi showed the hollowness of such theories; and from yet another perspective, colonialism began in 1947 with the removal of the formal supports of colonial culture, and is still at the centre of a cultural and ideological battle.

The position that I want to argue for here is that while it is always important to understand the frameworks of global exploitation that are imperialism, it is equally important to understand colonialism in cultural and discursive terms. There are a number of reasons for this position. First of all, I want to argue that although colonialism and imperialism were clearly economically driven, they are in fact far more complex. According to Said (1993):

> Neither imperialism nor colonialism is a simple act of accumulation and acquisition. Both are supported and perhaps even impelled by impressive ideological formations that include notions that certain territories and people *require* and beseech domination, as well as forms of knowledge affiliated with domination.
>
> (p. 8)

Similarly, Nandy (1983) suggests that 'It is becoming increasingly obvious that colonialism – as we have come to know it during the last two hundred years – cannot be identified with only economic gain and political power' (p. 1). For Nandy, colonialism is crucially a 'state of mind in the colonizers and the colonized, a colonial consciousness which includes the sometimes unrealizable wish to make economic and political profits from the colonies, but other elements too' (pp. 1–2). Colonialism was about far more than just economic and political exploitation.

In suggesting that the cultural and discursive domains be seen as crucial, I am not merely arguing that we need to look beyond economic and political control; I am also making an argument concerning the production of cultures, discourses and ideologies. Alatas (1977) argues that:

> The vigorous outburst of colonialism in the 19th century was accompanied by intellectual trends which sought to justify the phenomenon. Colonialism, or on a bigger scale, imperialism, was not only an extension of sovereignty and control by one nation and its government over another, but it was also a control of the mind of the conquered or subordinated.
>
> (p. 17)

Yet I also want to go beyond this argument about the colonial or imperial production of *justificatory* 'intellectual trends'. What I am suggesting is that cultural, ideological or discursive aspects of colonialism are not mere reflexes of the material domain. It is frequently suggested that the ideologies of colonialism, particularly its profound racism, were 'rationalizations' or 'justifications' for colonialism. I want to argue that this is only partially true, for my argument here is that the cultural and ideological domains have a certain autonomy: in some senses, colonialism can be seen as the material manifestation of the beliefs in racial and cultural superiority. Van Arkel (1982) makes a similar point when he suggests that the view that racism is a product of capitalism and imperialism is the result of 'a not unjustified but one-sided Marxist interpretation of racism as an excuse for exploitation' (p. 15). The argument I am making, then, does not see cultural developments as always based on prior material 'realities', particularly those in the socio-economic domain, but accords a greater sense of cultural independence and human agency to this process. At the very least, there is a reciprocal relationship here, with cultures and ideologies both enabling and being generated by colonialism.

Another reason for distancing myself from the functionalist ideology argument – ideologies are produced to justify certain actions – is that this suggests too easy a taking-up and a putting-down again of ideology: they are produced to explain or justify certain practices and then may be dropped once those practices no longer exist. While I am not trying to distance myself

entirely from the obvious way in which ideologies *are* used to justify behaviour, I want to argue that they emerge from a complex existing network of
discursive possibilities, that their deployment is far less functional than many
accounts allow (they can exist in apparent contradiction to more obvious
practical needs), and, most significantly for my argument here, they often
continue to exist well after the conditions of their production have changed.

The view that colonial ideologies are not mere servants to a larger economic or political goal also allows for more space to understand that such
ideologies were frequently contradictory (see Metcalf, 1995; Thomas, 1994;
Viswanathan, 1989). As Dirks (1996) suggests with respect to attempts to
construct too monolithic a view of colonial ideology in India, such an
understanding 'runs the risk of conflating cause with effect, or ascribing
intention as well as system to a congeries of activities and a conjunction of
outcomes which, though related and at times coordinated, were usually
diffuse, disorganized, and even contradictory' (p.xvi).

The view I am developing here, then, has important implications for how
colonialism and imperialism are understood. A view that takes the socio-
economic domain as primary seeks explanations and means for change in that
domain. As Nandy (1983) suggests, however, in many ways it is the cultural
and psychological effects of colonialism that matter, hence the title of his
book, *The intimate enemy: Loss and recovery of self under colonialism,* or the call
of others to 'decolonize the mind' (see for example Ngũgĩ, 1986). If we
develop this more psychological or cultural view of colonialism, then opposition, struggle or resistance to colonialism has to be fought as much in the
cultural or psychological domains as in the material or economic. A similar
distinction between a materialist and a non-materialist understanding of
'postcolonialism' may also be made: in the same way that it is useful to distinguish between postmodernity and postmodernism (Lyon, 1994), the
former being a term used to describe a current condition – the state of life
and thought in late capitalist society – while the latter is an intellectual and
cultural movement that seeks to deconstruct givens of dominant modes of
thought and to open a space for diversity, so it is useful to distinguish
between postcoloniality and postcolonialism (cf. Appiah, 1991), the former
being a material state after the end of colonialism and the latter a political
and cultural movement that seeks to challenge the received histories and
ideologies of former colonial nations and to open a space for insurgent
knowledges to emerge.

My understanding of colonialism, then, is not as a secondary phase of
imperialism but rather as a primary site of cultural production. My argument
is *not* that economic, physical, political and other material aspects of colonialism are inconsequential: the deaths, imprisonments, diseases, beatings,
economic deprivations of colonialism matter fundamentally. But my interest
in colonialism rather than imperialism derives from viewing imperialism as a
system through which the cultural constructs of colonialism have flowed

back into the hearts of empires rather than as a system of global capitalism (which it obviously also was). My focus will be on the cultural constructions, the discourses, of colonialism, not as rationalizations for imperial exploitation but as fundamental aspects of European culture that may predate colonialism and certainly have outlived its formal end. Once we start to take an interest in the longer-lasting cultural effects of colonialism, the economic and political distinction between colonialism and imperialism starts to collapse 'since the basic principles of this discourse, rooted in the very foundations of Western culture, also constitute the discourse of imperialism. Imperialism has survived the formal ending of colonial rule, but so has colonial discourse' (Spurr, 1993, p. 5).

### Structure, agency and good intentions

A critical view of colonialism confronts other problems, particularly issues of how the role of individuals is to be understood within the systems, cultures or ideologies of colonialism. I have already suggested that my interest here is not in a deterministic thesis of cultural imperialism whereby colonial culture is imposed on colonized people; rather, my interest is in the cultural productions of colonialism. But it is nevertheless important to consider where to place individual actors within this framework. Several of these problems can be found in Sweeting's (1990) book on colonial education policies in Hong Kong, in which he argues against a 'crude and simplistic "colonialistic" interpretation of educational development in Hong Kong' (p. 3) since such an analysis cannot account for the diversity of colonial ideas, actions and intentions or for the context in which they occur. In one sense, he is quite right in pointing to the dangers of simplistic cultural imperialism theses and of viewing Hong Kong people as *tabula rasa* on whom colonial education, culture and knowledge were imposed. But in another sense, his view is surely inadequate. First, he is adamant that a balanced and fair view can be achieved by presenting 'facts' rather than 'opinions' and thus warns against the writer who has 'intruded his or her own opinions and assumptions, or has unconsciously reflected the prejudices of the time' (p. 3). Quite how Sweeting believes that such opinions or prejudices are to be avoided, or how such a clear distinction between fact and opinion can be maintained, or how a presentation of historical fact rather than opinion can allow for free, unbiased interpretation, is unclear.

Second, he argues that we should consider the beliefs and intentions of the colonizers: 'The Governor [Hennessy] . . . believed, with some justification, that he was acting in the interests of the local Chinese who were fully convinced of the value of learning English' (p. 2) and:

> Missionaries may have sounded at times dismissive of traditional
> Chinese education and culture, but many of them worked hard and

sincerely in what they considered to be the interests of the Chinese, perhaps most notably in the field of female education; and some of them respected the culture sufficiently to become distinguished sinologues.

(p. 3)

This raises an extremely important question: Are we trying to judge the intentions and actions of individuals or to understand the historical location of actions and ideas? If we are interested in judging individuals and whether they acted ethically or honourably according to the ideologies of the time, Sweeting's arguments may be of interest. But if we are interested less in making judgements of individuals and more in understanding discursive frameworks and their effects, then Sweeting's position surely misses the point: however well-intentioned missionaries, colonial officers and the like may have been, those intentions cannot be removed either from the effects of their actions or from the ideologies within which they are constructed. A. Williams (1995) makes this point with respect to the forced removal of Aboriginal children in Australia from their homes. Many of those involved in this, he suggests, 'acted from what they saw as an impeccable motive – a desire to ensure better lives for the children they were replacing,' and yet in hindsight it is clear that the 'horrendous and destructive nature of this prac-tice' (p. 21) renders such good intentions unable to exculpate those involved from the consequences of their actions (and see, for example, McGrath, 1995a). Thus, while I think Sweeting is right that it is important to avoid a reductionist and deterministic view of colonialism and cultural imperialism – both because of what is missed by such analyses and because of the dangers of constructing a passive colonized Other – his own insistence on facts and good intentions leave no space for a critical understanding of how either of these are constructed.

An interesting parallel here can be found in recent discussions of Winston Churchill. Reviewing Andrew Roberts' *Eminent Churchillians*, for example, Deedes (1994) argues that Churchill should not be seen as racist simply because of his use of such terms as 'niggers', 'chinks', 'baboons' and 'blacka-moors'. Deedes argues, first, that Churchill cannot be judged by the current understandings of such terms, since these terms and the way they are now interpreted have changed greatly since Churchill's time; and, second, that since such terms were common during Churchill's time, he cannot be held accountable: 'Is a man who in the last century fought in African wars . . . and who then called his enemies "fuzzy-wuzzies", now to be accused of racism?' (p. 19). At one level, Deedes has a point to make here: such terms and their interpretation have indeed changed over time; the word 'Negro', for example, was a less racially marked term than it is today and it would be unjustified to assume that someone using this term twenty years ago was thereby necessarily racist. On the other hand, there are a lot more problems with the argument that because many people used such terms, we cannot single out one of them as racist. Churchill lived in times when racist ideologies abounded and himself espoused many racist ideas (see p. 64). To espouse currently held racist (or sexist, homophobic etc.) views does not make one less racist (sexist, homophobic), it merely shifts a degree of culpability from the individual to the cultural and ideological frameworks in which he or she lives. Sweeting seems to fall into the same trap: by arguing that theories of cultural imperialism may be too deterministic and that we need to consider the 'good intentions' of the individuals, he shifts the focus away from both the cultural-ideological context and the effects of colonialism, arguing instead for a kind of historical relativism whereby we cannot judge the past because it is different.

Thus, the argument that we should consider the good or bad intentions of colonialists is problematic for a number of reasons. If good or bad intentions are considered simply in terms of whether an individual honestly believed in what they were doing (they acted honestly in terms of their own beliefs), then anything can be justified as well-intentioned: it doesn't matter what you do, it matters that you believe that it is right. Even if we expand this notion to suggest that to act with good intentions must include not only action in accordance with one's beliefs but also beliefs that one's actions will be of benefit to others, we are still left in a closed circle. To judge people's intentions by whether they truly believed that what they were doing was in the interest of others still permits anything to be justified: if it was truly believed that killing Jews was to the benefit of a greater Germany and a greater Europe, then the 'good intentions' of some perpetrator of mass genocide may be excused because they believed they were doing good. Those who removed Indigenous Australian children from their homes, acted with good intentions: they thought this was the only way to give these children a good chance in life. Surely, simply to deal with an individual's belief in the righteousness of their cause is, at the very least, inadequate. Rather we need, first, to look at the cultural and ideological frameworks that produce those beliefs, and second, to look at the effects of those beliefs. That is to say, we need to be able to judge the discourses of colonialism on moral grounds and to evaluate the effects of colonial actions. By doing this we are able to separate judgements about individuals from judgements about beliefs. Thus, we can argue that a person acted in the belief that they were doing good, but were doing so within a way of thinking that was deeply problematic.

From this point of view I think we are able to avoid the pitfalls of individualism and historical relativism, of attempting to understand history in terms of individual intentions or of viewing historical periods and beliefs as cultures unto themselves and therefore not amenable to our criticisms. So, to look at the construction of racial superiority in colonial discourse is not necessarily to criticize the intentions of individual colonial actors (though the material realizations of such discourses must always be open to critical scrutiny): if that is one's interest, then one needs to consider the availability of alternative discursive positions and one needs to look at a person's actions and beliefs relative to their contemporaries. But an interest in the cultural and discursive constructs of colonialism allows for a far more critical assessment. The way forward here is to develop, first, a critical view that avoids economic and cultural determinism but never loses sight of the very real relations of social, cultural, political and economic domination; second, an understanding that intentions may, in some sense, exculpate the agent, but that ultimately it is more useful to attempt to understand the cultural constructs rather than the individual intentions of colonialism; and, third, a view of culture and discourse that shows how attitudes and intentions are constructed within certain discourses and how, for example, to be a sinologist, does not in the least remove one from relations of power and knowledge (see Chapter 3).

Sweeting's arguments about facts, opinions and intentions are closely tied to the insistence, commonly heard in Hong Kong, that the benefits of colonialism outweigh the drawbacks, or at least that one should always try to see 'both sides' of colonialism. This argument needs to be strongly resisted not because colonialism did not in some senses bring some positive aspects but because of the many problematic ideas that it puts into play. First, it tends to construct the colonized — and especially those who resist colonialism — as unappreciative and unable to understand the benefits that are being bestowed on them. As West (1906) commented:

> There is amongst too many of the educated classes in India a disposition to take all that has been done, all that has been conceded, as a mere matter of course, all that has been withheld as a just ground for discontent. . . . Worst of all, there is a tendency amongst clever but feather-headed Hindus to deem lightly and speak lightly of their obligations as subjects and citizens of the empire.
>
> (p. xxiv)

This view that the benefits of colonialism have gone unappreciated is an old colonial trope in constant need of resistance.

Second, this argument does not take into account the fact that the overwhelming mass of writing on colonialism has occurred in the colonisers' languages and has extolled the virtues of the colonial enterprise. Given the extent of this work, it hardly seems an imperative to reiterate the supposed benefits of colonialism. Third, this argument almost inevitably starts with the assumption that colonies had problems (poverty, backwardness, political despotism etc.) that could be solved by Western intervention, and furthermore defines the terms on which this balance sheet should be calculated. Thus, the comparison is always an unfair one in that on the one hand it starts with a list of advantages and then shows that these were lacking before colonialism,

43

and on the other it does not take into account the many other negative effects of colonialism. But Césaire, among many others, has made this point with far more passion and eloquence than I am able to:

> They talk to me about progress, about 'achievements', diseases cured, improved standards of living.
> *I* am talking about societies drained of their essence, cultures trampled underfoot, institutions undermined, lands confiscated, religions smashed, magnificent artistic creations destroyed, extraordinary *possibilities* wiped out.
> They throw facts at my head, statistics, mileages of roads, canals, and railroad tracks.
> *I* am talking about thousands of men sacrificed to the Congo-Océan [Brazzaville to Pointe-Noire railway]. I am talking about those who, as I write this, are digging the harbor of Abidjan by hand. I am talking about millions of men torn from their gods, their land, their habits, their life – from life, from the dance, from wisdom.
> I am talking about millions of men in whom fear has been cunningly instilled, who have been taught to have an inferiority complex, to tremble, kneel, despair, and behave like flunkeys.
> They dazzle me with the tonnage of cotton or cocoa that has been exported, the acreage that has been planted with olive trees or grapevines.
> *I* am talking about natural *economies* that have been disrupted – harmonious and viable *economies* adapted to the indigenous population – about food crops destroyed, malnutrition permanently introduced, agricultural development oriented solely toward the benefit of the metropolitan countries, about the looting of products, the looting of raw materials.
> They pride themselves on abuses eliminated.
> I too talk about abuses, but what I say is that on the old ones – very real – they have superimposed others – very detestable. They talk to me about local tyrants brought to reason; but I note that in general the old tyrants get on very well with the new ones, and that there has been established between them, to the detriment of the people, a circuit of mutual services and complicity.
> They talk to me about civilization, I talk about proletarianization and mystification.
>
> (Césaire, 1972, pp. 21–2)

### The disfigured colonizer

The final point I wish to emphasize here before moving on to look in greater detail at the cultural constructs of colonialism, is that colonialism is deeply bound up with European culture. The significant issue here is that although colonialism has generally fostered few close connections between colonized and colonizers, both are nevertheless indelibly linked by the colonial process. As Sartre (1957) put it in his introduction to Memmi's *The colonizer and the colonized*, 'A relentless reciprocity binds the colonizer to the colonized' (p. xxviii). Thus, as Nandy (1983) suggests, the colonizer should not necessarily be seen as 'the conspiratorial dedicated oppressor that he is made out to be, but a self-destructive co-victim with a reified life-style and a parochial culture, caught in the hinges of history he swears by' (p. xv). The important point here is that although we need on the one hand to acknowledge that these 'self-destructive co-victims' brought the very real oppressions of colonialism, on the other hand we need to see that by so doing they also had devastating effects on their own cultures. European and American culture has to no small extent been produced in the cradle of colonialism.

Colonization, says Memmi (1965), 'can only disfigure the colonizer' (p. 147). Césaire (1972) makes the point more strongly: 'colonization works to *decivilize* the colonizer, to *brutalize* him in the true sense of the word, to degrade him, to awaken him to buried instincts, to covetousness, violence, race hatred, and moral relativism' (p. 13). As I have already mentioned in the last chapter, Césaire argues that Nazism was but the inward turn of colonial practices on Europeans. Hitler, he suggests, 'applied to Europe colonialist procedures which until then had been reserved exclusively for the Arabs of Algeria, the coolies of India, and the blacks of Africa' (p. 14). Even if one accepts this argument, however, colonialism can still be seen, like Nazism, as an aberrant departure from the otherwise civilized cultures of Europe. But Césaire goes on to argue that 'a nation which colonizes, . . . a civilization which justifies colonization – and therefore force – is already a sick civilization, a civilization that is morally diseased . . .' (p. 18). What he is getting at here is that Nazism is colonialism revisited on Europe and that colonialism is an essential part of European culture, that is to say that European culture produced Nazism as surely as it produced those aspects of which it is more proud.

According to Fanon (1963):

> Europe undertook the leadership of the world with ardour, cynicism and violence. . . . That same Europe where they were never done talking of Man, and where they never stopped proclaiming that they were only anxious for the welfare of Man: today we know with what sufferings humanity has paid for every one of their triumphs of the mind.
>
> (p. 251)

As Young (1990, p. 9) suggests, it is this relationship between European enlightenment, with its 'grand projects and universal truth-claims', and the history of European colonialism that Césaire and Fanon brought to light. And thus it becomes clear that:

> humanism itself, often validated among the highest values of European civilization, was deeply complicit with the violent negativity of colonialism, and played a crucial part in its ideology. The formation of the ideas of human nature, humanity and the universal qualities of the human mind as the common good of an ethical civilization occurred at the same time as those particularly violent centuries in the history of the world now known as the era of Western colonialism.
>
> (p. 121)

I am concerned here with both the general European relationships to colonialism and the more specific British relationships. As part of Europe and as the major colonizing nation, Britain shares a great deal with the broad ideological climate of colonizing Europe. At the same time, however, the cultures and practices of different colonizing nations varied quite widely and it is thus important also to look at British colonialism in its own specificity. Indeed the temporal, political, economic and geographical magnitude of British colonialism would suggest that the effects of colonialism would be even greater on Britain than on other countries. Nandy suggests that:

> The experience of colonizing did not leave the internal culture of Britain untouched. It began to bring into prominence those parts of the British political culture which were least tender and humane. It de-emphasized speculation, intellection and *caritas* as feminine, and justified a limited cultural role for women – and femininity – by holding that the softer side of human nature was irrelevant to the public sphere. It openly sanctified – in the name of such values as competition, achievement, control and productivity – new forms of institutionalized violence and ruthless social Darwinism. The instrumental concept of the lower classes it promoted was perfectly in tune with the needs of industrial capitalism and only a slightly modified version of the colonial concept of hierarchy was applied to the British society itself. The tragedy of colonialism was also the tragedy of the younger sons, the women, and all 'the etceteras and and-so-forths' of Britain.
>
> (1983, p. 32)

In the next section I shall start to explore what I see as the crucial dimensions of these discourses of colonialism. Although the topic of this book is the relationship between English, English language teaching and colonialism, I shall not at this juncture be looking specifically at ELT. This relationship will be explored more specifically in later chapters.

## Colonial dichotomies

Given the 'relentless reciprocity that binds colonizer and colonized', it is hard to separate these constructs of Self and Other. Juxtaposed with every primitive savage there must be a civilized gentleman, for every despotic regime there must be a model of democratic government, every childlike, irrational, heathen native must have a mature, rational, Christian opposite. As Metcalf (1995) explains:

> as Europeans constructed a sense of self for themselves apart from the old order of Christendom, they had of necessity to create a notion of an 'other' beyond the seas. To describe oneself as 'enlightened' meant that someone else had to be shown as 'savage' or 'vicious'. To describe oneself as 'modern', or as 'progressive', meant that those who were not included in that definition had to be described as 'primitive' or 'backward'. Such alterity, what one might call the creation of doubleness, was an integral part of the Enlightenment project.
>
> (p. 6)

In this section I want to illustrate the diverse yet strangely homogeneous colonial constructs of colonialism. An important part of my argument is worth keeping in mind here: I want to consider these colonial constructs not merely as justifications for colonialism but rather as cultural conditions that both enabled and were generated by colonialism. Thus, although they figure massively in the writing and thinking of the central era of colonialism, their origins are not necessarily in that period and, most importantly, they have existed as cultural beliefs well beyond the formal end of colonial rule in most parts of the world.

### Europe and the Other: the Inside and the Outside

Returning for a moment to Hobson's (1902) critique of imperialism discussed above, it is clear that however critical he may be of imperialism as he saw it, he still subscribes to two of the most basic tenets of colonialism: the belief in the superiority of Europe and the existence of 'lower races'. At the heart of this belief is what Blaut (1993) has called 'Eurocentric diffusionism':

> Europeans are seen as the 'makers of history.' Europe eternally advances, progresses, modernizes. The rest of the world advances

more sluggishly, or stagnates: it is 'traditional society.' Therefore, the world has a permanent geographical center and a permanent periphery: an Inside and an Outside. Inside leads, Outside lags. Inside innovates, Outside imitates.

(p. 1)

Such Eurocentric diffusionism is 'quite simply the colonizer's model of the world' (p. 10). Chakravarty (1989) describes this 'Raj Syndrome' in similar terms: 'European attitudes towards the non-European societies were largely conditioned by a significant Euro-centric consciousness. To all intents and purposes Europe was presented, in sharp contrast to the non-European world, as the centre of the universe' (p. 217).

Thus, as Metcalf (1995, p. 34) suggests, 'The hierarchical ordering of societies on a 'scale of civilization' reflected not just the classifying enthusiasms of the Enlightenment, but was a way to reassure the British that they themselves occupied a secure position, as the arbiter of its values, on the topmost rung'. There are any number of examples of writing that celebrate colonialism and imperialism, urging Great Britain to fulfill its mission to civilize the world. I shall give a few examples here before looking in greater detail at this colonial discourse. Early in the nineteenth century, Thomas Arnold (1815) in his essay on 'The Effects of Distant Colonisation on the Parent State', argued that although the principal benefits of colonization were commercial, for many people the real benefits, 'the happy magic of Colonisation', lay in 'the glory and happiness of diffusing the light of the Gospel amongst poor and blinded Pagans' (p. 29). 'The Parent Country,' he continued, 'shall reflect with comfort, that when the course of human events shall have consigned it to oblivion, its name and language shall be perpetuated by its children in a far distant land' (p. 30). Happy are those, therefore, 'who crave the honour of being the channel of so much happiness to the world' (p. 30).

Caldecott (1901) is similarly clear about the right of Europe to have assumed 'the guidance of the world' (p. 5). Colonialism, he argues, has brought peace, security of persons and property, organization of industry and trade, and European science, literature, and religion to the world. 'We have won our way,' he suggests, 'not by weight of physical might, but by moral energy' (p. 69). Likewise, West (1906), discussing the 'sublime, civilising, humanising task apparently assigned to us' (p. xxiii), suggests that 'The British rule in India has been specially distinguished from all previous governments by the inestimable blessings it has conferred in security, justice and material development' (p. xiii) and urges that 'We must not halt in our onward march, or waver in that continual process of adaptation by which we have won, rather than commanded, co-operation and obedience' (p. xi). Finally (though one could fill another 50 pages with such examples), Alston (1907) argues that it is the moral duty of nations such as Britain to take up their civilizing mission to the world: 'It is not in our power to rest content in the midst of the countless hordes of lower beings, steeped in foul and degrading ideas of what man is and ought to be' (p. 4). Interestingly, Alston is quite critical of what he sees as the biased and unfair comparisons made by other writers between an idealized West and a decadent East, especially those made by the missionary who 'tends to contrast an idealised Christendom and the highest teaching of Christianity with the vileness of the darkened lives around him' (pp. 19–20). While criticizing such one-sided judgements of other races and trying hard to present a fair and balanced view, he remains nevertheless certain of European superiority:

> But while admitting the fallibility of our one-sided judgements on our own and other races' moral positions, it will be necessary to assume that our Western ideals, though not above criticism, and always susceptible of development, stand higher in the main than those which are at present effective elsewhere (except possibly in Japan).
>
> (p. 44)

Such Eurocentrism is perhaps so obviously part of colonialism that it would not seem to warrant much discussion. There are, however, three points I would like to make before moving on. First, as Blaut (1993) convincingly argues, this model of Eurocentric diffusionism is based on the 'myth of the European miracle'. There are two sides to his argument: on the one hand, he shows how, over the past five hundred years, Europe has constructed a view of itself as having always had qualities superior to the rest of the world, thus explaining colonialism as a result of European superiority; and on the other hand, he shows how this myth is in fact far from the truth, that in fact European development was a *result* of colonialism after 1492 and not a pre-1492 *cause* of development. Thus, he suggests, '*no* characteristic of Europe's environment, Europe's people, or Europe's culture, at any time prior to 1492, can be convincingly shown to have had anything to do with the fact that Europe developed while other civilizations did not do so' (p. 135). Rather, it was the economic boost brought about by colonialism as well as the benefits brought by greater trade and movement of ideas, cultures and technologies that brought about Europe's rapid development into a global economic and political power.

Second, I want to emphasize that although the focus here will be on ideas and beliefs that had their heyday during the era of mass colonialism, such ideas have many connections to current views of the world. From Eurocentric diffusionism to modern Eurocentrism, from views of racial superiority to current forms of racism, from academic complicity in providing a scientific rationale for racism and colonialism to more recent academic complicity in the 'Cold War', from nineteenth century views of the noble savage to the lush pages of *National Geographic,* from paternalistic views on education to modern concepts of modernization, there are many parallels to be drawn. Thus, although in its language and style we may find nineteenth and early twentieth century writing distant and faintly amusing, I want to argue for the need to take it very seriously and to seek the connections with more recent views on language, culture and race. Blaut (1993) argues that the modern concept of diffusionism still underlies the relationships that now exist between the First and Third Worlds. He goes on to argue that:

> our world-scale models, and many of our specific theories and factual truisms, are accepted mainly – and in some cases only – because of their conformality to the values of the European elites; . . . this has been the case since the beginning of the nineteenth century, and is true today.

> (p. 39)

Finally, as I shall discuss in the rest of this section, it is important to look beyond this general Eurocentrism at the more particular cultural constructions that were created by colonialism. Blaut (1993), for example, lists a series of dichotomies that were typical of diffusionist thought, the first characteristic in each pair belonging to Europeans, the second to non-Europeans: inventiveness vs. imitativeness, rationality/intellect vs. irrationality/emotion/ instinct, abstract thought vs. concrete thought, theoretical reasoning vs. empirical/practical reasoning, mind vs. body/matter, discipline vs. spontaneity, adulthood vs. childhood, sanity vs. insanity, science vs. sorcery, progress vs. stagnation (p. 17). Spurr's (1993) analysis of the 'rhetoric of empire' also emphasizes how 'the colonizer's insistence on difference from the colonized establishes a notion of the savage as *other*, the antithesis of civilized value' (p. 7).

Spurr identifies eleven tropes of colonial discourse: surveillance (the privileged vantage point), appropriation (rendering others' land and ideas as European), aestheticization (treating the Third World as material for sentimental human interest or melodramatic entertainment), classification (grouping colonized people into different categories, especially racial hierarchies), debasement (the constant description of the colonized as corrupt, dirty and dishonest), negation (viewing the Other in terms of absence, as lacking in language, culture and intellect), affirmation (the constant stress on European superiority), idealization (the view of native peoples as innocent, noble savages), insubstantialization (the description of colonized countries only as a backdrop for European voyages of inward discovery), naturalization (considering colonized people as following natural rather than cultural laws) and eroticization (comparing the relationship between colonizer and colonizer with that between men and women). Similarly, Singh (1996) points to the 'characteristic Orientalizing tropes of difference producing an ontological distinction between West and East, defining the Orient in terms of every-thing the Occident is not: decadent, weak, barbaric, feminine' (p. 59). It is worth observing that although in many respects these can be seen as forming part of a closely interwoven, Eurocentric view of the world, in other ways they also reveal a number of paradoxes and contradictions, as, for example, between the debasement and the idealization of colonized people. As I shall argue, such differences do not necessarily represent different periods of colonialism but rather coexist in an interesting tension with each other.

### Racial difference

The concept of race and the distinctions that were built around this concept are surely the most significant cultural construct of colonialism. According to Blaut (1993), racism 'had as its main function the justification of colonialism and all other forms of oppression visited upon non-Europeans, including minority peoples in countries such as the United States' (p. 62). As I have been suggesting, however, I prefer to treat this rather functional 'justification' position with some caution, arguing instead that although racism was central to colonialism, it had its origins earlier in European thought (Poliakov, 1982; Outlaw, 1990) and has outlasted the general demise of colonialism. Never-theless, it is certainly the case that racism is the cornerstone of colonial and imperial ideology, both enabling and being generated by colonialism. As Memmi (1965) puts it, racism is *not*

> an incidental detail, but . . . a consubstantial part of colonialism. It is the highest expression of the colonial system and one of the most significant features of the colonialist. Not only does it establish a fundamental discrimination between colonizer and colonized, a *sine qua non* of colonial life, but it also lays the foundation for the immutability of this life.
>
> (p. 74)

Simply put, from the eighteenth to the nineteenth century Europeans devel-oped a view of the world in which different people could be divided into so-called 'races' and that these races differed in terms of various mental and physical characteristics. By the middle of the nineteenth century, the writings of George Cuvier, Robert Knox (*The Races of Man*, 1850), Count Joseph de Gobineau (*Essay on the Inequality of Human Races*, 1854) and many others had established scientific theories of racial difference, apparently demonstrating differences in brain size, intelligence, character and so on. Once Darwin's theory of evolution was published, the already racist premises of many of his ideas were pounced upon by the social Darwinists and a full theory of racial struggle and survival was developed (see Curtin, 1971; Outlaw, 1990). As Curtin suggests, 'most imperial theory between the 1870's and the 1920's was based on racist assumptions with evolutionary overtones' (p. xvii). By this stage, the theory had developed to encompass a wide range of differences, based on the argument that since European culture is superior to non-European culture, and non-Europeans are racially distinct from Europeans, the cultural inferiority of non-Europeans is a genetically-based racial difference.

With this apparent scientific backing to the broader cultural beliefs in racial difference and hierarchies, many writers were able to write with confidence about racial characteristics. Alston (1907), for example, confidently ranks the races from the Europeans to the Chinese and Japanese to the Indians and finally the Negro. As we have already seen, colonial writing was full of these assumptions about 'lower races'. Lord Grey wrote in 1899 that:

> Probably everyone would agree that an Englishman would be right in considering his way of looking at the world and at life better than that of the Maori or Hottentot, and no one will object in the abstract to England doing her best to impose her better and higher views on those savages. . . . Can there be any doubt that the white man must, and will, impose his superior civilisation on the coloured races? The rivalry of the principal European countries in extending their influence over other continents should lead naturally to the evolution of the highest attainable type of government of subject races by the superior qualities of their rulers.
>
> (quoted in Hobson, 1902, pp. 165–6)

Always at the bottom of these fixed racial hierarchies was the African, labelled and fixed permanently in the European imagination as a savage 'Negro'. As Fanon (1963) describes it:

> Colonialism . . . has never ceased to maintain that the Negro is a savage; and for the colonist, the Negro was neither an Angolan nor a Nigerian, for he simply spoke of 'the Negro'. For colonialism, this vast continent was the haunt of savages, a country riddled with superstitions and fanaticism, destined for contempt, weighed down by the curse of God, a country of cannibals – in short, the Negro's country.
>
> (p. 170)

The construction of native people as cannibals was, of course, one of the most consistent of colonial constructs (see figure 3).

The nature of the debates that did occur at this time rarely questioned the characterization or hierarchies of race but rather focused on the causes of racial difference. A debate in 1849–50 between Thomas Carlyle and John Stuart Mill, for example, focused on whether African labourers in the British West Indies should be forced to work for whatever wages the white

*Figure 3* Images of cannibalism

plantation owners could afford or whether they should be granted certain rights. Carlyle's position was that the natural and inherited hierarchy of races, from the 'Wisest Man' (European) at the top to the 'Demarara Nigger' at the bottom, justified the extortion of whatever labour was required from such inferior peoples. Mill, by contrast, argued that this hierarchy was a product of different rates of development, and not immutable laws, and thus Africans could be improved if exposed to European civilization. Mill's much more liberal view does not question the hierarchy of races itself, only its causes (see Spurr, 1993, p. 66). And thus, from whatever point of view, the Black African slave remained at the very lowest rung of the evolutionary ladder and thus often compared to various animals:

> The slaves themselves, offspring of generations of slaves, were not fit to have freedom thrust upon them; they were, indeed, almost as unfit for immediate liberty as would be a kennel of dogs suddenly let loose into the midst of a poultry yard, without a master-hand to control them.
>
> (J. Lang, no date, p. 145)

It was John Stuart Mill's father, James Mill, who was famous for his massive *History of India* (1820). This

> six-volume bible which every aspiring Company cadet took with him on his first ship out, describes the natives of India, and the Chinese for good measure, as dissembling, treacherous, mendacious, cowardly, unfeeling, conceited, and unclean, the victims of despotism and witchcraft.
>
> (Thornton, 1965, p. 172)

The same issue as that discussed by Mill and Carlyle is also raised by Alston (1907). The crucial question, he suggests, is whether 'the present inferiority which we perceive in the lowest branches of the human race' is a result of environmental differences and therefore could be remedied, or whether 'between Negro and European there yawns a chasm similar in character (though not in degree) to that which divides us from brute creation' (pp. 4–5).

Again, it would be possible to discuss at far greater length the nature and significance of the colonial development of racist ideologies. The point I wish to make here is that on the one hand racism was, as Memmi put it, the *sine qua non* of colonialism, but on the other hand it has been the cultural construction that has best outlived the era of colonialism. Racism has in many instances changed from the overt statements of racial inferiority of the nineteenth century to a range of more covert beliefs about racial difference. Examining the racial views of John Buchan and Frederick Lugard (of whom more later), Spurr (1993) suggests that their views:

reflect an early form of the ideology of modernization that still governs the classification of Third World nations in the postcolonial era. Although the ideology of the modern has replaced an earlier ideology of the civilized, this newer system of value performs essentially the same function of classifying human societies according to Western standards of technological and political advancement.

(p. 69)

Racism still exists in both neocolonial definitions of third world populations and in many areas of daily life. And people of African descent are still generally the subjects of the worst aspects of racist discourse. It is also worth bearing in mind the very obvious, though I think nevertheless important, two-sided nature of racist views, that is that not only have other 'races' been seen as inferior but the 'Anglo-Saxon race' has been seen as superior: 'Buttressed by mythology, insensitivity and stupidity, by the end of Victoria's reign this belief in an Anglo-Saxon superiority was firmly established' (Mangan, 1985, p. 114). While twentieth century liberalism has made overtly racist views about 'primitive people' less acceptable, it has done far less to deconstruct the other side of the equation, European superiority. But without dealing with this second construct, the first cannot be removed either.

### Emptiness and absence

In the passage from *An Outline History of England* quoted in the previous chapter, Eyre (1971) described British settlers in Canada, Australia and New Zealand as 'true colonists who went to make their new homes in empty lands' (p. 150). As Sir Andrew Clarke, the British Governor-Designate for the Straits Settlements, commented in 1875 as he eyed the rich resources of the independent Malay states to the north, 'it only wants the protection and assistance of a civilised power here to fill all these empty waste lands with industrious and thriving settlements' (quoted in *The Straits Times*, 9 January 1875). This view of the emptiness of colonial lands was officially described in the doctrine of *terra nullius,* which denied the very existence of people in many countries (see, for example, McGrath, 1995a; Mudrooroo, 1995). The obvious and immediate upshot of this claim that these lands were unoccupied was that it made occupation easily rationalizable. As Singh (1996) suggests, the 'discovery motif has frequently emerged in the language of colonization, enabling European travelers/writers to represent the newly "discovered" lands as an empty space, a *tabula rasa* on which they could inscribe their linguistic, cultural, and later, territorial claims' (p. 1). But more than this, the idea of emptiness and absence was expanded not only to refer to land but also to the people themselves. Commenting on Darwin's description of Patagonia as a vast emptiness, Spurr (1993) suggests that this view served two purposes: it justified the colonization of the natural world by the scientific and it created a sense of foreboding at the empty chasm surrounding Europe. This Blaut (1993) calls 'the diffusionist myth of emptiness' (p. 15), a view starting with arguments about empty lands and indigenous people's lack of understanding of property and extending finally to the cultural and intellectual lives of the people. Once again this was often viewed on a comparative scale, with some Asian societies accorded a cultural history that was denied to African and Aboriginal people. Lugard (1926), for example, claimed that 'Unlike the ancient civilizations of Asia and South America, the former inhabitants of Africa have left no monuments and no records other than rude drawings on rocks like those of neolithic man' (p. 66).

Colonized people were seen as lacking history, culture, religion and intelligence and thus it became clear that it was a European duty to fill this void. It was Europe's role to bring history (both in terms of writing histories of colonies and helping those countries to start on the path of 'development' that was history as Europe saw it), culture (introducing better ways of understanding the world, especially through Europe's great store of literature), religion (introducing true belief in the European god [appropriated from the Jews] rather than superstition) and intelligence (European education could bring these people at least closer to the level of European intellect). This view of absence of religion and therefore of morality is encapsulated by Fanon (1963):

> Native society is not simply described as a society lacking in values. It is not enough for the colonist to affirm that those values have disappeared from, or still better never existed in, the colonial world. The native is declared insensible to ethics; he represents not only the absence of values, but also the negation of values. He is, let us dare to admit, the enemy of values, and in this sense he is the absolute evil.
>
> (p. 32)

One of the central tenets of this view has been that only Europeans have history: the rest of the world has been locked in stagnant, timeless, non-history. As Metcalf (1995) suggests, whatever tensions and disagreements existed within the British view of colonialism, they never questioned the 'fundamental British vision of India as a land lost in the past, whose people were shaped by the heat of their climate, the distinctive character of their religion, and the immemorial antiquity of their social institutions' (p. 27). As Spurr (1993) argues, 'This way of defining the African, as without history and without progress, makes way for the moral necessity of cultural transformation. The colonizing powers will create a history where there was none' (p. 99). Such a view has a central place in European thought, having been articulated most strongly by Hegel: 'What we properly understand by Africa, is the Unhistorical, Undeveloped Spirit, still involved in the conditions of mere nature, and which had to be presented here only as on the threshold of the world's history' (quoted in Spurr, p. 98).

This view was then taken up by Marx, who 'shares with his fellow Victorians the need to deny a significant history to the colonized' (Spurr, p. 100). Describing village life in India (where, of course, like many of the writers on colonial people, he had never been), Marx warned that:

> these idyllic village communities, inoffensive though they may appear, had always been the solid foundation of Oriental despotism, that they restrained the human mind within the smallest possible compass, making it the unresisting tool of superstition, enslaving it beneath traditional rules, depriving it of all grandeur and historical energies . . . We must not forget that this undignified, stagnatory, and vegetative life, that this passive sort of existence evoked on the other part, by contradistinction, wild, aimless, unbounded forces of destruction, and rendered murder itself a religious rite in Hindustan.
>
> (Marx, 1853, pp. 40–1)

For Marx, then, colonialism was justifiable and correct since it helped to destroy the fixed, unhistorical nature of primitive societies and to move them towards capitalism, a crucial step on the inevitable path towards communism (see Avineri, 1968). Thus, as Young (1990) puts it, 'the dominant force of opposition to capitalism, Marxism, as a body of knowledge itself remains complicit with, and even extends, the system to which it is opposed' (p. 3). The significant point here is that Marxism remains 'collusively Eurocentric' (ibid) as a body of knowledge that has denied history to the rest of the world. In the same way, then, that a retrospective look at the so-called 'Cold War' starts to suggest that the two 'Superpowers' shared more similarities than they did differences, it becomes clear that the different ends of the so-called 'ideological spectrum' have also shared more than they have disputed by dint of their fundamental Eurocentrism.

### The cultured and the natural

As the above discussion suggests, if the colonized lacked history, they also lacked culture. This argument, however, had some interesting paradoxes: on the one hand, culture was simply contrasted with absence of culture and thus the moral imperative of the Europeans was to bring their culture to the rest of the world; on the other hand, culture was contrasted with nature, and thus, with the rise of European romanticism and pastoralism, the colonized were idealized in their 'uncultured' naturalness. As Spurr (1993) suggests, this idealized view of the 'noble savage', which is associated particularly with Rousseau and other eighteenth-century European Romantics, was constructed as an abstract ideal through which social, cultural and political institutions in eighteenth-century Europe could be criticized. As in its later manifestations, such as Gauguin's paintings in Tahiti (see Tatlow, 1993), it never signalled any real interest in or admiration for native people but rather an idealized backdrop against which European institutions could be shown in a certain light. 'It is no accident,' suggests Spurr, 'that the idealization of the savage from the beginning has always accompanied the process of Western imperial expansion, for this idealization simply constitutes one more use that can be made of the savage in the realm of Western cultural production' (p. 128).

A variant of this 'noble savage' construct was adapted for agricultural populations, so that, as Savage (1984) suggests, the 'British administration in the early halcyon days of colonialism in Malaya pictured the Malays as "noble peasants"' (p. 289). This view of the Malays as noble peasants whose lifestyle should be preserved under colonial rule led to the implementation of education policies aimed at maintaining the inequitable structures of colonial rule: 'Much of the primitive Malay education that continued to be supplied by the British Government was in no small degree due to this attempt to preserve the Malay as a Malay, a son of the soil in the most literal sense possible' (Loh Fook Seng, 1970, p. 114).

### The industrious and the indolent

In his book *The Myth of the Lazy Native*, Syed Hussein Alatas (1977) shows how the cultural construction of the 'lazy native' developed during colonial rule. This idea that native peoples were lazy 'was an important element in the ideology of colonial capitalism. It was a major justification for territorial conquest, since the degraded image of the native was basic to colonial ideology' (p. 215). As Alatas demonstrates, the image of lazy Malays, Indonesians and Filipinos (the main focus of his detailed analysis, though not of course the only people to be subjected to this view) was a view that developed under colonial rule as colonists combined their derogatory images of native peoples with the view that they were lazy if they did not participate in the colonial economy. Hugh Clifford lamented that the Malay 'never works if he can help it, and often will not suffer himself to be induced or tempted into doing so by offers of the most extravagant wages' (1927, p. 19). Swettenham's view was that 'the leading characteristic of the Malay of every class is a disinclination to work' (1907/1955, p. 136). Or as W.H. Treacher, Resident-General of the Federated Malay States, remarked in 1902: 'The Malay, with his moderate wants, and rooted disinclination to steady work of any kind, will give his labour neither to Government undertakings nor to mines or plantations' (*Reports on the Federated Malay States*, 1902). This last quote clearly shows how the construction of the 'lazy native' was in the context of the Malays' refusal to engage in the exploitative labour of tin mines and rubber plantations. Sir Harry Johnston's views in his *History of the*

*Colonisation of Africa by Alien Races* (quoted in Hobson, 1902) show a similar view of the naturalness of certain types of labour and the indolence of native people:

> In this world natural law ordains that all mankind must work to a reasonable extent, must wrest from its environment sustenance for body and mind, and a bit over to start the children from a higher level than the parents. The races that will not work persistently and doggedly are trampled on, and in time displaced, by those who do. Let the negro take this to heart; let him devote his fine muscular development, in the first place, to the getting of his own rank, untidy continent in order. If he will not work of his own free will, now that freedom of action is temporarily restored to him; if he will not till, and manure, and drain, and irrigate the soil of his country in a steady, laborious way as do the Oriental and the European; if he will not apply himself zealously under European tuition to the development of the vast resources of tropical Africa, where hitherto he has led the wasteful, unproductive life of a baboon; then force of circumstances, the pressure of eager hungry, impatient outside humanity, the converging energies of Europe and Asia will once more relegate the negro to a servitude which will be the alternative – in the coming struggle for existence – to extinction.
>
> (Cited in Hobson, 1902, pp. 286–7)

On the one hand, then, there are natural laws that govern how and how much we should work. On the other hand, there is an inherent laziness of many people around the world which leads them to ignore such laws and thus to expose themselves to the results of the natural racial struggle for survival. Another argument that was linked to this notion of laziness and which became a dominant aspect of colonial thought was the view that the environment determined work habits and development. There were a number of different aspects to this argument, though its principal elements were that the supposed static and despotic nature of Oriental civilizations was a result of the nature of their climate and more particularly their agricultural practices; that hot, tropical climates on the one hand produced abundant and easy living conditions so that native people were not induced to work hard and on the other hand the heat and humidity led to idleness and lethargy; and that the temperate climate of Europe and its concomitant agricultural practices had brought Europe to the pinnacle of global development: 'some diffusionist arguments were built on the idea that tropical conditions induce sloth, indolence, etc., in everyone, and thus the need for control-at-a-distance from temperate-climate civilizations' (Blaut, 1993, p. 70). As Blaut clearly shows, furthermore, these views once again are not merely ideas that are now lost in the colonial past; rather, they can be found in many recent books on history and geography. Alatas (1977) also demonstrates how this myth of the lazy native has continued down to the present.

### The adult and the child

A further significant polarity mapped onto and then developed through colonialism is that between adult and child. Linking together the idea of a process of development from primitive to advanced with the nineteenth century interest in the extent to which ontogeny recapitulates phylogeny (the development of the individual mirrors the development of the species), it was a short step to see colonized people as children and the colonizers as adults. Arnold (1815) articulated an early version of this view when he spoke of the pride that colonizers could feel at 'changing at once by their exertions the infancy of the world into its maturity; of elevating the savage to the rank of civilised man; of founding a new nation of Englishmen and Christians' (p. 27). Or as Winstedt was to remark later: 'The malay is still a child of nature in a sophisticated world that awaits his exploration' (1956, p. 50). Or as J. Lang (no date) remarks, 'The negroes, childishly ignorant and unstable, were easily moved and liable to be worked up to a high pitch of excitement' (p. 147). Nandy (1983) argues that the modern European concept of childhood came into being in the seventeenth century. Whereas before, children had been seen as a smaller version of adults, now children were seen as an inferior version, one that was in need of strict moral training and education in order to ensure its upward progress to maturity. Interestingly, the same divide between the Rousseauian view of the 'noble savage' and the view of natives as uncultured brutes applied to the views on children: for some, children were innocent and happy creatures unspoilt by the bonds of society; for others, they were irrational and immature beings in need of strict moral discipline and extensive education. This distinction Nandy describes as 'childlike' or 'childish': 'What was childlikeness of the child and childishness of immature adults now also became the lovable and unlovable savagery of primitives and the primitivism of subject societies' (pp. 15–16). Both states, of course, required European correction: childlike innocence could be reformed into maturity through education and introduction to Western civilization; childish rebellion required strict control and authoritarian rule. Colonial tutelage also brought native people from childlike states to adolescence, a time requiring particularly firm control and discipline: 'The child we have reared, though not robust, has grown mature and active and exacting' (West, 1906, p. xi). As Mangan (1985) suggests, 'The outcome of an adherence to the "child-race" theory was the Schoolmaster Syndrome' (p. 112), a view that colonized people needed a good dose of British public school style discipline. And today, European teachers still spread across the world to bring enlightenment (often through English) to the child-like races of the world.

A further important result of this view of colonized people as children and the colonizers as adults was that it was then linked to the concept of rationality. If, phylogenetically, Europeans had become more rational as history progressed, and if, ontogenetically, the child progressed from irrational childhood to rational adulthood, then clearly the same model applied to colonial people: 'Non-Europeans . . . were seen as psychically *undeveloped*, as more or less *childlike*. But, given the psychic unity of mankind, non-Europeans could of course be brought to adulthood, to rationality, to modernity, through a set of learning experiences, mainly colonial' (Blaut, 1993, p. 96). This concept of rationality and the childlike state of the colonized has a host of more recent correlates, having been adopted by Marx, Freud, Jung and many others since then. The idea of colonial tutelage was adopted into modernization and development theory and surely underlies much of how education in Hong Kong is understood. It has also received considerable backing from psychology. Piaget (1971), for example, mapped his concept of stages of development onto a belief in this adult/child view of the world: 'It is quite possible . . . that in many societies, adult thought does not go beyond the level of 'concrete' operations, and therefore does not reach that of propositional operations which develop between the ages of twelve and fifteen in our milieus' (p. 61; cited in Blaut, 1993, p. 99). These ideas were then taken up by a broad range of psychologists who 'used the tests of cognitive ability that Piaget had used with European children and, scarcely modifying them, administered these tests to non-European children and adults and found, predictably, that these people do not have full adult cognitive abilities' (Blaut, 1993, p. 99). This same problem of ethnocentric tests being administered inappropriately and showing cognitive or other deficits has continued down into psychometric and standardized testing, from a long history of psychological research into 'cross-cultural' difference (according to Blaut, about ten per cent of all empirical articles in the first 16 years (up to 1985) of *The Journal of Cross-Cultural Psychology* were by white South Africans claiming to show cognitive inferiority of black Africans) to tests such as SAT and TOEFL.

### Masculine and feminine

Not surprisingly, perhaps, if colonizers constructed themselves as rational and the colonized as irrational, it was not long before this view became linked to one of gender: rational man colonized, penetrated, took authority over irrational woman. According to Singh (1996), the category of 'woman' became an important marker in colonial discourse, the foundation for colonial demarcations between so-called Western modernity and Eastern backwardness' (pp. 89–90). Discussing a passage from Kipling, Spurr (1993) points out how he 'translates the difference between colonizer and colonized into a conventional distinction between rational man and irrational woman'

(p. 172). In opposition to images of the feminine – irrationality, hysteria, nature – Kipling constructs a view of masculine reason and order: 'Colonial domination thus is seen to have a beneficial, cathartic effect, like the dash of cold water in the face of the woman who has lost her senses' (ibid). Nandy (1983) explains this relationship thus:

> The homology between sexual and political dominance which Western colonialism invariably used – in Asia, Africa, and Latin America – was not an accidental by-product of colonial history. It had its correlates in other situations of oppression with which the West was involved, the American experience with slavery being the best documented of them. The homology, drawing support from the denial of psychological bisexuality in men in large areas of Western culture, beautifully legitimized Europe's post-medieval models of dominance, exploitation and cruelty as natural and valid. Colonialism, too, was congruent with the existing Western sexual stereotypes and the philosophy of life which they represented. It produced a cultural consensus in which political and socio-economic dominance symbolized the dominance of men and masculinity over women and femininity.
>
> (p. 4)

This is perhaps one of the clearest examples of how such images can feed off each other in a constant reciprocal relationship. Once a particular image of women and men is mapped onto colonial relationships between colonizer and colonized, this then not only has implications for this colonial relationship but also for gender relations: other aspects of the cultural construction of the colonized – despotic, irrational, dirty, backward, inferior, simple-minded, cannibalistic, dangerous, innocent etc. – start to attach themselves to the concept of femininity, while other aspects of the construction of the colonizers – rational, mature, superior, clean, authoritative, cultured etc. – attach themselves to the concept of masculinity. Thus, the effect of this use of a masculine/feminine metaphor is not only to ascribe already negative and positive views of femininity and masculinity to the colonized and colonizers but also to further develop the nature of negative and positive stereotypes attached to the two genders. This is one of the crucial ways in which colonialism has come to construct European culture.

Another aspect of this analogy between gender and colonialism was that it both produced and was generated by direct sexual relationships. What emerges from Hyam's (1990) documentation of sexuality in the British Empire is the very close relationship between the two. The huge number of sexual relationships (and documented reports can only be the tip of the iceberg) between colonizer and colonized (nearly all British men in the first case; a mixture of men, women and children in the second) reveals not only that the supposed sexual restraint of Victorians was certainly not practised in the Empire (if indeed it really was in Victorian Britain) but also that the colonies provided something of a sexual outlet for the frustrated sons of Empire. More importantly, it shows how sexual relationships were a significant part of colonialism. As Nandy noted above, sexual relations had also been a central aspect of slavery, and Hyam quotes W.E.B. Du Bois (1920) as saying he could forgive the White South much in its final judgement day, including slavery, but there was one thing he could not forgive: 'its wanton and persistent insulting of the black womanhood which it sought and seeks to prostitute to its lust' (Hyam, 1990, p. 4). Sexual relationships in the colonies were both produced by and themselves produced gendered and colonial relationships. The large extent of paedophilia (particularly with young boys – one autobiographical account cited in Hyam lists sexual relationships with 129 boys in India between 1897 and 1917) is also symptomatic of these relations (and note here the adult/child, masculine/feminine, colonizer/colonized pairings).

Linked to these sexual relationships were very particular constructions of masculinity. It was this version of masculinity that would then save the feminized colonies from their passive inertia. Metcalf (1995) describes the construction of India as 'a "changeless" India inhabiting a past that endured in the present; an India of racial "decline" . . . ; and an India of a gendered "effeminacy" which made its women and men alike dependent on British "masculinity"' (p. 110). As Hyam (1990) and Mangan (1985) point out, the late nineteenth century saw a major change in what counted as masculinity: there was a shift from a more sensitive 'maleness' to a hardened, militarized, physical games-oriented masculinity that was linked to physical prowess, a spartan existence, a rejection of all that came to be defined as 'feminine' (caring, intellectual pursuits), and patriotism, a 'neo-Spartan virility as exemplified by stoicism, hardiness and endurance – the pre-eminent virtues of the late-Victorian English public school' (Mangan, 1985, p. 147). The games ethic that grew up in the British public schools of the late nineteenth century had particular implications for the construction of British masculinity. It was linked not only to aspects of imperial command – courage, endurance, assertion, control and self-control – but also to aspects of imperial 'manliness' – both dominance and deference, the ability to take command and the ethic of loyalty and obedience. It was therefore 'a useful instrument of colonial purpose. At one and the same time it helped create the confidence to lead and the compulsion to follow' (Mangan, 1985, p. 18). British public schools, as well as other contemporary and like-minded organizations such as the Boy Scouts, with their cult of 'moral muscularity' expanded massively during this period, producing generations of boys ready to take up their positions in the colonial service and expound their ethics of masculinity, sportsmanship, 'muscular Christianity', unswerving loyalty, anti-intellectualism, and belief in God and Empire: 'Once the Empire was established, the public schools sustained it' (p. 21). Not only were the playing fields of Eton seen as the best preparation for colonial service but the Empire was seen as one vast playing field.

Once again, the British public school remains one of those central sites of production of colonial constructs. As someone with the misfortune to have spent seven years in one of these misogynous, homophobic, racist, brutal, and élitist institutions, I can attest to the continuing existence of such constructs of masculinity as evinced in the games ethic: a view of masculinity as dominant, uncaring, unemotional and superior; a deep fear and suspicion of homosexuality; an utter disregard for and ignorance of women; and an unshakable sense of social and cultural superiority. The deeply damaged products of British public schools were perfectly suited for the all-male world we were designed for, the world of rugby, men's clubs, the army and colonial service. For those of us who have emerged into a different world and have tried to live our lives differently, it has been a struggle against the deep-seated codes of masculinity in which we were brutally raised.

### Cleanliness and dirt

A constant theme that runs through writing from the colonial era and beyond is one in which the colonies and their people were seen as dirty and diseased. 'From the beginning,' suggests Metcalf (1995), 'the British conceived of India as a land of dirt, disease, and sudden death' (p. 171). The opposite side of this, of course, constructed Europe as the continent of health and cleanliness. 'Calcutta, one might say, became filthy only as London became clean' (p. 173). Blaut (1993) sees as one of the axioms of Eurocentric diffusionism the 'counterdiffusionist' fear of the spread of death and disease from the colonies back to the metropolitan countries. This fear was constantly strengthened by the tales of death and disease that circulated back from the colonies, reinforced by 'the reports of upper-class European travelers about the, to them, dirty, disgusting, diseased communities they found outside of Europe' (p. 77). As a correspondent for the *Daily Telegraph* in 1897, Winston Churchill described the Mohmand tribes of the Indian Northwest frontier in these terms:

> Their habits are filthy; their morals cannot be alluded to. With every feeling of respect for that wide sentiment of human sympathy which characterises a Christian civilisation, I find it impossible to come to any other conclusion than that, in proportion as these valleys are purged from the pernicious vermin that infest them, so will the happiness of humanity be increased, and the progress of mankind accelerated.
>
> (Cited in Spurr, 1993, p. 82)

Clearly the images of 'filth' and 'vermine' here, contrasted with the superior virtues of a Christian civilization and seemingly implying a threat of dirt and disease to this civilization, are being used to justify the same type of action that is reserved for 'vermine', in this case genocide.

This view was then linked to the assumptions about tropical climates and seen as a fixed quality of colonial regions, thus ignoring the facts that Europe had until recently had similar scales of disease and epidemic, that it was the Europeans that suffered from any diseases more than the native peoples, who were often fairly immune, and that, as Alatas (1977) points out, it was quite often colonial projects such as road building and plantation clearing that contributed to the spread of diseases such as malaria. As Metcalf (1995) shows, this view of India as diseased and dirty was to have great influence on colonial architecture, with buildings and even cities constructed to keep the white population separate from the death, dirt and disease around them. Houses were built with broad verandahs, set in large, fenced compounds, located where possible in the 'Civil Lines' (separate areas designated for Europeans; this area in Delhi is still known by this name), or, even better, located on a hill, or, better still, located in hills far away from the cities. As we shall see in Chapter 4, 'The Peak' in Hong Kong was one such exclusionist European settlement. Once again, this is one of the many cultural constructs of colonialism that has outlived the colonial era. Travel writing up to the modern day is full of similar images of dirt and depravity (see Chapter 6). Furthermore, as both Blaut (1993) and Spurr (1993) argue, this discourse in which the civilized West is threatened by the diseased rest has recently re-emerged in writing about the AIDS virus and the attempt to locate its 'origins' in Africa or among Third World populations such as Haitians.

## Conclusion

I have tried in this chapter to give a background to the colonial contexts that I shall be discussing in subsequent chapters. I have not attempted to give any historical overview of colonialism but rather to map out some of the cultural constructs that were central to the colonial project. The main argument here has been that colonialism was both made possible by and itself made possible a range of beliefs and views about the colonized Other and the colonising Self that have had a fundamental impact on European culture. To paraphrase Fanon, in some ways Europe is a product of colonialism. What I have been trying to show, then, is that beyond the economic exploitation and political domination that were in many ways the most obvious aspects of colonialism, there were also crucial cultural effects. And it is these that have survived colonialism and that still live on in many forms today. It is important to understand one other important upshot of the argument I am making here.

My focus is principally on the effects of colonialism on European culture, rather than on the effects of colonialism on colonized people. While this may seem a strangely Eurocentric direction to take, I want to argue that it is important both because I, as a European, am looking critically inward to examine some of the cultural constructs that govern my and other European/Western lives, and because in so doing I am not trying to suggest on behalf of colonized people how they have experienced colonialism.

One last concluding remark is worth making here with respect to the scope of colonialism as a metaphor. In many ways I have suggested a fairly traditional sense of colonialism as the embedded site of imperialism. My interest in culture and knowledge has also suggested, however, that this definition needs broadening into the non-material domain. As Cohn (1996), Metcalf (1995), Niranjana (1992), Singh (1996) and others have argued, a central part of the colonial project was concerned with the production of knowledge of and over colonial subjects. Through the work of Orientalists and other scholars and administrators, local domains of culture and knowledge were colonized by the British. It is this act of so-called discovery of the cultures and knowledges of the Other that it is also crucial to include in an understanding of colonialism. Thus, although I do not wish to use colonialism here as an all-encompassing metaphor for any type of cultural and political power, the arguments I am making here will clearly have strong resonances for understanding other sites of oppression, such as patriarchy (see Showalter, 1981).

# 3

# ANGLICISM, ORIENTALISM AND COLONIAL LANGUAGE POLICY

Thus superior, in point of ultimate advantage does the employment of the English language appear; and upon this ground, we
give a preference to that mode, proposing here that the communication of our knowledge shall be made by the medium of our
own language. . . . The first communication, and the instrument
of introducing the rest, must be the English language; this is a
key which will open to them a world of new ideas, and policy
alone might have impelled us, long since, to put it into their
hands.

> (Grant, 1797, cited in Bureau of Education 1920, p. 82)

I shall merely observe that the greatest difficulty this Government suffers, in its endeavours to govern well, springs from the
immorality and ignorance of the mass of the people, their disregard of knowledge not connected with agriculture and cattle
and particularly their ignorance of the spirit, principles and
system of the British Government.

> (W. Fraser, 1823, cited in Bureau of Education 1920, p. 13)

I am aware that there are some (perhaps I might say many)
learned and distinguished individuals, for whose judgment I feel
a very high respect, who entertain an opposite idea, and who
hold that English alone is the proper and all sufficient instrument
for the desired end; but I must in that respect decidedly express
my dissent, because my belief is, that an education solely attained
through English, instead of fitting a native of India for general
worldly intercourse with his fellowmen, or being likely to
render him a good and valuable member of the community, and
an efficient servant of the state, should his fortune lead to his
being so employed, has directly a reverse tendency.

> (Governor Pottinger, 1851, cited in Bureau of Education
> 1922, p. 205)

> In a word, knowledge must be drawn from . . . the English language, the Vernaculars must be employed as the media of communicating it, and Sanscrit must be largely used to improve the Vernaculars and make them suitable for the purpose.
> (Captain Candy, 1840, cited in Bureau of Education 1922, p. 2)

I have argued in the first two chapters that colonialism is a crucial site of cultural production, that many of the cultural constructs that still operate in the contemporary world are products of colonial contexts. Furthermore, I suggested that such constructs adhere to English, that the centrality of English and English language teaching at the heart of the colonial enterprise, and the significant role played by English in the contemporary world, have brought about an intertwining of English and certain discourses. While later chapters (5 and 6) will focus on contemporary constructions of Self and Other as they operate in relationship to English language teaching, this and the next chapter will be concerned with the development of language policies under British colonialism. This focus has two principal elements: on the one hand, it aims to illuminate the complexities of language policies in their relationship to colonial governance; on the other hand, it aims to show how such language policies were part of the production of the cultural constructs of colonialism.

Colonial language policies can be seen as constructed between four poles: first, the position of colonies within a capitalist empire and the need to produce docile and compliant workers and consumers to fuel capitalist expansion; second, local contingencies of class, ethnicity, race and economic conditions that dictated the distinctive development of each colony; third, the discourses of Anglicism and liberalism with their insistence on the European need to bring civilization to the world; and fourth, the discourses of Orientalism with their insistence on exotic histories, traditions and nations in decline. From amid these often competing demands emerged colonial language policies of many different hues that worked generally to bolster the economic and political position of Britain but which also operated along particular ideological positions that gained sway in particular contexts.

This chapter, then, explores ways in which colonial ideologies were reflected in language education policies. Thus, I am interested in showing how different policies on the medium of education were constructed as part of colonial governance. We therefore need to understand education policy within the larger material and discursive positions that surround it; we need to understand both broad background ideological positions as well as particular material (economic, political, social) conditions of education. But not only do we need to understand this embeddedness – how educational discourses reflected wider social and ideological conditions – but we also need to see the educational context as *productive* of colonial discourse. Thus, I am

68

interested in showing how such policies not only reflected colonial ideology but also produced it; that is to say I am arguing that language policy and language education were (are) crucial sites of colonial cultural production. Education and education policy were a crucial site of colonial encounter and of the production of colonial discourse. As a result they both helped to produce colonialism more generally and also have had lasting effects into the present.

Colonial language policy thus became another site of colonial knowledge production. Such knowledge, suggests Metcalf 'could effectively subordinate and contain the Company's Indian underlings' (1995, p. 23). But the effects of such knowledge went beyond their role in the control of the Indian populace. India, as Viswanathan (1989) argues with respect to the development of the English canon of literature, was a key site for the development of policies that then flowed back to England. As I suggested in Chapter 2, one crucial way in which I view the notion of empire is as a system that allowed the flow of knowledge and culture produced in the colonial encounter to flow back to the imperial centre. Similarly, in terms of general administrative and educational policies, India became a laboratory for liberal reforms, 'a laboratory for the creation of the liberal administrative state, and from there its elements – whether a state-sponsored education, the codification of law, or a competitively chosen bureaucracy – could make their way back to England itself' (Metcalf, 1995, p. 29).

As I suggested in Chapter 1, one of my concerns here is also to shift a common representation of colonial history in which a simple past is contrasted with a complex present. The point here, then, is not to try to show the negativity of colonial discourses in order to efface such negative constructions. Rather, we need, as Thomas (1994) points out, 'a pluralization and historicization of "colonial discourse", and a shift from the logic of signification to the narration of colonialism – or rather, to a contest of colonial narratives' (p. 37). One of the crucial arguments of this chapter, therefore, will oppose those overly simple accounts of the triumph of Anglicism and the rabid rhetoric of Macaulay. Too often (see, for example, Kachru, 1986; Phillipson, 1992) the history of colonial language policy has been cast as a victory for English, which explains the current role of English (generally a good thing in Kachru's view) or the need to develop policies to oppose its spread (in Phillipson's view). Thus, Kachru sees the resolution passed as a result of the Minute as 'epoch-making' and resulting in the 'diffusion of bilingualism in English on the subcontinent' (p. 35). Phillipson argues that 'Macaulay's formulation of the goals of British educational policy ended a protracted controversy which had exercised planners both in India and in the East India Company in London' (p. 110). Yet, without understanding the relationships between support for English or vernacular languages and other material and discursive forces of colonialism, we will not have an adequate appreciation either of colonialism or of current language policies.

## *1882 and the state of education in India*

I shall start this discussion of language policy with the massive *Report of the Indian Education Commission* of 1882. My purpose in this is to break up the order of colonial narrative (I shall be dealing mainly with policy prior to this date in later parts of the chapter) and to make a point about the production of colonial knowledge. Regarding this second point, it is interesting to compare this report with an educational document produced in Hong Kong in the same year (of which more in the next chapter). In 1882, Hong Kong was still a relatively young colony and language policy was only vaguely formulated. The 1882 document in Hong Kong, therefore, is a series of interviews with influential people in Hong Kong in an attempt to develop a coherent policy for the colony. The 1882 Indian report (*Report, 1883a*), by contrast, is a massive documentation of education in India: some 717 pages of documentation, 193 'witnesses' interviewed, 323 submitted 'memorials', and so forth. Such a document is an excellent example of 'colonial knowledge', the vast accumulation of knowledge over the other. Such a document needs to be seen as part of the larger process of colonial knowledge production. As Cohn suggests, Europeans:

> took control by defining and classifying space, making separations between public and private spheres; by recording transactions such as the sale of property; by counting and classifying their populations, replacing religious institutions as the registrar of births, marriages and deaths; and by standardizing languages and scripts.
>
> (p. 3)

It is, however, the centrality of language and schools in the colonial project that is of primary interest here since, as Cohn goes on to suggest, 'schools became the crucial civilizing institutions and sought to produce moral and productive citizens' (p. 3).

The 1882 document takes as its primary goal the evaluation of how educational policy had successfully implemented the 1854 Despatch from the Directors of the East India Company (to which I shall return). This Despatch, and the 1859 Despatch, which confirmed the policies outlined in 1854 following the transfer of authority from the former East India Company to the British Government, 'stand out from all later documents as the fundamental codes in which Indian education rests' (p. 24). The Report's summary of the position on language of the 1854 Despatch, with its huge increase in support for education, is that 'The English language is to be the medium of instruction in the higher branches, and the vernacular in the lower. English is to be taught wherever there is a demand for it, but it is not to be substituted for the vernacular languages of the country' (p. 23). Here, then, is the basic position laid out in the 1854 Despatch and confirmed through the rest of the century. The Report of 1882 goes on to report, favourably or unfavourably, the extent to which these basic goals had been met.

The Report's own recommendations include the following: First, that 'primary education be regarded as the instruction of the masses through the vernacular in such subjects as will best fit them for their position in life . . .' (p. 174). This, then, is a clear enunciation of the general position that education should be for the masses, should be in the vernacular, and should be aimed at educating people to better fulfill their position in the social order. Primary education is clearly defined as practical and to do with basic requirements; secondary education, by contrast, which was largely in English, is associated with 'liberal education, and with the exercise of the higher faculties of thought' (p. 177). It is not my intention to map out the educational implementation of such views, but rather to look at how such policies emerged from amid the competing ideologies of Orientalism and Anglicism, and the needs to run and develop a colony within the larger structures of the British Empire.

### Education, control and language

We might start this discussion of educational policy by asking 'Why educate?' 'What were the reasons for providing education in colonial India and elsewhere?' Early educational provision in India had been on a small scale and generally haphazard. It was only at the end of the eighteenth century that various British thinkers, especially members of the Clapham Sect, which included Charles Grant and Henry Wilberforce, and from where Macaulay's views were to emerge, started to urge educational responsibility on the East India Company. In 1813 the first clause was written into the East India Company Act stating that education should be funded through public revenues. Nevertheless, education in the early part of the nineteenth century was generally made up of local initiatives predominantly in local languages but increasingly in English (for example the opening of the Hindu College in Calcutta in 1817); missionary or other private activity; and limited government support and supervision. According to the 1882 Report, however, the demand for English started to grow in the early part of the nineteenth century as 'An English education started to be recognized as an assured means of livelihood' (p. 15). Early educational endeavours were still almost always directed towards a small élite. From 1823, however, consideration was given to broadening education to larger sections of society. Nevertheless, the lack of funds and the difficulties faced in developing a broader-based educational endeavour, meant that in practice educational provision remained within the model of downwards filtration of knowledge.

There were a number of different reasons for providing such an education. First of all, was the argument that education was a crucial means for more effective governance of the people. As W. Fraser wrote in a letter to the Chief Secretary, W.B. Bayley, on 25 September 1823:

> It would be extremely ridiculous in me to sit down to write to the Government or to you a sentence even upon the benefit of teaching the children of the Peasantry of this country to read and write. I shall merely observe that the greatest difficulty this Government suffers, in its endeavours to govern well, springs from the immorality and ignorance of the mass of the people, their disregard of knowl- edge not connected with agriculture and cattle and particularly their ignorance of the spirit, principles and system of the British Govern- ment.
>
> (Bureau of Education, 1920, p. 13)

Similarly, Holt Mackenzie, in a Note dated 17 July 1823 (Bureau of Educa- tion, 1920), explicitly rejects the argument that an ill-educated and ignorant population is beneficial for colonial rule: '. . . to keep the people weak and ignorant that they may be submissive is a policy which the Government decidedly rejects' (p. 58). Rather, he argues, the Government must seek to provide education for the people. Noting, however, the impossibility of pro- viding education for the majority of the population, and lamenting the impossibility of providing religious instruction, he is pessimistic about the overall efficacy of the education they are able to provide:

> The education indeed of the great body of the people can never, I think, be expected to extend beyond what is necessary for the busi- ness of life; and it is only therefore through religious exercises, which form a great part of the business of life, that the labourer will turn his thoughts on things above the common drudgery, by which he earns his subsistence. Hence it is under the Christian scheme alone, that I should expect to find the labouring classes really edu- cated. . . . We have no such instrument with which to work bene- ficially on the lower orders here.
>
> (p. 59)

Clearly, then, for this colonial administrator, the problems with educa- tional provision at this period were, first, its small scale, but, second, its inability to provide a moral grounding without religious instruction. As we shall see, this need for some form of a moral education remained a central concern for colonial educators. And, as Viswanathan (1989) shows, the development of a canon of English literature was in part a direct response to this problem.

Beyond the general concern for producing a well-ordered and docile population, therefore, there was also the feeling that colonial education should provide instruction in moral behaviour. This view was also part of a larger concern that colonial subjects should benefit from European knowledge. At this point, then, we immediately confront the arguments over which languages would best suit the teaching of European knowledge. The argument that generally won out here was in favour of an education in the vernacular languages. Following the guidelines of the 1854 Despatch, the Provincial Committee of Bombay Report (in the 1882 *Report 1883a*) argues that:

> the vernaculars would be enriched by translations of European books or by the compositions of men imbued with the spirit of European advancement, and that the only method of thus bringing European knowledge within the reach of the masses is to give every pupil a thorough grounding in the vernacular, and to keep his attention upon it even up to the college course. In pursuance of this policy English is rigidly excluded from the primary school course.
>
> (pp 124–5)

In a Minute on education in Madras, 6 June 1851, Sir Henry Pottinger (Governor of Madras, 1848-54, and a former Governor of Hong Kong, 1843-4), presented his view on these issues:

> After much reflection, and careful reference to the educational reports of all parts of India, including both Government and private schools, I have come to the conclusion, that in the Provincial schools useful knowledge and a moderate scale of general education should only be aimed at, without entering on the higher grades of learning and science, or introducing as a necessary ingredient the acquirement of refined literature. An education such as I refer to may doubtless be, with great advantage, partly taught through the medium of English books, adapted to that purpose; but my own firm persuasion is, from past personal experience, as well as from inquiry and reading the reports to which I have adverted above, that good and careful translations from English into the vernacular dialects must, after all, be the chief channel of instruction, and of the communication of knowledge to the great body of the population of Southern India.
>
> (Bureau of Education, 1922, p. 205)

At the same time, however, there was also the question of English, and particularly the need to respond to the widespread demand for access to English. Although Niranjana (1992) argues that this demand was more a construction of colonial rule than a reality, it does seem that beyond the need for a limited body of people able to work as clerks, translators and administrators, the

British spent much of their time trying to resist the demand for English. Commenting on whether English should remain optional or should become compulsory for the pupils of the Sanskrit College (Calcutta), the Report from the Select Committee of the House of Commons on the affairs of the East India Company, 16 August 1832 (Bureau of Education, 1920, pp. 38–44) suggests that it should remain optional:

> The inducement to acquire the language of the rulers of the country is already so vastly extended and so greatly productive of effect among the Hindus, that it does not require any addition, whilst any appearance either of coercion or of a political or religious design on the part of the Government would alarm those Hindus who preserve a somewhat too rigid and exclusive adherence to their ancient and sacred language and customs.
>
> (Bureau of Education, 1920, p. 43)

Later, the 1882 Report suggested that:

> The demand for English instruction in the south of India is so strong that the large attendance in primary schools is said to be due in no small measure to the popular demand for English. In Bombay, on the other hand, the Department has systematically resisted every attempt to introduce the study of English until a boy has completed Standard IV and reached the point where secondary education commences. Even then an English class is not attached to a purely primary school unless those who require it are prepared to pay for the extra cost.
>
> (*Report*, 1883a, p. 124)

As Frykenburg (1988) notes, in South India the move towards provision of English education dates back to the late eighteenth century and increased from that point on. Similarly, further north, the Bengali bourgeoisie, frustrated at their exclusion from the institutions of British rule, set up their own college, The Hindu College, in 1816, which was designed to provide an education in English language and literature, Western philosophy and the social and natural sciences. Rahim (1986) remarks that, 'English and Western education became a powerful agent of change at the initiative of the Bengali middle class in Calcutta who found it essential in gaining advantage in their unequal power relationship with the British' (p. 235). Indeed for many, the issue went beyond the question of whether it was necessary to provide English education, but rather questioned the effects of education in English. As Governor Pottinger argued in 1851:

I am aware that there are some (perhaps I might say many) learned and distinguished individuals, for whose judgment I feel a very high respect, who entertain an opposite idea, and who hold that English alone is the proper and all sufficient instrument for the desired end; but I must in that respect decidedly express my dissent, because my belief is, that an education solely attained through English, instead of fitting a native of India for general worldly intercourse with his fellowmen, or being likely to render him a good and valuable member of the community, and an efficient servant of the state, should his fortune lead to his being so employed, has directly a reverse tendency.

(Bureau of Education, 1922, p. 205)

Summarizing very briefly these views, it can be seen that education was seen as a means to enlighten the Indian population and to make them aware of the system and benefits of colonial rule. It was a means to produce a well-ordered, docile and co-operative population, but it was also a moral and imperial duty to bring to the Indian population the benefits of European knowledge. In order to understand the terms of the arguments over which languages should be used to convey such educational goals, it is important at this juncture to look further into the heated debate between the Anglicists and Orientalists. Much has been written about these arguments (see, for example, Singh, 1996; Viswanathan, 1989), and I do not intend to repeat these points here. Rather, I want to show briefly how these positions were significant both to language policy and to the cultural constructions that are a major theme of this book. I also intend to point to three other important considerations: first, that neither position was as monolithic as it is sometimes made out to be; second, that both coexisted for a significant part of the colonial era; and third, that both were equally complicit with colonial governance.

## Anglicism and Orientalism

In trying to understand Orientalism, it is worth returning to Said's (1978) classic discussion of Orientalism:

as the corporate institute for dealing with the Orient – dealing with it by making statements about it, authorizing views about it, describing it, by teaching it, settling it, ruling over it: in short, Orientalism as a Western style for dominating, restructuring, and having authority over the Orient.

(p. 3)

Crucially, then, following Foucault, Said argues that the construction of knowledge of the Other must be seen as a crucial site for the operation of colonial governance: 'without examining Orientalism as a discourse one cannot possibly understand the enormously systematic discipline by which European culture was able to manage – and even produce – the Orient politically, sociologically, militarily, ideologically, scientifically, and imaginatively during the post-Enlightenment period' (p. 3).

This understanding of Orientalism, then, opens a significant space for examining how work on Indian languages was a central part of the colonial enterprise. According to Cohn (1996), British studies of Indian languages, literatures, science and thought developed into three major projects: 'the objectification and use of Indian languages as instruments of rule to understand better the "peculiar" manners, customs and prejudices of Indians, and to gather information necessary to conciliate and control the peoples of India'; the 'discovery' of Indian traditions in order to 'construct a history of the relationship between India and the West, to classify and locate their civilizations on an evaluative scale of progress and decay'; and to patronize individuals and institutions who would produce what the 'British conquerors defined as the traditions of the conquered' (p. 46). In all three projects we can see how Orientalist scholarship was intertwined both with colonial rule and with constructions of Indian Otherness. 'Acquiring historical and linguistic knowledge of India's classical past was not simply a disciplinary activity, but also an administrative imperative of colonial rulers mapping and securing a new political and cultural terrain' (Singh, 1996, p. 70).

Looking particularly at the development of work on Indian languages, Cohn (1996) argues that the development of grammars, dictionaries and translations from Indian languages 'began the establishment of discursive formation, defined an epistemological space, created a discourse (Orientalism), and had the effect of converting Indian forms of knowledge into European objects' (p. 21). Halhed's English grammar of Bengal (1778), therefore, was 'part of a large project that would stabilize and perpetuate British rule in Bengal' (p. 30). Singh (1996) similarly suggests that the well-intentioned work of the sanskritist William Jones was 'aimed at the "discovery" of Indian tradition and the reform of its society' and 'fed into a larger liberal, yet colonial, discourse of civilization and rescue that interpellated the Indian subject' (p. 69). According to Cohn, the command over Indian languages was intimately linked to the development of a language of command. Thus looking at conversations in Hindustani in the *Oriental Linguist* revised and republished in 1809, Cohn shows how 'in almost all the dialogues the mishap, mistake or stupidity of the Indian servant is the theme: soup is served without a spoon, food is either too hot, cold, thick, or thin' (p. 40). Meanwhile the image of the Englishman that emerges from these dialogues is of 'the one who commands, who knows how to give orders and how to keep the natives in their proper place in the order of things through practical, not classical knowledge' (p. 41). It is in such constructions that we can start to see the connections between the development of language policies, dictionaries, and teaching materials and the construction of images of Self and Other.

There are some important points to note, however, in the particular relationships between Orientalism and language policy. First, it needs to be understood that for most of the Orientalists there was never much doubt about either the superiority of Western knowledge or the importance of Oriental knowledge for effective colonial rule. Indeed, in the same year as Macaulay's famous Minute, the Orientalist W.C. Taylor, clinched his argument for more funding for Orientalist scholarship with the aphorism 'KNOWLEDGE IS POWER' (Capitals in original; cited in Cohn, 1996, p. 45). It is also interesting that according to Macaulay, in making his sweeping dismissal of Indian literature ('a single shelf of a good European library was worth the whole native literature of India and Arabia') he claims to be taking 'the oriental learning at the valuation of the orientalists themselves' (Macaulay, 1835, p. 241). In fact, a crucial aspect of Orientalist language policy was to use vernacular languages in order to promote Western knowledge. As Edward Bayley, Vice Chancellor of the Calcutta University, observed in a Minute on 13 August 1870 (Government of India, 1963, p. 101), Orientalism 'was an attempt to make the Classical Languages of the East the media for conveying European knowledge'.

On the other hand, it is also important to understand a diversity of positions within Orientalism. First, in general terms, as Metcalf (1995) has observed, two different Orientalist discourses converged in India: 'one derived from the European encounter with Muslim Middle East; the other an attempt to describe distant Asian lands where a tropical climate shaped passive and effeminate people' (Metcalf, 1995, p. 138). Thus, it is important, as I shall be arguing particularly in Chapters 4 and 6, to distinguish clearly between different versions of Orientalism. In this chapter I am trying to show how the genesis of this work intertwined with colonial language policy in India. Later I shall argue that this took on different forms in relation to Malaya, Hong Kong and China. Second, it is also important to observe some of the paradoxes in the Orientalist position. Singh describes it thus:

> on the one hand, the Orientalists as civil servants shared the standard colonial belief in the superiority of Western knowledge and institutions. On the other hand, these Indologists 're-discovered' a glorious India by identifying a certain resemblance between East and West in a shared ancient past.
>
> (1996, p. 71)

Metcalf (1995) suggests that such contradictions lay at the heart of colonial ideology.

Finally, there were deep tensions between those whose interests centred on the study of (and construction of) classical Indian languages, and those who took a more pragmatic stance and urged more work in the vernaculars. As Cohn (1996) puts it, 'the battle between the classicists and the vernacularists in relation to Hindustani was to continue throughout the nineteenth century' (p. 44). Indeed it was eventual victory of a vernacularist view of education rather than a classicist line that would be more significant than any supposed victory of Anglicism over Orientalism. Within these competing Orientalist arguments, several positions on language policy can be discerned. First, was what we might call the purist Orientalist, who favoured education in the Asian classics and little else (this was also suggested for both colonized and colonizers). This view on the one hand revered some distant ancient past and on the other saw India in the present in disarray and decline. The way to return to a golden (and, of course, as it turned out, Arean) past was via the classics. Second, two slightly different versions of this position argued that the end goal must nevertheless be to spread Western knowledge, which could be, as a common phrase put it, 'grafted on' to the Eastern knowledge already gained; or, more simply, Western knowledge should be spread via the classical languages of Asia. A third position saw the spread of Western knowledge as the key aim of education but considered the best route to be the vernacular languages. Finally, a fourth position was most concerned with education as moral discipline, and was content to use local forms of moral education taught through the vernacular as the best means of achieving this. It is these last two more pragmatic versions of Orientalism that gained sway in nineteenth-century India.

Turning now to Anglicism – the vehement support for educational intervention through the medium of English – it is worth noting that it emerged at a similar time. Charles Grant (1746–1823), a member of the Clapham Sect, made his position clear towards the end of the eighteenth century in his article entitled: *Observations on the state of society among the Asiatic subjects of Great Britain, particularly with respect to morals, and on the means of improving it* (written chiefly in 1792; dated 16 August 1797; Bureau of Education, 1920, pp. 81–6):

> The true cure of darkness is the introduction of light. The Hindoos err, because they are ignorant, and their errors have never fairly been laid before them. The communication of our light and knowledge to them, would prove the best remedy for their disorders, and this remedy is proposed, from a full conviction that if judiciously and patiently applied, it would have great and happy effects upon them, effects honourable and advantageous for us.
>
> There are two ways of making this communication: the one is, by the medium of the languages of those countries, the other is by the medium of our own. In general, when foreign teachers have pro-

posed to instruct the inhabitants of any country, they have used the vernacular tongue of that people, for a natural and necessary reason, that they could not hope to make any other mean of communication intelligible to them. This is not our case in respect of our eastern dependencies. They are our own, we have possessed them long, many Englishmen reside among the natives, our language is not unknown there, and it is practicable to diffuse it more widely.

(pp. 81–2)

Grant's arguments are interesting since, first, they emerge from the influential context of the Clapham Sect; second, this is one of the earliest clear enunciations of what was to become the Anglicist position; third, it is clearly an argument in favour of education for enlightenment; and fourth, it appears to put the argument for education in English in largely practical terms.

Grant goes on to argue that 'Thus superior, in point of ultimate advantage does the employment of the English language appear; and upon this ground, we give a preference to that mode, proposing here that the communication of our knowledge shall be made by the medium of our own language.' (p. 82). Rather than the Orientalist position, which for many was an issue of how best to spread European knowledge through the languages of India, Grant argued fervently for the importance of English as the language through which such benefits would reach the Indian populace: 'The first communication, and the instrument of introducing the rest, must be the English language; this is a key which will open to them a world of new ideas, and policy alone might have impelled us, long since, to put it into their hands' (p. 83). With English, he suggested, a whole world would open up to the native population:

With our language, much of our useful literature might, and would, in time be communicated. The art of Printing, would enable us to dissemble our writings in a way the Persians never could have done, though their compositions had been as numerous as ours. Hence the Hindus would see the great use we make of reason on all subjects, and in all affairs; they also would learn to reason, they would become acquainted with the history of their own species, the past and present state of the world; their affections would gradually become interested by various engaging works, composed to recommend virtue; the general mass of their opinions would be rectified; and above all, they would see a better system of principles and morals. New views of duty as rational creatures would open upon them; and that mental bondage in which they have long been holden would gradually dissolve.

(p. 84)

This is, of course, a splendid example of the arrogance of this line of thinking, with its arguments that Indian beliefs and customs would not only be
changed but would also be corrected by Western knowledge. Yet, as I
argued above, it was not in many ways different from the Orientalist position. It is also worth observing here too the argument that teaching through
English would lead to the development of rational thought, an issue to
which I shall return in later chapters. Nevertheless, although we can see here
a clear line to the arrogance of Macaulay and his infamous Minute described
below, I also want to argue that to cast this line of thought as the black
sheep of colonialism is both to fail to see the liberal and ameliorative intentions that lie behind it (and thus, as I shall argue, to fail to see the arrogance
that often lies behind such liberal humanism) and also to contrast this too
easily with an apparently less arrogant Orientalism (and thus to fail to see the
arrogance and will for social control that may lie behind apparently benevolent policy decisions in favour of local languages).

From arguments such as those of Grant, we finally arrive at Macaulay's
Minute, with its sweeping dismissal of Indian thought and culture, its pragmatic insistence that while they could not hope to educate all the people,
they should nevertheless 'do our best to form a class who may be interpreters
between us and the millions we govern – a class of persons Indian in blood
and colour, but English in tastes, in opinions, in morals and in intellect'
(1835, p. 240), and finally its argument in favour of English:

> It stands pre-eminent even among the languages of the West. . . .
> Whoever knows that language has already access to all the vast intel-
> lectual wealth which all the wisest nations of the earth have created
> and hoarded in the course of ninety generations. It may safely be
> said that the literature now extant in that language is of greater value
> than all the literature which three hundred years was extant in all
> the languages of the world together. Nor is this all. In India, English
> is the language spoken by the ruling class. It is spoken by the higher
> class of natives at the seats of Government. It is likely to become the
> language of commerce throughout the seas of the East.
>
> (Bureau of Education, 1920, p. 110)

One important point I wish to make before turning to the effects of the
struggles between Anglicism and Orientalism is the location of Anglicism
within liberal humanism. In spite of the arrogance of his rhetoric, Macaulay
represented a liberal view of progress – India was to come under the tutelage
of England and was to progress towards a European model and the best way
for this to be achieved was via education in English. Thus it was the arguments of Macaulay, Trevelyan, Bentham and others that were at the fore-
front of the 'frenzy of liberal reform known as the "civilizing mission"'

(Singh, 1996, p. 89). This liberalism, as Metcalf (1995) points out, was informed by a 'radical universalism':

> Contemporary European, especially British, culture alone represented civilization. No other cultures had any intrinsic validity. There was no such thing as 'Western' civilization; there existed only 'civilization'. Hence the liberal set out, on the basis of this shared humanity, to turn the Indian into an Englishman.
>
> (p. 34)

And this liberal interventionist view of civilization was to form one of the central discourses that continued through the colonial period: 'Macaulay and Mountbatten, the last viceroy, were . . . linked indissolubly together as the beginning and the end of a chain forged of liberal idealism' (Metcalf, 1995, p. 233). As I shall argue, however, there are also good reasons for not viewing Mountbatten as the final link in this chain.

Anglicism is often taken as the stereotypical colonialist position. There were also, however, contradictions in this position since, as Singh (1996) points out, the 'agents of empire were faced with a dual task of justifying colonialism on the ground that backward societies need to be civilized and insisting that only Europeans could do this, ironically implying both that the liberal principles were universally valid and that they were uniquely European in their origin' (p. 85). More importantly, however, it is worth noting that the Anglicist position shared many similarities with the various Orientalist positions: the main point of disagreement was the medium through which India should be civilized. Thus, although Macaulay's condescending and disdainful attitude may seem particularly obnoxious, it is not much worse than the view of Asian despotism and static history held by many Orientalists. In this view, India was stuck in an immutable past and was irredeemably corrupt, despotic and diseased. Macaulay's patronizing colonialism was at least more liberal and optimistic, even if it implied a cultural imperialism more threatening than the cultural imprisonment implied by the Orientalists.

### The complementarity and complicity of Orientalism and Anglicism

Much has been made of Macaulay and his Minute. Certainly the debates between Orientalists and Anglicists that had increased in force since 1823 came to a head in the debates of 1834–5. What I want to argue, however, is that, first, the Anglicist view never won out over the Orientalist position; second, that both discourses have continued in various forms down to the present; and that, third, each position was equally complicit with colonialism. It is important to note, however, that although, as Sharpe observes, 'The famous minute was not generally known at the time' (Bureau of Education,

1920, p. 102) and as Frykenberg suggests 'it seems clear from all records and sources of data so far uncovered, that the Minute made virtually no impact in the south' (p. 312), the Minute nevertheless had important short-term implications. Governor Bentinck, the Governor-General, entirely concurred with Macaulay (as we shall see, educational policy was often determined, at least in the short run, by the particular stance of influential administrators and governors), and in a resolution on 7 March 1835 urged that 'all the funds appropriated for the purpose of education would be best employed on English education alone' (Bureau of Education, 1920, p. 120). Others, such as H.T. Prinsep (member of the Council of the Governor General, Director of the East India Company in 1850, an Orientalist and strenuous opponent of Macaulay) strongly opposed both the Minute and Bentinck's hasty endorsement of it. It is nevertheless worth noting that Prinsep concurs on issues such as the superiority of English – the issue is whether English and the knowledge gained via a Western education *can* actually be taught (see Note by H.T. Prinsep, 15 February 1835; Bureau of Education, 1920, pp. 117–29).

Bentinck's endorsement of Macaulay's position by no means ended the controversy, either in terms of the debate over education or in terms of the practical outcomes. First, in any case, implementing the proposed educational change almost inevitably involved a process of compromise between the two camps. Second, with Lord Auckland's succession to the Governorship in 1835, the process of compromise was further extended. (Macaulay, who was in India only from 1834 to 1838, devoted much of the rest of his time to drafting the penal code that was to become the basis of India's criminal law.) Auckland's Minute of 24 November 1839 (and see also discussion of this in the 1882 Report), signalled a compromise between increased provision for English education (while lamenting limited funds) and the maintenance of existing provision for vernacular education. Thus, although it by no means signalled an increase in vernacular provision, neither did it in fact signal a particularly significant increase in English education. Again, emphasis was placed on an education for a small number of Indians of higher class. Auckland did not support, however, translation of European literature and science since, quoting Hodgson on education, although he saw translation and investing in the development of translators as 'an infinitely better disposal of the Parliamentary grant than the present application of it to the training of a promiscuous crowd of English smatterers, whose average period of schooling cannot, by *possibility*, fit them to be the regenerators of their country . . .' (Bureau of Education, 1920, p. 157), he nevertheless saw translation as an impossible task.

Auckland goes on to argue that 'I would then make it my principal aim to communicate through the means of the English language, a complete education in European Literature, Philosophy and Science to the greatest number of students who may be found ready to accept it at our hands and for whose instructions our funds will admit of our providing' (Bureau of Education, 1920, p. 157). Auckland takes into account the many dissenting views, including those who argued that the central issue was the diffusion of Western knowledge and that poor education in English was not beneficial for this. He cites in his Minute the concerns expressed in the education report from Bengal (*Reports on Vernacular Education in Bengal and Behar* (by Mr Adam), cited in Bureau of Education, 1920, p. 158):

> Extraordinary efforts have been made to extend a knowledge of the English language to the Natives, but those who have more or less profited by the opportunities presented to them do not find much scope for their attainments which on the other hand little fit them for the ordinary pursuits of native society. They have not received a good Native education, and the English education they have received finds little, if any, use.
>
> (p. 158)

Here, then, are three of the main arguments against English: first, that the object of education is to impart Western knowledge and to instill morality and discipline in the native population; second that this is more efficiently done in vernacular languages than in English; and third, that an English education often ill-suits a native for work or for continued integration into society.

Meanwhile, other educational administrators had in any case chosen to interpret Macaulay's and Bentinck's position in their own way. The Report of the General Committee of Public Instruction (Bengal) for 1835 provides an interesting contemporary alternative to the Macaulay/Bentinck position:

> We are deeply sensible of the importance of encouraging the cultivation of the vernacular languages. We do not conceive that the order of the 7th of March (Governor Bentinck's Resolution – 7th March, 1835) precludes us from doing this, and we have constantly acted on this construction. In the discussion which preceded that order, the claims of the vernacular languages were broadly and prominently admitted by all parties, and the question submitted for the decision of Government only concerned the relative advantage of teaching English on the one side and the learned Eastern languages on the other. We therefore conceive that the phrases 'European Literature and Science', 'English education alone', and 'imparting to the native population a knowledge of English literature and science through the medium of the English language', are intended merely to secure the preference to European learning, taught through the medium of English language, over Oriental learning, taught through the medium of the Sanskrit and Arabic

languages, as regards the instruction of those natives who receive a learned education at our seminaries. These expressions have, as we understand them, no reference to the question through what ulterior medium, such instruction as the mass of the people is capable of receiving is to be conveyed.

(Bureau of Education, 1922, pp. 71–2)

In terms of practical policies, then, it can be seen that the prominence given to the Anglicist position as representing colonial discourse is surely misguided. Importantly, however, just as I have suggested that Anglicism by no means won out over Orientalism, neither was this a victory for Orientalism. Rather, the two positions continued alongside each other, and indeed it becomes clear that Anglicism and Orientalism were complementary rather than antagonistic aspects of colonial discourse. Loh Fook Seng (1970) argues that Macaulay's dismissal of Indian culture and scholarship should not be seen as oppositional to the Orientalist position: 'They are but two sides of the same colonial coin sharing the same rationale, to bring light into the native darkness as well as facilitate the exigencies of trade and government' (p. 108). Similarly, Viswanathan (1989) argues that the two positions should be seen 'not as polar opposites but as points along a continuum of attitudes toward the manner and form of colonial governance' (p. 30). Ultimately, she suggests, 'both the Anglicist and the Orientalist factions were equally complicit with the project of domination' (p. 167). With these two discourses in a complementary relationship with each other, and with both deeply complicit with colonial rule, colonial language policy can thus be seen to both reflect colonial ideologies and to be a crucial site of their production.

## Towards a policy of pragmatic vernacularism

Lord Auckland's Minute (24 November 1839) is generally regarded as having settled the 'Anglo-Orientalist controversy' by taking a balanced view. This is certainly true up to a point since it aimed to strike a balance between the two sets of arguments and to develop a policy that accommodated some of the demands from both sides. In two significant ways, however, it did not settle this controversy. First, of course, the debates continued. The Reverend A. Duff of the Church of Scotland Mission, for example, wrote several letters to Auckland criticizing the continued provision of education in Oriental languages, while others continued their arguments against English. And second, because of the limited provision of education, such debates and their supposed resolutions did not have great practical outcomes. As we shall see, it was not until the crucial 1854 Despatch that education turned fundamentally towards widespread provision of vernacular education, and thus in very real terms tipped the argument in one direction. Nevertheless, one can trace from Bentinck's Anglicist position in 1835 a gradual move via Auckland's position in 1839, and the Despatch of the Court of Directors on 20 January 1841, which confirmed Auckland's position, the gradual development of a pro-vernacular line of thinking culminating in the 1854 Despatch.

It is nevertheless instructive to look at how arguments around English and vernacular education developed at this time. Captain Candy, Superintendent of the Poona Sanskrit College, wrote in his 1840 report:

> It seems to me that too much encouragement cannot be given to the study of English, nor too much value put upon it, *in its proper place and connection*, in a plan for the moral improvement of India. This place I conceive to be that of *supplying ideas and the matter of instruction,* not that of being the medium of instruction. The medium through which the mass of the population must be instructed I humbly conceive must be their *Vernacular Tongues,* and neither English nor Sanscrit. . . . In a word, knowledge must be drawn from . . . the English language, the Vernaculars must be employed as the media of communicating it, and Sanscrit must be largely used to improve the Vernaculars and make them suitable for the purpose.
>
> (Bureau of Education, 1922, p. 2; emphasis in original)

This is an intriguing example of a number of key arguments: first, the continued acknowledgement of the importance of English; second, the clear view that its role should nevertheless be limited; third, the conviction that education is about the moral improvement of India; fourth, the emphasis on the vernaculars as the media of education; fifth, the view that English is a storehouse of knowledge, rationality and morality; and finally, the view that the vernaculars need to be improved by drawing on older languages (and that, of course, the British should get involved in such an ameliorative project).

Another way of framing the concerns about using English emerge in a Minute by Colonel Jervis (Member of the Board of Education of the Bombay Presidency, 1844–1849) (24 February 1847) when he criticizes the idea that effective education can be conducted through English:

> '. . . the conclusion appears incontrovertible, that, in proportion as we confine Education to the channel of the English language, so will the fruits be restricted to a number of scribes and inferior Agents or Public and Private Offices, and a few enlightened indi-viduals, – isolated by their very superiority, from their fellow countrymen.
>
> (Bureau of Education, 1922, p. 12)

Jervis goes on to argue that 'The project of importing English literature along with English Cottons into India, and bringing it into universal use, must at once be felt by every reasonable mind as chimerical and ridiculous' (Bureau of Education, 1922, p. 13). While Sir Erskine Perry, President of the Board of Education in Bombay, strongly disagreed with Jervis (a member of the Board), and argued that people wanted education in English, another member of the Board, Juggonath Sunkersett, argued that '. . . the Vernacular languages possess advantages superior to English, as the medium of communicating useful knowledge to the people of Western India' (Bureau of Education, 1922, p. 16). 'If our object is to diffuse knowledge and improve the minds of the natives of India as a people, it is my opinion that it must be done by imparting that knowledge to them in their own language' (p. 17).

In a letter, 5 April 1848, from the Government of Bombay to the Board of Education, the Government's position was put that:

> any one, who observes and compares the proficiency attained by the pupils in the English and Vernacular schools, cannot fail to be convinced of the superiority which the latter manifest in sound and accurate understanding of the subject of their studies. He [the Hon'ble the Governor in Council] has no hesitation in declaring his acquiescence in the view of those who give the preference to the Native languages, in so far that he considers the main efforts for the general education of the people should be exerted in the language familiar to them in infancy; at the same time he would unquestionably afford them the means of acquiring the higher branches of education – the English languages [sic].
>
> (Bureau of Education, 1922, p. 19)

The government position was reaffirmed in a Minute from the Hon'ble J.P. Willoughby (1798–1866; Chief Secretary, Bombay, 1835; Member of Bombay Council, 1846–57) on 12 January 1850, that 'in the opinion of the Government, too much attention is at present paid to English, and too little to Vernacular instruction and that our Educational funds are too unequally apportioned between these two branches of Education' (Bureau of Education, 1922, p. 25).

According to Willoughby, the pro-vernacular arguments, which he shared, 'correspond with those constantly and emphatically avowed by almost all the distinguished men who have taken a part in the administration of India' (Bureau of Education, 1922, p. 26). After producing a list of these distinguished men (Macaulay, Bentinck, Trevelyan and a few other die-hard Anglicists are conspicuously absent from this list), Willoughby goes on to express his surprise that anyone could view this differently:

> It is indeed extraordinary that any difference of opinion should have arisen on the subject, for it seems to me to be perfectly chimerical to suppose that a sound and practical education can be imparted to a

large body of the natives of India speaking so many different tongues and dialects through the medium of a foreign and very difficult language.

(Bureau of Education, 1922, p. 26)

Thus, while allowing for a degree of hyperbole here, it seems that by the middle of the nineteenth century the dominant view, and the view that was claimed to have been dominant historically was one that favoured vernacular education. This was not the more radical Orientalist view that had promoted an élite education in Oriental classics but rather a pragmatic Orientalism, that on the one hand acknowledged the superiority of English and Western knowledge, but on the other sought to develop and control India through as efficient and practical education as possible.

### The 1854 Despatch

The crucial Despatch of 1854 *(Despatch from the Court of Directors of the East India Company, to the Governor General of India in Council* (No. 49, dated 19 July 1854), in a number of ways articulates a position on language education that had already become the standard view in India. The significance of this document (recall that in the 1882 document cited above it was viewed as the key policy document in Indian education) nevertheless warrants looking at some of its key arguments. One of the first interesting points is the language in which the document now couches the moral responsibility of the British to provide education, and to bring light to the darkness of Indian ignorance: 'It is one of our most sacred duties to be the means, as far as in us lies, of conferring upon the natives of India those vast moral and material blessings which flow from the diffusion of useful knowledge, and which India may, under Providence, derive from her connexion with England' (Bureau of Education, 1922, p. 364).

A second and crucial part of the argument, however, displays a much more material reason for providing education to the Indian population, arguing that such an education:

will teach the natives of India the marvellous results of the employment of labor and capital, rouse them to emulate us in the development of the vast resources of their country, guide them in their efforts and gradually, but certainly, confer upon them all the advantages which accompany the healthy increase of wealth and commerce; and, at the same time, secure to us a larger and more certain supply of many articles necessary for our manufactures and extensively consumed by all classes of our population, as well as an almost inexhaustible demand for the produce of British labor.

(Bureau of Education, 1922, p. 365)

Alongside the stance on the British moral imperative to civilize India, then, there exists a far more pragmatic argument. A central issue here is to provide education in order to make Indians greater (and more docile) contributors to colonial capitalism, both as producers of goods for European markets (needing therefore a cheap, minimally educated but docile workforce) and as consumers of European goods (requiring therefore a consumer society with interests in imported goods and the money to buy them).

In light of the above, therefore, it is no surprise that the Despatch signals an intention to provide for 'more extended and systematic promotion of general education in India' (p. 366). The view of education is that it should be centrally concerned with 'European knowledge'. The question is how best to diffuse such knowledge, and thus the document turns to a lengthy exposition on the issue of the medium of instruction:

> We have next to consider the manner in which our object is to be effected, and this leads us to the question of the *medium* through which knowledge is to be conveyed to the people of India. It has hitherto been necessary, owing to the want of translations and adaptations of European works in the vernacular languages of India and to the very imperfect shape in which European knowledge is to be found in any works in the learned languages of the east, for those who desired to obtain a liberal education to begin by the mastery of the English language as a key to the literature of Europe, and a knowledge of English will always be essential to those natives of India who aspire to a high order of education.
>
> (p. 367)

The Despatch goes on to warn of the dangers around the larger towns where:

> a very moderate proficiency in the English language is often looked upon by those who attend school instruction as the end and object of their education rather than as a necessary step to the improvement of their general knowledge. We do not deny the value in many respects of the mere faculty of speaking and writing English, but we fear that a tendency has been created in these districts to neglect the study of the vernacular languages.
>
> (Bureau of Education, 1922, p. 367)

The Despatch goes on to point out, in a phrase that was often to be quoted in subsequent documents that:

> It is neither our aim nor desire to substitute the English language for the vernacular dialects of the country. We have always been most sensible of the importance of the use of the languages which alone

are understood by the great mass of the population. . . . It is indispensable, therefore, that, in any general system of education, the study of them should be assiduously attended to, and any acquaintance with improved European knowledge which is to be communicated to the great mass of the people – whose circumstances prevent them from acquiring a higher order of education, and who cannot be expected to overcome the difficulties of a foreign language – can only be conveyed to them through one or other of those vernacular languages.

(Bureau of Education, 1922, p. 367)

Having made its position clear on the primacy of vernacular education, the Despatch goes on to discuss how to deal with an acknowledged demand for English: 'In any general system of education, the English language should be taught where there is a demand for it, but such instruction should always be combined with a careful attention to the study of the vernacular language of the district, and with such general instruction as can be conveyed through that language' (pp. 367–8). Interestingly, the Despatch goes on to argue that English is indeed 'the most perfect *medium* for the education of those persons who have acquired a sufficient knowledge of it to receive general instruction *through* it', but it should never be given preference over the vernacular languages, which:

will be gradually enriched by translations of European books or by the original compositions of men whose minds have been imbued with the spirit of European advancement, so that European knowledge may gradually be placed in this manner within the reach of all classes of the people.

(p. 368)

The Despatch thus argues for a dual role for English and the vernacular languages:

We look, therefore, to the English language and to the vernacular languages of India together as the *media* for the diffusion of European knowledge, and it is our desire to see them cultivated together in all schools in India of a sufficiently high class to maintain a school-master possessing the requisite qualifications.

(Bureau of Education, 1922, p. 368)

In its summary of objectives, the Despatch concludes:

We have declared that our object is to extend European knowledge throughout all classes of the people. We have shown that this object must be effected by means of the English language in the higher branches of instruction, and by that of the vernacular languages of India to the great mass of the people.

(Bureau of Education, 1922, p. 392)

In this document, then, we can see a rejection of hardline Orientalism and Anglicism, and an adoption of a position informed by both. European knowledge remains the key goal of education, and while English may be the exemplary language for its promotion, the vernacular languages remain the more efficient way to spread such knowledge. The dangers of allowing limited English education are warned against while the Despatch overall underscores its new emphasis on education as a moral duty and as a means to promote colonial capitalism.

### Policy after 1854

The Despatch brought about a number of significant changes and developments, including a major emphasis on vernacular education. It also was responsible for the creation of an Education Department with school inspectors, the establishment of Calcutta, Bombay and Madras Universities in 1857, a development of the grants–in–aid scheme whereby private and missionary schools could apply for state funding subject to regular school inspections, and the establishment of normal schools for teacher education.

Following the abolition of the East India Company in 1858 (after the so-called Indian Mutiny) and the shift of colonial administration directly to the British Government, the recommendations of the 1854 Despatch were confirmed by the *Educational Despatch, No 4*, India Office, London, 7 April 1859, for the Secretary of State for India. Following this consolidation of policy in 1854 and 1859, education reports tend to be large factual reports of the state of education in India, culminating in the huge 1882 report (see p. 70). These are of course interesting as forms of knowledge of the Other (see Cohn, 1996; Metcalf, 1995), but they are less interesting in terms of the debates over educational issues. Nevertheless, there were many interesting discussions in the latter half of the nineteenth century and I would like to briefly point to a few of them.

First, the concern raised above about students aiming for a simple knowledge of English for quick gain resurfaces a number of times. In his *Note on the State of Education in India* (1862) A.M. Montreath, Under Secretary to the Government of India, decries the 'evil tendency which has shewn itself more especially in the immediate vicinity of the Presidency Towns to substitute a study of the English language in place of the acquisition of general knowledge through the vernacular'. This refers generally to the practice that the report goes on to lament of many students opting for 'as much knowledge of English and no more as is sufficient for becoming inferior clerks, copyists, salesmen, hawkers, &c' (Government of India, 1960, p. 106). What I think is interesting here is the emerging concern – described in terms as strong as an 'evil tendency' – that the lure of English will lead students to get a short-term education in the language without the necessary cultural and ideological load supplied by a proper education. As we shall see, this was one of the emerging fears about the implications of widespread English use.

This concern re-emerges in a slightly different form in an 'Explanatory Memorandum by the Government of the Punjab' on 7 July 1877. Discussing the proposal to raise the Punjab University College to the status of a full university, Lepel Griffin (Officiating Secretary to the Government of the Punjab) remarks that 'what is intended in the Punjab is to place higher education in sympathy with the people, and not in opposition to them'. This, he argues, would be achieved by retaining English only for the highest while disseminating 'the truths of science and art and history through the medium of the vernacular languages'. This would not lead to any neglect of English, he suggests, since it is recognized generally as the key which opens the door to all the higher kinds of employment under the British Government' (Government of India, 1963, p. 202). The real danger, he warns, would be to make English compulsory and deny access to vernacular languages, for if 'the study of the English language is forced upon a very large class of students for whom the Government is unable to provide employment,' there is the danger that such people, 'becoming unfit for their own natural and heredi-tary professions, remain discontented and disloyal members of the com-munity' (Government of India, 1963, pp. 202–3). Here, then, is an argument that was to echo through colonial discourses on education: the fear that too much English would lead to a class of 'discontented and disloyal members of the community'.

Interestingly, too, there was not universal agreement that higher education should aim so completely at education in English. The three universities established in 1857, Bombay, Calcutta and Madras, had all adopted English as their medium of instruction and emphasized almost exclusively Western science and culture. From the mid-1860s however, a controversy developed, with a number of influential groups arguing that Indian languages should be used and more emphasis should be placed on Indian culture and learning. This debate was started by a 'Memorial from the British Indian Association, North-Western Provinces, to the Viceroy and Governor General of India . . .' on 1 August 1867. While acknowledging the importance of English in edu-cation in India, the petition argues that such education still only touches a tiny minority of the people. What is needed is a more accessible education so that people 'will no longer be the ready recipients of those false notions and idle terrors which occasionally confuse and alarm the public mind and lead to the disturbance of general tranquility and order' (Government of India, 1963, p. 22). They go on to argue that:

The country as a whole is in its original state of uncivilised ignorance, and has tasted none of the advantages of learning and civilisation. We have said that in offering our present petitions, our object is not to revive the dead learning and refinement of Asia, but to supplant all this by the introduction of the truer and more recently acquired knowledge of Europe, while we desire to benefit not the few only but the large masses of the people, and to spread over the whole country the blessings of good morality and sound wisdom.

(p. 23)

At present an acquaintance with the higher branches of knowledge can be obtained only by a study of the English language, and it is this which presents the greatest obstacles to the general and rapid propagation of useful knowledge in the country, and which delays the approach of any change for the better in the ideas and morals of the people. By this the growth of Public Education is stunted and withered, and a few only, through a medium difficult of access, can cull the fruits of learning, which should be easy of approach to all.

(Government of India, 1963, p. 23)

What they propose is that 'instead of English alone, the vernacular also may be made the channel for the instruction of all the people alike in the very highest subjects of culture and education' (p. 24). Thus:

while maintaining and promoting English education, can we not adopt a vernacular language, as a medium better suited than a strange tongue for the general diffusion of knowledge and the general reform of ideas, manners and morals of the people – cannot European enlightenment and civilisation be better taught through a language which is understood, than through one which is foreign and unknown and can never be acquired by the vast majority of the 140 millions of British India?

(Government of India, 1963, p. 25)

One other element in these arguments is also worth noting. In a note (3 June 1885) on emphasizing classical languages and literatures in the proposed university for the North-Western Provinces and Oudh, Dr G. Thibaut, Principal of Benares College, argues (Government of India, 1963, pp. 405–18) that students educated only in English and European thought are often unable to properly value their own traditions, and, therefore, despite their supposed better knowledge, morality and rationality, are vulnerable to be taken in by the growing tendency towards Indian nationalism. Their lack of knowledge of their languages and cultures then leads such English–educated individuals to overstate the past traditions of their country. A good education in vernacular languages and literatures would enable such students to come to a fairer and better balanced understanding of the relative merits of the different cultures and forms of knowledge. Here, then, to conclude, is Orientalism turned against itself, or rather a pragmatic version of Orientalism being prescribed as an antidote to a growing nationalism.

## Conclusion

In this chapter I have been trying to show how colonial discourses on language education are interwoven both with broader colonial discourses and with modes of colonial governance. The need to provide education for Indian people became framed among sometimes competing and sometimes complementary discourses: the liberal discourse of the civilizing mission and the moral obligation to bring enlightenment to backward peoples, the need to provide a productive and docile workforce who would also become consumers within colonial capitalism, the various Orientalist positions, including an exoticization and glorification of a distant Indian past and a belief that vernacular languages were the most efficient way to spread European knowledge in India, and the Anglicist insistence that English should be the language of education.

A crucial element of the argument has been the attempt to show the significance of going beyond the simple belief that Anglicism is the archetypal version of colonialism. This has several implications. First, as I suggested in Chapter 1, it helps us readdress relations between simple pasts and complex presents. By focusing on Anglicism, by labeling Macaulay as the designer of educational policy and showing his bigotry, modern day liberals, leftists, and conservatives alike are able to distance themselves easily from colonial complicity. Second, this argument has shown the complicity of various forms of Orientalism in colonial governance. As I shall discuss later, there are important implications for contemporary language policy of understanding how support for vernacular languages was integral to the colonial project.

And third, the significance of my attempt to dislodge what Frykenberg (1988) terms the 'Myth of Macaulay's Minute' (p. 305) has major implications for understanding the development of the cultural constructs of colonialism. It is interesting to observe that in A.P. Howell's (1872) *Education in British India, 1870–71,* (Government of India, 1960), Howell laments the arguments still prevalent that would promote English: 'On the subject of studies in India it is not unusual, especially in papers written in England, to hear a lament that English is not introduced into our schools as the *lingua franca* of the country – a measure of which the advantages are triumphantly insisted on. To such laments I need only offer the consideration of the statistics of area and population and of the millions whose only acquaintance with English is derived from an occasional glimpse of the Collectors' tents in a cold weather tour' (Government of India, 1960, p. 532). What this clearly suggests is that it was in England, not in India, that Anglicism was most rife.

As Frykenberg argues, the effects of the Minute were very limited in India, but as Macaulay's fame grew in England in subsequent years, 'the influence of this Minute was probably cumulative, so that it became more pervasive with each successive generation' (p. 315). That is to say, the significance of Anglicism was not in determining educational policy in Britain's colonies, but rather in developing a discourse about English as the crucial medium for the purveyance of knowledge. Thus, as I shall argue further later, the effects of Macaulay's Minute and colonial Anglicist discourse were far less significant within colonial language policy than they are today within global institutions of support for English. Anglicism has been able to re-emerge in a new world order in which promotion of English has become a far more viable option.

I have focused particularly on India here because of its significance as the major site of production of colonial ideology. As I suggested in Chapter 2, from my point of view, one of the central roles of Empire was to allow colonial ideologies and discourses to flow back to the centre or to flow across to other colonies. As Metcalf (1995) explains:

> The British Raj in India did not of course exist by itself, or solely in its relationship to Great Britain as the metropolitan power. It participated as well in a larger network of relationships that defined the entire British Empire. Ideas and people flowed outward from India, above all to East and South Africa and to Southeast Asia.
>
> (p. 215)

In subsequent chapters, therefore, I shall be looking at how these colonial ideologies flowed through this imperial network. In Chapters 5 and 6 I shall look at how Anglicist and Orientalist discourses have adhered to English in contemporary contexts, re-emerging in different forms in the modern world. In the next chapter I shall explore how colonial language policy developed in Malaya and the Straits Settlements, and Hong Kong. Focusing particularly on Hong Kong, Chapter 4 will show that while on the one hand colonial ideologies flowed across the empire and informed language policies, on the other hand the particular material circumstances of different colonies also produced their own ideological orientations.

# 4

# HONG KONG

## Opium and riots, English and Chinese

I don't see why the English Government should encumber itself
with the teaching of Chinese. . . . I maintain the English
government should teach English. . . . I maintain the English
Government should anglicise its subjects.

(E.R. Belilios, 1882, cited in Report 1883b)

In conclusion I would emphasize the value of English as the
medium of instruction. If we believe that British interests will be
thus promoted, we believe equally firmly that graduates, by the
mastery of English, will acquire the key to a great literature and
the passport to a great trade.

(Lugard, 1910, p. 4)

Boys strongly imbued with European civilization whilst cut away
from the restraining influence of Confucian ethics lose the benefits of education, and the practical experience of Hongkong is
that those who are thoroughly imbued with the foreign spirit,
are bad in morals.

(Eitel, 1882, cited in Report 1883b)

Money spent on the development of the conservative ideas of
the Chinese race in the minds of the young will be money well
spent, and also constitutes social insurance of the best kind.

(R.H. Kotewall, 1926, CO 129/489)

The focus of the last chapter was on how the competing forces of empire,
colonial context, Anglicism and Orientalism together produced the discourses of language education policy. There were three principal focuses to
this argument: first, that it was important to move beyond some simple view
whereby English had been imposed on Indian people. Rather, it was clear
that once a colonial administration was in place, and once it became evident
that English was a gateway to social and economic prestige, the colonized
demanded access to the language. Indeed, colonial governance was pursued
far more through the provision and regulation of local languages than

through the promotion of English. Second, Orientalism and Anglicism, rather than being competing discourses, were both complementary with each other and complicit with colonialism. And third, while these discourses had varying effects on colonial language policy, they also had important effects in terms of the production of the cultural constructs of colonialism. While the proper role for English was being debated, constructions of Self and Other were constantly produced, and as the debates wore on, such constructions came increasingly to adhere to English.

The last chapter focused entirely on India as the crucial site of early production of colonial imagery. In this chapter I want to move on to look very briefly at policy in the Straits Settlements and Malay States before turning in more detail to Hong Kong. The purpose of this investigation is both to develop the arguments of the last chapter further and to point more clearly to the particular contexts of development of colonial discourse. Although in the last chapter I tried to show in general terms how colonial language policies were interwoven with colonial discourses and colonial governance, the breadth of the discussion led to a generality concerning the production of colonial discourse. In this chapter, therefore, by focusing on particular moments in Hong Kong history, I shall try to make the production of colonial discourse more concrete.

There are, as I have already suggested, also more personal reasons for returning to Hong Kong as a site of study, for it was while working in Hong Kong as an English teacher that I became increasingly convinced of the power and continuity of colonial discourses. It was while on the one hand reading colonial documents in Hong Kong libraries and, on the other hand, participating in discussions of English language teaching in Hong Kong, that I started to formulate my concerns about the adherence of discourses. Returning to the context of Hong Kong also allows me to develop another theme I have been trying to emphasize: the importance of achieving an understanding of the complexities of colonial rule in order to readdress both a simplistic view of the past and a distancing from a supposedly complex present. I have been arguing, by contrast, for an approach to history that can work critically and yet tolerate ambiguity. One general example of this may be useful here.

A good example of the complexities and ambiguities of colonial rule can be found in the colonial attitude towards the education of women. A common theme in colonial documents, both in Hong Kong and elsewhere, emphasized the need for far more provision of education for girls. The education report for 1892 proudly shows an increase for girls attending school from 13 per cent of pupils in 1873 to 36 per cent in 1891. In 1893 Belilios School was opened (named after E.R. Belilios, who provided a substantial donation) to provide both primary and secondary education for girls. What is interesting here is that while the British colonial view may be seen as more 'enlightened' in terms of seeing schooling as a moral right for both men and women, this education was also clearly not aimed so much at changing the status of women in society but rather at maintaining the same status for them. As the Director for Education in the Straits Settlements commented in 1934:

> The curriculum of the girls' schools is no longer dead and uninspiring. Cookery, clay-modelling, paper-cutting, drawn-thread work, hygiene taught by Lady Medical Officers, are romantic subjects for the little Malay girl compared with what her elder sisters learnt a few years ago.
>
> (Straits Settlements, 1934)

Thus, as with the general idea that education for men should make them more efficient, law-abiding and so on, so education for women was seen as playing a role in making them better wives and mothers. Since the mothering role was also seen as crucial in educating future generations, this enthusiasm for educating women can be seen as yet another aspect of fostering a more receptive, obedient and hard-working population. According to Addis (1889) 'It is evident that no scheme of education can be considered complete which does not lay special stress on the importance of female education, and no system is adequate which does not provide a careful training for the future wives and mothers of the race' (p. 207). The issue of the medium of education for girls was also an important one. According to Smith (1985) there was a reluctance to provide Chinese girls with an English education lest this made them too attractive to the male European community. Eitel also points to this problem when he recounts the closing of the Diocesan Female Training School in 1865 because 'almost every one of the girls, taught English in that School, became on leaving school, the kept mistress of foreigners' (CO 129/242, p. 80). Eitel goes on to argue, however, that 'by excluding Chinese girls from the onward movement of English education in the Colony,' the government had 'methodically prevented the spread of the English language in Chinese families' (p. 81). He urged greater education for girls in English so that English – and morality – would be more widely spread. Thus, while colonial rule certainly provided more girls with a formal education than would presumably have been the case in the Chinese school system, the content and purposes of that education remained oriented towards using these 'wives and mothers' to further foster the colonial enterprise.

And there is a further complication. As discussed in Chapter 2, one of the major constructs of colonialism was the masculine colonizer and the feminized colonized. One upshot of this construction was that the British came to see themselves as the protectors of native women. By so doing, the colonizers 'could not only, as they saw it, "rescue" these unfortunate creatures; they could also make manifest their own "masculine" character and proclaim their moral superiority over the Indian male' (Metcalf, 1995, p. 94). Probably the most focused of these attempts to save colonized women was the campaign against such practices as sati in India (see Lata Mani, 1989). The setting up of girls schools should also be seen within this production of gendered colonial roles. Thus, even a brief examination of the practices and discourses of colonial education for girls reveals how colonial discourse was both reflected and produced in this encounter.

## Playing safe: language policy in Malaya

I have written fairly extensively elsewhere about language policy in colonial Malaya (1994a, 1994b), so I shall only briefly raise some salient issues here. As I argued in the last chapter, it may at first be tempting to assume that language policies in the empire favoured a massive spread of English around the globe, that the zeal of imperialistic discourse, the call to bring British culture and language to the rest of the world, had led to the teaching of English being as extensive and widespread as possible. Such a view might be bolstered by the rhetoric of many nineteenth-century writers on language, who praised the spread of English as something ordained by God, as a matter of destiny, as something beneficial to the human race. Soon, some writers suggested, English would be the universal language, swallowing up other languages and becoming the international medium of communication (see also Chapter 5). If one lets oneself be seduced by the imperialistic passion of such writing, it is not hard to believe that English had indeed been so widely spread during the colonial era that the subsequent spread in more recent years was but a natural product of this earlier missionary zeal.

Just as the colonial history of India renders this interpretation impossible, so discourses on language education in Malaya suggested a tendency to 'play safe' and promote local languages rather than English. In the 1884 report on education (Straits Settlements, 1884), E.C. Hill, the Inspector of Schools for the colony, explained his reasons against increasing the provision of education in English:

> The objections to teaching English in all the Malay schools would be – (1) that the cost would be very great; (2) that it would be impossible, at once, to obtain teachers with the necessary qualifications; (3) that as pupils who acquire a knowledge of English are invariably unwilling to earn their livelihood by manual labour, the immediate result of affording an English education to any large number of Malays would be the creation of a discontented class who might become a source of anxiety to the community. A certain number of Malays educated in English are of course required to fill

clerical appointments and situations of the kind which do not include manual labour.

(p. 171)

This last argument concerning the creation of a 'discontented class' through education in English clearly echoes statements from the preceding chapter. These views in turn are echoed by the influential figure of Frank Swettenham, Resident of Perak (later, Sir Frank, High Commissioner of the Federated Malay States and Governor of the Straits Settlements), when he commented in the *Perak Annual Report* for 1890 that:

the one danger to be guarded against is an attempt to teach English indiscriminately. It could not be well taught except in a very few schools, and I do not think that it is at all advisable to attempt to give to the children of an agricultural population an indifferent knowledge of a language that to all but the very few would only unfit them for the duties of life and make them discontented with anything like manual labour.

(p. 16)

Four years later in the *Perak Government Gazette* (6 July 1894), he wrote: 'I am not in favour of extending the number of 'English' schools except where there is some palpable desire that English should be taught. Whilst we teach children to read and write and count in their own languages, or in Malay . . . we are *safe*' (emphasis in original). Thus, as Loh Fook Seng (1970) comments, 'Modern English education for the Malay then is ruled out right from the beginning as an unsafe thing' (p. 114).

The other side of this policy – the promotion of vernacular education for the Malay population – although frequently couched in terms of a 'moral duty', was closely linked to questions of social control, colonial capitalism and a desire among many colonial administrators to maintain local populations in a state of 'happy innocence'. Here again we can see the intersection of Orientalist discourses and colonial capitalism. As George Maxwell (Chief Secretary to the Government of the Federated Malay States, 1920-26) said in a speech in 1927, the main aims of education in Malaya were 'to improve the bulk of the people and to make the son of the fisherman or peasant a more intelligent fisherman or peasant than his father had been' (Maxwell, 1927, p. 406). In an article on vernacular education in the State of Perak, the Inspector of Schools, H.B. Collinge, explained that:

Thousands of our boys are taken away from idleness, and whilst learning to read and write their own language, to cipher a little, to know something of geography, to write Malay in the Roman character, and to take an active interest in physical exercise and manly sports, they at the same time acquire habits of industry, obedience, punctuality, order, neatness, cleanliness and general good behaviour. . . . After a boy has been a year or two at school, he is found to be less lazy at home, less given to evil habits and mischievous adventure, more respectful and dutiful, much more willing to help his parents, and with sense enough not to entertain any ambition beyond following the humble home occupations he has been taught to respect. . . . The school also inspires a respect for the vernacular; and I am of the opinion that if there is any lingering feeling of dislike of the 'white man', the school tends greatly to remove it, for the people see that the Government has really their welfare at heart in providing them with this education, free, without compulsion, and with the greatest consideration for their mohammedan sympathies.

(Perak Government Gazette, 4 January 1895, pp. 4–7)

Clearly, then, one aspect of this vernacular education was to promote loyalty, obedience, and acceptance of colonial rule. Another dimension of the promotion of vernacular education was tied to the Orientalist interests of many of the scholar-administrators who were closely connected to educational policies. Swettenham, Loh Fook Seng suggests, 'earned his Knighthood on the strength of his ability to understand the ignorant unspoilt Malays' and Wilkinson 'believed as many an Englishman has believed before him and since that the native must not be taken away, must not be uprooted from his fascinating environment, fascinating to a brilliant Malay scholar' (1970, p. 114). Thus, as Loh Fook Seng goes on to suggest, 'Much of the primitive Malay education that continued to be supplied by the British Government was in no small degree due to this attempt to preserve the Malay as a Malay, a son of the soil in the most literal sense possible' (p. 114).

These policies in Malaya were to have serious effects for the colonized, increasing class and ethnic divisions in the country, dividing the different ethnic groups (Malay, Chinese and Indian) and developing a more inequitable social structure:

The vernacular educated remained as a substratum of the new Malayan society; while the Malay aristocracy learned that their duty was to get on in the world created by the British, the mass of the Malays remained untouched by Western culture and had no share in the enormous wealth produced by the country.

(Chai Hon-Chan, 1964, p. 278)

Thus, while both Anglicist and Orientalist factions contributed in their different ways to the maintenance of colonial rule, they also left a country more sharply divided along class and ethnic lines than before. English education 'had emerged as a new basis for the achievement of elitist status' (Loh Fook Seng, 1975, p. 85) while the vernacular educated remained divided and disenfranchized. These divisions are still being struggled over today.

And, as I have been arguing, the effects of colonial language policies can be seen not only in the legacies of ethnic and class divisions that the British used and broadened for colonial governance, but also in their productive force as constructs of colonialism. Here again we can see how the native Other and the exclusive English are constructed within colonial discourse. It is with these concerns in mind that I shall now turn to look at colonial education in Hong Kong. Once again, this is not intended to be a complete or linear documentation of this period but rather an attempt to show how different colonial discourses operated to construct education in certain directions. My interest then is to look at educational policy as a cultural construction of colonialism and to trace its legacies – both material and discursive – down to the colonial present in Hong Kong.

## Hong Kong: opium, riots and myths

As I suggested at the beginning of this chapter, I want to work towards a more contextualized account of colonial discourse than I was able to do in the last chapter. To this end, it is important to provide a clearer account of the historical background to colonial education. In this very brief overview of various aspects of Hong Kong's history, I want to emphasize certain features that are frequently downplayed. One of the immediate difficulties in dealing with Hong Kong history is that so much of it (and especially the histories written in English) could by and large be categorized as colonial history. Such histories not only frequently reproduce that old colonial trope of suggesting that history began with the coming of the White Man (1842) but also present a history of benevolent and beneficial rule. Although there are a number of different types of colonial history, from the new genre of coffee-table history book spawned by the 1997 handover to the serious academic book, many echo loudly with the discourses of colonialism. An example of the first type is Robson's (1992) *The Potent Poppy*, which announces on its cover that 'Clippers laden with opium launched a golden age of adventure, trade and treachery for merchants and mandarins – and shaped the glittering prize of Empire: Hong Kong'. A slightly more serious but nevertheless celebratory approach can be found in books such as Mellor's (1992) history of Frederick Lugard's period as Governor of Hong Kong (see pp. 117–22). While this style of overtly colonialist history is less common today, the colonial discourses on which they draw can still be found at work in the more serious works of history.

More recent and more subtle approaches to colonial history tend to equivocate a great deal on how to interpret the colonial past, suggesting that we need to see 'both sides' of colonialism. Sweeting's (1990, 1992) work on

101

educational history is a good example of this. Arguing against what he calls the 'more simplistic versions of the colonization-as-cultural-imperialism thesis' (1992,p. 42; and compare 1990, p. 48), he suggests that:

> It is not fair to conclude . . . that the process of colonization yielded in an unvariable and uniform manner ethnically harmful or culturally imperialistic results. Whether one refers to society in general or focuses on specific educational developments, cases can be quoted of racial cooperation, relatively harmonious side-by-side coexistence, or at least the emergence of a symbiotic relationship between the Chinese and the British in Hong Kong.
>
> (p. 44)

Later, while acknowledging that colonization 'contributed to the generation of a range of patronizing or, at least, paternalistic attitudes', he suggests that it nevertheless 'brought some advantages for the territory's educational policies and practices' and 'thus, the colonization strand in Hong Kong's historical tapestry appears, on deeper analysis, multihued, not uniformly black in color' (p. 47). The point here is not so much that Sweeting is wrong about this 'multihued tapestry' – indeed I have also been arguing for a more complex treatment of colonialism – but that this argument is used to oppose a critical form of analysis. By taking up a stance against the sometimes simplistic versions of cultural imperialism, Sweeting is able to emphasize harmony and stability.[1]

In Sweeting's constant attempts to refute a view of cultural imperialism, he quotes from the preface to the 1907 edition of the *Chambers' English Cantonese Dictionary*, which tells of a group of men (including Dr J. Chalmers, the head of the London Mission, G.H. Bateson-Wright, Headmaster of Queen's College and A. Falconer, former Second Master of the old Government Central School) assiduously discussing translations of Chinese classics. Sweeting comments that:

> the existence of a group of sinologues, similar in ways to the 'Orientalists' of the British Raj, composed of missionaries, government officials of varying rank and businessmen . . . may also suggest that, in Hong Kong's case, a revision needs to be made to interpretations based upon concepts of Colonialism as Cultural Imperialism.
>
> (1990, p. 48)

Once again, on one level he is right: this does not accord with a simplistic thesis of cultural imperialism. On another level, however, without taking up the far more interesting implications of Orientalist scholarship, Sweeting is able to do little more than paint a glowing picture of these assiduous scholars. Yet, as the discussion of Orientalism in the last chapter made clear, such

Orientalist scholarship was also deeply complicit with colonialism. Translating the classics from Chinese is seen here as an engagement with Chinese culture, an alternative to Anglicism. And yet, translation must also be understood within the context of colonial relations of culture and power: 'Translation as a practice shapes, and takes shape within, the asymmetrical relations of power that operate under colonialism.' (Niranjana, 1992, p. 2). In the context of India:

> the famous Orientalist attempt to reveal the former greatness of India often manifests itself as the British or European task of translating and thereby *purifying* the debased native texts. This Romantic Orientalist project slides almost imperceptibly into the Utilitarian Victorian enterprise of 'improving' the natives through English education.
>
> (ibid, pp. 16–17)

The views of colonialism that many of these histories put into place downplay the background of colonial exploitation, disdain and racism and stress instead a history of colonial benevolence, stability, and docility. As Yee (1992) argues, the imperialist belief that whatever was done in the name of freedom and trade was good, as well as the negative stereotypes of China produced a very distorted version of the history of the opium trade:

> With such anti-China thinking from leading writers and the abundant stereotypic reports of ship crews and missionaries, the truth of the Chinese side of the argument never came across until long after negative attitudes were solidified in the West . . . This unhealthy lack of understanding would continue well into the present century with a lingering effect even today.
>
> (p. 9)

What I want to focus on, then, in this brief historical overview are two aspects of Hong Kong's history that I think are crucial to an understanding of the colony but which have been constantly downplayed by colonial historians: the role of opium and the long succession of riots. As Trocki (1990) points out, British colonial historians have constantly neglected the role of the opium trade in Britain's history as a colonial power in Asia: 'The story of the opium trade and its role in the entire imperial century has been almost totally neglected' (p. 5). With respect to the history of anti-colonial riots and demonstrations in Hong Kong, Young (1994) suggests that 'the common view that Hong Kong has always enjoyed political stability is a historical myth' (pp. 135–6). Furthermore, when this view is coupled with another common theme in historical and contemporary writing that Hong Kong people are politically docile (see e.g. Miners, 1981), it is important to ask what interests such a version of history serves: 'If to suggest that there had been no political reform in Hong Kong because of the Hong Kong people's lack of interest in political matters is not to make apologies for British colonial rule, then the attempt must be to ignore the history of Hong Kong's recent past' (Young, 1994, p. 145).

## The opium city

The first aspect of Hong Kong's colonial history that I want to emphasize, then, is its role in the opium trade. As Yee (1992) argues, the magnitude and importance of this trade, indeed what he refers to as the 'opium holocaust' has frequently been played down: 'Compared to the infamies of World War II, which still prey upon the Germans and Japanese, the supply of opium to China which led to the addiction and death of countless hundreds of millions has been neglected' (p. 47). Hong Kong developed as a direct result of the imperial trade in opium. In a similar fashion to the triangular slave trade before it (ships left England with cheap goods for barter off the African coast, sailed across the Atlantic to the Caribbean or American ports to sell their cargoes of slaves, and returned to England laden with cotton, sugar and other goods from the American colonies), the British (and others, including the Americans) developed a lucrative route from England to India, where they traded for opium, across the Indian ocean to the coastal ports of China, where they traded opium for tea, silk and other Chinese goods in demand in Europe, and then back to England. These two trade triangles in fact interlocked through the cotton mills of North England, where the new industrial labour force of Britain turned the cotton from North America into finished articles for export to India. According to Freuchen (1957, cited in Yee), it would be more appropriate to refer to the famous and romanticized giant sailing ships of the nineteenth century not as tea clippers but as 'opium clippers'. Criticizing the 'flagrant self-contradiction of the Christianity-canting and civilization-mongering British government' (1858b, p. 219), Karl Marx quotes Montgomery Martin's comparison of the slave and opium trades:[2]

> Why, the slave-trade was merciful compared with the opium trade: We did not destroy the bodies of the Africans, for it was our immediate interest to keep them alive; we did not debase their nature, corrupt their minds, nor destroy their souls. But the opium seller slays the body after he has corrupted, degraded and annihilated the moral being and unhappy sinners, which every hour is bringing new victims to a Moloch which knows no satiety, and where the English murderer and Chinese suicide vie with each other in offerings at his shrine.
>
> (Cited in Marx, 1858a, pp. 213–14)

This trade soon took on immense proportions 'though few realise the magnitude and extent of opium trade through most of the territory's history' (Yee, 1992, p. 37). As a result of the first 'Opium War' (1840–42), during which the British attacked Guangzhou in retaliation for the destruction of large quantities of opium, Hong Kong was 'ceded' to the British, along with a six million dollar reparation. Hong Kong developed fast as a trading port, with many of the large and famous companies directly involved in the opium trade. According to the Auditor-General's report for 1845, there were 80 opium clippers registered in Hong Kong, 19 belonging to Jardine, Matheson & Co and 13 to Dent & Co (Yee, 1992, p. 37). Hong Kong became 'the world's opium centre handling 75% of India's opium crop' (p. 38). The Treaty of Nanjing (29 August 1842) had formally ended the First Opium War and reconfirmed British possession of Hong Kong. The Second Opium War (1857–58) led to further financial reparations and territorial gains, notably the cession of the Kowloon peninsula to the British in 1860. The trade in opium was to remain dominant in Hong Kong's development until the Japanese invasion in 1942: 'The deliberate application of its cultivation within the territory and in Singapore and other British colonies: its sale locally and as an export staple for more than two thirds of Hong Kong's history (1841–1942) cast an indelible blight upon British history in the territory and Asia' (Yee, 1992, p. 41).

The main points I wish to make here are that, as Yee says, although 'the history is abundantly clear on the prolonged official profiteering from opium in Hong Kong . . . it is a history not generally realised today' (p. 41). There has been a constant tendency to deny this history and to blame the Chinese for the rapacious Opium Wars. Cantlie's (1906) version of the Opium Wars is a good example: the war of 1840 'is frequently styled the Opium War, but that is a mere misnomer. The war was the result of 200 years of insult, injury, and wrong heaped upon British subjects by the Chinese. It was not, in fact, until starvation and annihilation stared the British community in the face that the Government came to their aid.' (Cantlie, 1906, p. 503). The similarities between this version of history and the book quoted in Chapter 1 are clear in terms of their explanation of British aggression as caused by its victims. It is interesting to compare this version with Karl Marx's (1857) description of 'English ferocity in China' in an article in the *New York Daily Tribune*: 'The unoffending citizens and peaceful tradesmen of Canton have been slaughtered, their habitations battered to the ground, and the claims of humanity violated, on the flimsy pretence that "English life and property are endangered by the aggressive acts of the Chinese!"' (p. 114).

Despite claims that the British authorities were opposed to the opium trade, this is simply not borne out by the evidence. Indeed, Trocki (1990) speaks of the 'incredibly determined efforts by the Colonial Office . . . and the British economic community in the colonies to oppose anything that might decrease the opium revenue or otherwise shift the tax burden'. 'Any argument', he suggests, 'that the imperial system did not rely on opium and was not, in the pathogenic sense, systematically dependent on the drug is simply not in accordance with the facts' (1990, p. 237). It is against this background of imperial trade and interests that the governance of Hong Kong needs to be seen. Hong Kong had become a crucial trading post in the Imperial system, with vast amounts of opium passing one way, and silk, tea and other goods in the other direction. What the colonial government would see as its moral duty to the shifting Chinese population in Hong Kong has to be seen in that context.

### Riots and resistance

The other theme I want to point to here is the frequent acts of resistance to colonial rule in Hong Kong. A common colonial discourse is one that constructs the colonized as willing and passive recipients of colonial rule. Acts of resistance are dismissed as acts of childishness, barbarity, foolishness, disloyalty and ingratitude. Discussing acts of resistance to colonial rule in India, West (1906) wrote:

> There is amongst too many of the educated classes in India a disposition to take all that has been done, all that has been conceded, as a mere matter of course, all that has been withheld as a just ground for discontent. . . . Worst of all, there is a tendency amongst clever but feather-headed Hindus to deem lightly and speak lightly of their obligations as subjects and citizens of the empire.
>
> (p. xxiv)

This view in Hong Kong has led to a tendency to stress the social and political stability of the colony, the political acquiescence and passivity of the population, and the supposedly ubiquitous interest in financial rather than political questions. According to Tsai (1994), however, this assertion tells only half the story since 'there was a long series of tensions and crises in which the Chinese people in Hong Kong expressed their displeasure with and hostility toward the British colonial authorities' (p. 9).

Indeed, as Tsai (1994), Chan (1994) and Young (1994) make clear, the history of colonial relations in Hong Kong is marked by a long series of 'riots' and demonstrations: the strikes in the 1840s and 1850s; the 1884 insurrection (a boatman's strike in sympathy with the Chinese conflict with the French which escalated after police intervention into large-scale riots and attacks on foreigners); the mass celebrations after the 1911 Revolution in China (which, as Tsai suggests, marked a shift from anti-foreign sentiment to Chinese nationalism); the tramway boycott of 1912–13; the 'May Fourth' boycott of 1919 (sparked off by protests in China as a result of the refusal of the European powers to return Qingdao to China at the Versailles Treaty);

the mechanics' strike of 1920; the 1922 seamen's strike; the massive general strike and boycott of 1925–26, which came close to ruining Hong Kong financially; and on to the postwar strikes, riots and demonstrations in 1952, 1956, 1967 (these violent clashes leading to an official account of 51 dead, almost 100 wounded, 5,000 arrested and many deported); and the peaceful pro-democracy demonstrations in May 1989. All these large-scale incidents suggest a fairly turbulent history and a populace that is anything but docile and acquiescent.

Many of these incidents have been dismissed either as the products of purely economic concerns or as the result of 'outside agitation'. Yet, the elements of anti-foreign, anti-government, and anti-colonial politics in many of these demonstrations suggest otherwise. Discussing the 1925–26 strike/boycott, for example, Chan (1994) argues that 'In all its essential aspects, the 1925–26 movement was a nationalistic protest against imperialism, using economic means for political ends, not vice versa' (p. 46). Chan warns that 'the British in the sunset years of their governance in Hong Kong should be more aware of the true nature of their colonial rule, which has been characterized by an acute lack of representative mandate, public accountability, and, above all, popular legitimacy among the majority of the people of Hong Kong' (p. 28). The history of colonial government in Hong Kong has therefore been anything but smooth and the people of Hong Kong have been far from acquiescent. And yet this myth continues until the present.

Not only is it important to grasp this in order to get a better understanding of Hong Kong's past, but it is also important to see this history of unrest as the background to educational policies. The setting up of Hong Kong University (1912) by Governor Lugard, for example, needs to be seen against the background of the 1911 revolution in China. Indeed this revolution and the increased sense of nationalism amongst the Chinese was to have profound effects on Hong Kong's schools. As Chan (1994) points out:

> To counter the Chinese revolution's undermining impact on the conservative ideas and traditional values taught by Hong Kong's several hundred vernacular schools, which to that point had remained unassisted and uncontrolled by the government, Governor May enacted in August 1913 the Education Ordinance, which required every school to register with the director of education, conform to government regulations, and submit to official inspection.
>
> (p. 32)

According to Sweeting (1992), this educational ordinance 'represents in some ways the high-water mark of colonial power and authority over education' (p. 45). Following the 1919 boycott, the Education Department promoted 'ultraconservative values and Confucian orthodoxy in the local school curriculum' (Chan, 1994, p. 36).

As I shall discuss at much greater length in the next section, educational policies must be seen against this background of, on the one hand, a strong imperial interest in maintaining Hong Kong as a trading port (with a major interest in opium) and, on the other, the need to maintain social order in a population that frequently showed violent anti-foreigner and anti-colonial sentiments. As my discussion at the beginning of this chapter and in previous chapters has also suggested, however, it would be simplistic to try to understand education policies only in such terms of material interests and social control. Rather, as I argued in the previous chapter, we need to understand the intersection between material concerns (both colonial and imperial), discourses of Anglicism and Orientalism, and the particular material and discursive context of Hong Kong, including the particular ways in which Chinese people were being put into discourse (see Chapter 6).

## Discourses of Hong Kong education

As I have been suggesting, colonial educational policies need to be understood in terms both of their relationships to the flow of colonial discourse through the empire, and of their particular construction in different contexts. In spite of the requirement to receive permission from the Colonial Office in London for any major policy initiative and thus to follow more general colonial policies, the directions that education policies took are frequently the result of the educational philosophies of certain influential figures in the colony. Therefore, although it is possible to determine certain trends in the educational policies across the empire, it is important to locate orientations in Hong Kong in the particular nature of Hong Kong, the actual individuals that determined these policies and the educational discourses available to them. With this in mind, I shall use as a central focus for this section a fascinating document from 1882 in which the discussions and debates of the Commission for Education (1880–82) are transcribed and thus the different battles over educational policies can be clearly seen. As I suggested in the last chapter, while the 1882 education report in India was a massive exercise in colonial knowledge, its contemporary in Hong Kong was a much more exploratory document.

### The 1882 Education Commission

The development of schools in Hong Kong had at first been slow, since the status and future of this trading port were uncertain. Gradually, however, various schools were established so that by the early 1860s there was a mixture of privately run Chinese schools, missionary schools and government-run or assisted schools. The Central School, a Government 'Anglo-Chinese' school offering seven years of upper primary and secondary education to boys from the colony, was opened in 1862, with Frederick Stewart as its first headmaster. Stewart was also appointed as Inspector of Government Schools and was to have a major influence on the early development of education in Hong Kong, emphasizing as he did that schools should be secular and should give strong support first to Chinese education (the Central School curriculum was divided into four hours in English and four hours in Chinese every day). In his education report for 1877, Stewart (*Hong Kong Government Gazette,* 1878) reported 3,144 students registered in schools subject to government supervision: 610 at the Central School, 1,151 at 16 government-supported 'Native Schools', 387 at 12 government-aided Native Schools, and 996 at 15 Grant-in Aid Schools (Missionary schools which, from 1873 onwards, received government grants subject to performance; the majority of these provided a Chinese education, though some provided a Western education in Chinese and others a Western education in English or other European languages).

Soon after his arrival in Hong Kong in 1877, Governor Hennessy visited the Central School and was later to describe with disappointment what he had seen. In a speech at the Central School Prize Giving on 25 January 1878, he recalled how he had been struck by the lack of knowledge of English and then shocked when he had asked how many boys spoke English and received the reply 'under fifty or sixty, and this small number imperfectly' (*HKGG*, 1878, p. 312). These comments were widely published and commented upon and there then ensued a series of correspondences between Hennessy and Stewart which were published in the *Gazette*. Hennessy later visited several village schools and commented that 'I found the Schoolmasters could not speak a word of English, and as far as I could ascertain, none of the pupils had any knowledge of English' (ibid, p. 51). In a series of letters, Stewart explained that only the Central School taught English and that his comments about the English ability of the students there had been misconstrued: he had been referring specifically to their ability to speak, not to their knowledge of English, which was far better. But Hennessy was far from satisfied and on 25 February held a conference on education at which he presided and six members of the Legislative Council as well as Stewart and Dr Eitel (of whom more on pp. 113–14) attended. The conference decided first and foremost 'That the primary object to be borne in view by the Government should be the teaching of English' (p. 90). It was therefore recommended that the Central School should teach five hours per day of English and only two and a half of Chinese, that these Chinese classes should be optional (Eitel and four others voted for this, Stewart and two others voted for compulsory Chinese), and that more emphasis should be put on English in the other government schools.

In March of that year, Stewart left on long leave and the posts of headmaster of the Central School and Inspector of Education were split into two, being taken by Falconer and Eitel respectively. When Stewart returned, he took over the position of headmaster again but resigned in 1881. But his chance to influence education and to turn back the dual moves to promote religion and English in the schools had come again when (now as Acting Colonial Secretary) he was appointed chair of the Education Commission in 1880 to look into the feasibility of building five new government schools and making the Central School a Collegiate Institution giving a higher education in English and science. This, then, was the background to the Education Commission. While ultimately it was relatively unimportant in terms of educational policy – the report was published after Hennessy's departure and generally did little more than advise against these new proposals – the discussions during the different sessions of the hearings are most revealing as regards educational discourses of the time.

Stewart's view of education seems to have been a broadly liberal one. He supported education in Chinese for three main reasons: first, because he felt that any student should have a solid education in their first language; second, because he believed that in order to learn another language, students must have a good grounding in their mother tongue; and third, because he reasoned that students would need a good command of Chinese for whatever work they took up after leaving school. It is important to recall, however, that, as we shall see in Chapter 6, Stewart's views on Chinese education were little different from many of his contemporaries. His support for English was based on the feeling that first, it was a practical need for educated students in Hong Kong and second, that it was only through English that students could receive a broad Western Liberal education, a goal which remained central to his educational mission. During the discussions of the Commission on Education, he insists he is an 'educationist not an instructor', arguing that he understood his purpose to be 'to give an education, and it occurred to me it would be impossible to do that, unless the boys had a proper knowledge of their own language' (p. 82). Although it does not seem to have been a principal element of his views on English education, he was also aware of the argument that teaching English might raise people above their social stations, an argument he himself used with respect to an English education for girls, suggesting that they should get a Chinese education 'without turning their heads by teaching them English or any other so-called accomplishment which would give them a distaste for their future humble sphere of life' (1865, p. 140).

For a nineteenth-century colonial educator, Stewart held some remarkably enlightened and liberal views on education, which indeed would benefit recent educational debates in Hong Kong. On the need for Chinese education as a base before English, for example: 'without it, it would be difficult, if not impossible, for the boys to acquire the knowledge of their own language which is so necessary for the acquisition of another' (1865 education report, *HKGG*, 1866, p. 138). Or his insistence on children 'being taught the *meaning* as well as the *forms* and *sounds* of what they read' (ibid. p. 140).

It is probably largely due to his influence that the suggestion of the Commission included anti-elitist statements '. . . while the public funds to be devoted to educational purposes are limited, and while the great need of the majority of the population is a sound elementary education, it is not the province of the Government to establish, at the cost of the ratepayers, an Institution that would be mainly for the advantage of the wealthier members of the community' (1883b, p. vii); the argument that to improve English 'it is essential that great attention should be paid by the scholars to the study of Chinese during the earlier years of their attendance' (p. vii); and a statement that the object of the Central School was 'not merely the training of the boys in English, but the imparting to them of a sound and liberal education' (p. viii). Some of his views were certainly supported by people interviewed by the Commission. Rev. Dr Chalmers, for example, argued:

> I don't think that much could be expected from a class of Chinese in this Colony who had an English education and knew little or nothing of their own written language. I would not advocate the producing of such a class of Chinese. I think they would be a very inferior class, and I think a Chinaman ought to have a fair acquaintance with his own written language.
>
> (p. 32)

It is worth observing, however, that although Stewart's policies seem enlightened when compared with many of his contemporaries and indeed when compared with many educators a century later, his policies favouring balanced bilingualism were also in clear accord with general colonial policy. As experiences in other colonies had shown, English education had produced mixed results: on the one hand, it was felt that widespread but poor quality English education led to the development of a discontented class of people. As we saw in the last chapter, this concern over the detrimental effects of teaching English had already been frequently alluded to in India. And warning the colonial administration in Malaya against the errors committed in India, H. B. Collinge suggested that 'It is the mere smattering of English and English ideas that is harmful, and which in India causes the country to "swarm with half-starved, discontented men, who consider manual labour beneath them, because they know a little English"' (cited by Hill in Straits Settlements, 1894). On the other hand, a small élite with a good education in English also seemed to pose possible problems by being alienated from their linguistic and cultural backgrounds and at the same time well versed in the colonizers' language and culture. According to Viswanathan (1989), it was felt that instead of producing the docile colonial subjects that they had hoped for, English education was in fact producing a new group of people armed with a sense of 'moral autonomy, self sufficiency and unencumbered will that caused more problems for British rule than expected' (p. 143). But an education only in local languages did not produce the class of bilingual intermediaries that the colonial administration needed to operate efficiently. The ideal education, then, provided a vernacular education to the majority of the population in order to maintain social control and educate workers better able to work under colonial capitalism, and a bilingual education for a small élite. Stewart's policies, therefore, although apparently based on liberal educational ideals, suited the colonial administration better than the more extreme Anglicist or Orientalist policies advocated by others.

Although he did not participate in the Commission, the educational agenda had been set by Hennessy who 'adopted an entirely pro-English attitude. He thought that the government should concentrate more on the provision of English education and leave vernacular education to voluntary or private efforts' (Ng Lun Ngai-ha, 1984, p. 69). In his despatch to London on 11 February 1878, Hennessy spoke of 'the importance of encouraging an English speaking community of Chinese in Hong Kong'. He then goes on to quote from a recent speech of his in which he said that he 'would like to see no Government School whatever in this Colony in which the children are not taught English'; and finally a stronger version of the previous statement, that 'we should have here an English-speaking Chinese Community' (CO/129/181/pp. 167–8).[3] His views were supported generally by the Bishop of Victoria, who argued that English should be taught and Chinese should be dropped. The Chinese would not regret the loss of their language because 'Their ambition is to get into a position to make money, and to make money at the open ports, and I don't think they would care much for any loss they might have as Chinese subjects in the country' (p. 8). This theme of the mercantile orientation of the Hong Kong Chinese is another common one that runs through these and other discussions (see Chapter 7). In his 1865 education report, Stewart remarked that:

> Before any real good can be effected the Chinese must have learnt to appreciate the value of education, and of their *own* education, such as it is. Nothing seems to find favour with them which does not bear a market value. Hence, the comparative success of the Central School, English being convertible into *dollars*; hence, also, the neglect of the Vernacular Schools, Chinese being *unsaleable*. . . . Engrossed in the pursuit of gain, the Chinese who have flocked to Hongkong have left behind them their traditional regard for education, and allowed themselves to settle into an apathy characteristic only of barbarism.
>
> (Annual Report, 1865, p. 141)

Support for English was given most bluntly by one of the members of the Commission, E.R. Belilios, who proclaimed: 'I don't see why the English

Government should encumber itself with the teaching of Chinese' (1883b, p. 11); and later: 'I maintain the English Government should teach English. . . . I maintain the English Government should anglicise its subjects' (p. 34). Belilios, basing his arguments on his experiences in India, suggests that the widespread teaching of English would also be a means of 'opening up China' (p. 35). Interestingly, in an ensuing argument between Stewart and Eitel over Macaulay's intentions in India, Stewart claims that Macaulay 'holds it as one of the first principles of education, that a boy who does not know his own language is not educated at all' (p. 35).[4] Doubts about the emphasis on Chinese at the Central School were also expressed by the recently-arrived new Headmaster, Bateson Wright, who wonders why so much time is spent on Chinese when 'one of the objects of the school was to train Chinese to know sufficient English to be useful in the Government offices and so on' (p. 104). Interestingly, in the summary of the Commission's findings, support for English also came from the one Chinese member of the Commission, the first Chinese member of the Legislative Council, Ng Choy (who had been educated in England). Dissenting on the question of supporting Chinese, on the grounds that it was a waste of time, he argued that on admission, Chinese students should show a competent knowledge of their own language but thereafter their attention 'should be confined to the study of English' (p. viii).

Eitel's position is an interesting one (and an important one – he was Inspector of Schools from 1879 to 1897). A German missionary, a 'sound orientalist and sinologist' (Lethbridge, 1983, p. vii), who had written a dictionary of Cantonese and books on Buddhism and *Feng Shui*, and now an educationalist, Eitel was most concerned that education should give students sufficient grounding in morality. Indeed, although he clearly supported the teaching of English, he also argued that students in the village schools were getting a better education than those receiving a secular education in English. By studying Chinese classics, students learn 'a system of morality, not merely a doctrine, but a living system of ethics.' Thus they learn 'filial piety, respect for the aged, respect for authority, respect for the moral law'. In the Government schools, by contrast, where English books are taught from which religious education is excluded, 'no morality is implanted in the boys' (p. 70). Thus, the teaching of Chinese is 'of higher advantage to the Government' and 'boys strongly imbued with European civilization whilst cut away from the restraining influence of Confucian ethics lose the benefits of education, and the practical experience of Hongkong is that those who are thoroughly imbued with the foreign spirit, are bad in morals' (p. 70).

This view of the underlying purposes of education emerge when Eitel asks the Bishop whether the Government schools produce 'a better individual, a better citizen' than the Chinese schools. Clarifying his question, he asks if they are 'better fitted to benefit the State' and ultimately whether they are better suited to serve 'the English Government' (p. 15). For the influential Eitel, education was for moral development and for preparing students to be good citizens of the empire. In the introduction to his book, *Europe in China* (1895), he expresses an interesting view on the role of Asian cultures on the West, but is nevertheless clear about the direction in which things were by then moving:

> For the last two thousand years, the march of civilization has been directed from the East to the West: Europe has been tutored by Asia. Ennobled by Christianity, civilization now returns to the east: Europe's destiny is to govern Asia. Marching at the head of civilization, Great Britain has commenced her individual mission in Asia by the occupation of India and Burma, the Straits Settlements and Hong Kong.
>
> (pp. iv–v)

According to Eitel's education report for 1891 (*Hong Kong Government Gazette*, 19 November 1892), there were in all 215 schools with 10,119 students in Hong Kong, leading him to estimate that 'in Hong Kong, as in England, about one half of children of school-going age actually come under instruction in public or private schools' (p. 965). Of these, 119 (8,103 students) were under government supervision and received some form of government aid and 96 (2,016 students) were private. Of the 117 schools under government supervision (two are excluded from his analysis), 81 (5,132 students) were voluntary Grant-in-Aid schools providing a Christian education, while the other 36 (2,540 students) were government-run schools providing a secular education. Overall, about 13 per cent of the students received an education purely in English, 25 per cent education in English combined with instruction in Chinese classics, two and a half per cent in Portuguese, two per cent a European education in Chinese, and 58 per cent a Chinese education in Chinese. Under Eitel, there was a gradual move away from vernacular education: in 1892, 11 vernacular schools were closed, and this trend continued throughout the decade. Between 1889 and 1900, numbers of students in government-supported English District (formally 'Village') schools rose from 398 to 899, while the number in Chinese schools fell from 862 in 28 schools to 527 in 7 schools (Ng Lun Ngai-ha, 1984, p. 76). Meanwhile at Queen's College (the renamed Central School from 1894), in 1896 the status of Chinese was changed from a medium of education to a subject.

The report of a Committee on Education in 1902 (*Report of the Committee on Education, The Hongkong Government Gazette*, 11 April 1902) reports 12 government-supported district schools, of which four were Anglo-Chinese and seven vernacular, and the other Belilios' public school for girls. There were 78 grant schools and 95 private vernacular schools. The report lists 7,737 students in school; 1,557 in government schools (894 in Queen's

College) – 1,181 in Anglo-Chinese schools altogether (Queens plus four others); 3,197 in Grant schools – 836 in English, 435 in Anglo-Chinese, 1,926 in vernacular; 2,938 in private schools – 2,457 in vernacular. Thus: 946 in English schools, 2,142 in Anglo-Chinese, 4,649 in vernacular. This report, signed by A.W. Brewin, Ho Kai (the only Chinese member of the Legislative Council) and E.A. Irving (the new Inspector of Schools and Director of the Education Department), is perhaps more interesting, however, for some of its strong statements about education (the Chair of the Committee, Bishop Hoare, had resigned over some of these statements). In discussing who should get what sort of education, the report was very clear on the basic goals of this education: '. . . in Imperial interests it is desirable to offer instruction in the English Language and Western Knowledge to all young Chinese who are willing to study them, even though they are not residents of the colony: provided that the instruction can be furnished at reasonable cost.' (p. 498) According to the report, the majority of boys at Queen's College were from mainland China. After studying Chinese at elementary school, they were now coming to Hong Kong to study English, a practice approved of because of the 'gain to British interests in China by the spread of English and of friendly sentiments towards our Empire' (p. 498). The committee expressed concern, however, that although the spread of English was crucial, it was the spread of Western knowledge that was most important:

> The Committee are fully alive to the extreme importance of spreading the English language among the Chinese: but they maintain that the spread of knowledge is no less essential. Their opinion that a knowledge of English has not always proved sufficient in itself to ensure a feeling of goodwill towards the Empire, is supported by the authority of Lord Cromer, who writes in his Report upon Egypt for 1900, page 51:- 'The Egyptians, as a rule, think that they will have a better chance of obtaining Government employment if they know English than if they are ignorant of that language. Within certain limits, they are probably right. The English on the other hand, provided they are really acquainted with Egyptian circumstances and requirements, regard the matter wholly from an educational point of view. * * * They wish to confine the study of foreign languages, whether English or French, to what is really necessary and useful to the Egyptians themselves. They are not led away by the superficial, and, in my opinion, generally erroneous view, that the study of French and English necessarily connotes the creation of French or English proclivities.' It is highly desirable that a fair exposition of our policy in the East, and of China's relations with the other Powers, should be presented to every Chinese scholar: but these

ideas can be conveyed in the Chinese language no less well than in English.

(p. 499)

The reason for ensuring literacy in Chinese seems to be that 'however learned in English and Western knowledge', Chinese could not be of influence in China without good knowledge of Chinese. It was proposed that scholarships should be set up in order that some poorer children could receive an education, though once again for very clear political rather than educational reasons: 'With the shifting and very ignorant population of Hong Kong, the most that can be done is to pick out and encourage all promising material, and so contrive things that the ablest men of the next generation shall be on our side' (p. 501). As regards vernacular schools, 'it is essential that Western Knowledge should be a compulsory subject in every Standard' (p. 501). It is this stress on Western knowledge that remains central in this report, suggesting that it should take precedence where necessary over English: 'Very important as the study of English is, Western Knowledge is still more so; and where the two studies cannot be conducted at the same time, Western Knowledge must take precedence' (p. 501). Indeed, English appears almost as a bait: it is suggested 'to use the eagerness of the Chinese to learn English, as an inducement to them to submit themselves longer to educational influences' (p. 502).

One other interesting aspect of this document is that a number of its views were not condoned by the Colonial Office in London. The report also recommends, for example, that children of British parentage should be educated separately because first their education is 'retarded by the inevitably slower progress of their classmates, to whom English is a foreign language' and, second, 'they have to consort during their most impressionable years with the offspring of alien beliefs and other ethical standards' (p. 498). This drew the following response from the Secretary of State for the Colonies, Joseph Chamberlain:'I am not at all prepared to accept as a general principle that education should follow the lines of race; and I cannot consent to exclude any nationality from the main school of the Colony – the Queen's College' (CO/129/311/p. 45). The final paragraph of the report argues that:

The committee hold that what Education is given should be thorough, and that better results will be obtained by assisting to enlighten the ignorance of the upper classes of Chinese than by attempting to force new ideas on the mass of the people. Civilized ideas among the leaders of thought are the best and perhaps only means at present available of permeating the general ignorance: for this reason much more attention has been paid to the Anglo-Chinese Schools than to the Vernacular.

(p. 518)

The response from London, however, is that this is unacceptable because the first responsibility is to education in the vernacular: 'It would need very strong grounds to justify withholding Government assistance from Vernacular education in a large native community such as exists at Hong Kong' (CO/ 129/311/p. 49).

Summarizing this report, however, another colonial administrator, Sir W. Gascoigne, seems to accord much more with the views expressed by the writers of the report:

> whether the point of view is Imperial or Colonial, the thorough education of a comparatively small number of Chinese will work more good than a smattering given to the many. . . . There is no doubt that neither the Chinese themselves, nor the object of the advancement of Western knowledge derive much benefit from the existing system, which apparently teaches the Chinese boy to be an inferior Chinaman without providing him with the intellectual or moral equipment of the average European.
>
> (CO 129/311, p. 30)

Here, then, we can see many of the dominant discourses of colonial education interwoven. The particular context of Hong Kong as a trading port with a shifting population, the importance of using Hong Kong to influence China, and the role of certain influential administrators led to a relatively strong pro-English line. Where other colonies had developed much stronger arguments for vernacular education, there was still a strong feeling in Hong Kong at the beginning of the twentieth century in favour of English for a small élite. At the same time, however, there were clearly competing discourses, both within the colony and from outside. These favoured education in Chinese as a duty of the imperial power, as a means to develop a loyal workforce in Hong Kong, as a tool for providing a better moral education, or as a medium for spreading European knowledge more generally. While these arguments had gained sway in other colonies, however, they remained less influential in Hong Kong.

### Lugard and Hong Kong University

At this point, it is worth looking in some length at the views of Frederick Lugard, who was Governor of Hong Kong from 1907 to 1912, and who was largely responsible for the founding of Hong Kong University. Despite his relatively short stay in Hong Kong (he is far better known for his time as Governor of Nigeria) and his preoccupation with the proposed closing of Hong Kong's opium shops and the implications of the Chinese revolution in 1911, Lugard is an important figure because he stands as one of the most influential articulators of a particular version of colonial ideology. In Mellor's

*Figure 4* Group photograph of British and Chinese commissioners

(1992) glowing account of Lugard's years in Hong Kong, he is described as 'one of Britain's most distinguished builders of paternal Empire' (p. xiii). Mellor goes on to explain that Lugard:

> was an imperialist and the first of that special breed to develop and apply a philosophy of 'trusteeship' as governing the relations between advanced and less advanced peoples. Colonial and protected territories were held in trust for the benefit of their inhabitants, who were never to be exploited solely for their rulers' or protectors' benefit.
>
> (p.xiv)

Lugard was best known for his development of the colonial philosophies of indirect rule and the 'dual mandate'. In his most important work, *The Dual Mandate in British Tropical Africa* (1926), Lugard pointed to the importance of understanding 'that Europe is in Africa for the mutual benefit of her own industrial classes, and of the native races in their progress to a higher plane; that the benefit can be made reciprocal, and that it is the aim and desire of civilised administration to fulfill this dual mandate' (p. 617). He remained steadfastly convinced of this idea that while Britain could gain materially from its colonies, the trusteeship of the world had been left to Britain in order that Britain could spread the benefits of its civilization: 'I am profoundly convinced that there can be no question but that British rule has promoted the happiness and welfare of the primitive races . . . We hold these countries because it is the genius of our race to colonise, to trade, and to govern' (pp. 618–19). In the same book, he also describes at length how colonial rule can best operate indirectly through the use of local rulers. His development of this form of indirect rule gave rise to a whole tradition of anthropological work aimed at facilitating colonial control through the co-option of a small minority, an orientation endorsed by many anthropologists such as Malinowski (Niranjana, 1992, p. 75). The International Institute of African Languages and Cultures, under the directorship of Lugard, sponsored colonial administrators to study anthropology. Here, then, we can see the direct links between Orientalist knowledge, its development into anthropological and linguistic knowledge, and the colonial need for better governance.

The first aspect of Lugard's view of education was that nations such as Britain should provide a secular education for 'backward' nations: 'It is not consonant with the traditions of Englishmen to stand aside and refuse secular help to 'a nation rightly struggling to be free' from the trammels of ignorance and superstition' (Lugard, 1910, quoted in Mellor, 1992, p. 4). As Mangan (1985) suggests, Lugard 'believed strongly in the civilizing role of British Imperialism' (p. 101) and was convinced that native people were inferior and childlike (Mangan, p. 112). He was a strong advocate of the need for racial segregation, disengenuously arguing that this policy 'favored neither race, for the European was as strictly prohibited from living in the native quarter as a native was from living in the European quarter' (Spurr, 1993, p. 87). When in 1908 the chief justice of Hong Kong, Sir Francis Piggot, proposed to let his house on the Peak (which by then was designated by law as a European reserve) to Robert Ho Tung, Lugard refused to grant exemption for this 'illegitimate half-caste' (Wesley-Smith, 1994, p. 99).

The key problem, as Lugard saw it, was that as students were gradually influenced by this Western education, they would lose touch with their cultural and moral roots. In a speech at a congress for universities of the British Empire in 1912, he expressed this view clearly:

> The result of Western Education is admittedly to undermine eastern beliefs, and thereby to disorganize much of the social life which among Eastern peoples is so intimately bound up with religion. The impact of a purely secular Western Education upon Eastern peoples has therefore a tendency to deprive students of their national religion and to substitute nothing for it, while the study of the philosophic theories of the West, of political economy, and of Western History with its outstanding examples of the emancipation of the people

from oppressive control, are all apt to fire the immature imaginations of imaginative races, and to impel them to conclusions destructive alike of the family influence on which the social system is so largely based, and of all constituted authority.

(cited in Mellor, 1992, p. 172)

For Lugard, then, the university needed to provide an education that would counter the deleterious effects of Westernization, materialism and, as Perham (1960) suggests, 'not only materialism, but the revolutionary and even socialistic influences which good Chinese parents must reprobate as sternly as he did himself' (p. 340). This emphasis on a non-materialist education, as Mangan (1985) points out, 'illustrated class prejudice as much as colonial altruism' (p. 104). Like many people educated in British public schools, he had a deep-seated class-based scorn for those who made their living through commercial trade. It is interesting to bear this in mind when one considers the other comments cited above that deride the Hong Kong Chinese for their mercantile nature. A discourse that is still commonly heard in Hong Kong today, this view of local people as 'only interested in money' must be seen in terms of these class origins.

The central difficulty lay in finding a means to provide a secular education with a strong moral foundation: 'The problem before us in opening a University in Hong Kong is how to train character, and how to create moral ideals which shall have a vital and compelling force in the formation of character and the conduct of daily life, without introducing compulsory religious teaching' (ibid, p. 173). His ideas were based in part on his reaction to (and discussions with the author of) *Indian Unrest* (Chirol, 1910), in which the author discussed problems in the Indian education system that had led to 'unrest' there. These included the lack of government control over education (not a problem for Hong Kong University, Lugard points out, since, amongst other things, the Governor is Chancellor), concentration on higher education at the expense of elementary and secondary (not the case in Hong Kong, Lugard highlights), the use of English as a medium of education (this criticism cannot apply to universities, Lugard asserts, since 'it is necessary that Western knowledge should be conveyed in a Western tongue' (p. 174)), and the neglect of moral education, one cause of which, according to Chirol, was the large proportion of Indian to British staff. On this last point Lugard concurs and asserts that 'In the Hong Kong University the staff will be wholly British' except perhaps for a few Chinese specialists (ibid).

Lugard's solution was to develop 'two main safeguards': the university was to be 'entirely residential and the British staff must be chosen for their moral as well as their academic distinction' (Perham, 1960, p. 341). He therefore stressed that textbooks should be carefully selected so that only good examples of morality should be presented, that religious bodies be allowed to establish university hostels, and that the remainder of the students would come under the influence of the British staff in the other residential halls: 'By bringing the best influence to bear on the remaining students, who will be compelled to reside in the University under the close control of a carefully selected staff; and by encouraging outdoor sports, in which the staff will find opportunities of associating with the students' (ibid. p. 173). Lugard's view of education, as a necessary corrective to the childlike immorality of native people was thus based on an image of British public school discipline:

> Within this civilizing process the English public school system and its games ethic held pride of place. Lugard's certainty in the moral inferiority of the native races of the empire stimulated in him an intense interest in education as a means of moral improvement. . . . Lugard was one of a band of imperial diffusionists who loyally attempted to take the values of the English upper-class system of education to 'less-favoured peoples' with an ethnocentric certainty in the soundness of their offering.
>
> (Mangan, 1985, p. 101)

Indeed, it is interesting to observe that in the original plans for the university, ample room was given to playing fields behind the main building, an emphasis which becomes more significant when one realises the scale of the work involved to construct level playing fields on the lower slopes of Victoria Peak.

Finally, it is interesting to observe Lugard's views on the importance of English as a medium of education. In his proposal for the development of the university, Lugard (1910) once again stresses the importance of moral education and then turns to the importance of English:

> In conclusion I would emphasize the value of English as the medium of instruction. If we believe that British interests will be thus promoted, we believe equally firmly that graduates, by the mastery of English, will acquire the key to a great literature and the passport to a great trade. On the one hand we desire to secure the English language in the high position it has acquired in the Far East; on the other hand since the populations of the various provinces in China speak no common language, and the Chinese vocabulary has not yet adapted itself to express the terms and conceptions of modern science, we believe that should China find it necessary for a time to adopt an alien tongue as a common medium for new thoughts and expressions – as the nations of the West did when Latin was the language of the savants and of scientific literature – none would be more suitable than English.
>
> (Lugard, 1910, p. 4)

The university, then, was to be one in which 'especial efforts will be made to train character, and to exert an effective moral discipline' and in which English would not only afford the students access to English literature and science but would also serve as a means by which 'British influence in the Far East may be extended' (1910, p. 5). As he observed in his speech at the laying of the foundation stone in 1910, the graduates of the university would be 'missionaries of Empire' (p. 30).

There are several significant points worth observing about Lugard's view of education. For myself, of course, it provides certain clues about the establishment and continuing cultures of Hong Kong University, this 'Oxford and Cambridge of the East', whose fulfilment of that dream has more to do with the maintenance of British racism and class prejudices than it does with the academic excellence that is also associated with those universities. But more generally, Lugard's early thinking on the notion of the dual mandate and the trusteeship of backward peoples emerges here in the context of a moral education through English. Clearly signalling the possibility that English might come to replace other languages such as Chinese, he insisted that it would be through English that a secular, Western and moral education could best bring civilization to Chinese people.

### Emphasizing and regulating vernacular education

But alongside his high ideals and his enthusiastic campaigning for an English-language university, Lugard also had to face the practical realities of running this restive colony on the coast of China. Against the background of political unrest in China, Lugard had announced the formation of the Board of Chinese Vernacular Primary Education in 1911. Set up as a body to raise funds for and improve Chinese education in the colony, it had little effect since it lacked official powers. The colonial government was becoming increasingly concerned, however, since nationalist sentiment was growing in the Chinese schools in the wake of the 1911 Revolution. Lugard had left his position as Governor by the time these fears led to the Education Ordinance of 1913, the first legislation throughout the British Empire to make school registration mandatory: apart from government, military and other schools that the Governor may exempt at his discretion:

> every school in the colony whether such school is in existence at the date of the coming into operation of this Ordinance or whether such school comes into existence after the date of the coming into operation of this Ordinance shall be registered under the provisions of this Ordinance and any school not so registered shall be deemed to be an unlawful school.
>
> (*The Hong Kong Government Gazette*, 8 August 1913, p. 345)

The reasons for this severe policy were clear: fearing further social unrest and the growth of Chinese nationalism, the government was now intent on bringing all Chinese schools under much closer supervision.

This process was to take a new turn in 1926 in response to the massive 1925–26 strike and boycott of British goods. A discussion in 1925 as to whether the position of Inspector of Vernacular schools should be maintained in light of diminishing school attendance made it abundantly clear how the Colonial Office viewed this schooling. Comparing the situation to that in Malaya (where the rise in Chinese nationalism had brought about a sudden new attention to Chinese education), a Colonial Office Minute suggests that 'experience in Malaya has proved the wisdom of maintaining a strict watch over the teaching in such schools, and I should have thought that in these days of anti-British propaganda, the wise policy would be to increase rather than to abolish the European inspectorate in Hong Kong' (CO 129/489, p. 179). This sentiment was echoed in the (draft) reply to the Governor from the Secretary of State for the Colonies, who suggested that 'I should have thought European inspectorate essential to prevent spread of anti-British teaching' (CO 129/489, p. 183).

At this time of strikes and anti-British feeling, however, there was not only a stress on careful monitoring of vernacular education but also a new emphasis on more direct intervention in the Chinese school curriculum. In his memorandum on the 1925 strike and boycott, R.H. Kotewall (CO 129/489) pointed directly to the schools as the source of problems and recommended increased supervision: 'Obviously the first remedy is an increased watchfulness in the schools. Special care should be exercised in the supervision of the vernacular schools in particular, for these can the more easily become breeding grounds for sedition' (p. 455). His recommendations go beyond this, however, for he then goes on to recommend particular orientations for Chinese school curricula:

> The Chinese education in Hong Kong does not seem to be all that it should be. The teaching of Confucian ethics is more and more neglected, while too much attention is being paid to the materialistic side of life . . . In such a system great stress should be laid on the ethics of Confucianism which is, in China, probably the best antidote to the pernicious doctrines of Bolshevism, and is certainly the most powerful conservative course, and the greatest influence for good.
>
> (pp. 455–6)

Thus, 'money spent on the development of the conservative ideas of the Chinese race in the minds of the young will be money well spent, and also constitutes social insurance of the best kind' (p. 456).

This idea was supported most actively by the Governor, Sir Cecil Clementi, a long term colonial administrator in Hong Kong (as Clerk of Councils he had written the Education Ordinance of 1913), and a scholar of Chinese folk songs. Inviting senior Chinese literati to Government House in 1927, Clementi addressed them in Cantonese and asked them to help him to develop a curriculum that would emphasize traditional morality and scholar-ship, a curriculum based on orthodox Confucianism accentuating social hier-archy and subservience to patriarchal authority (Luk, 1991). This initiative also led to the establishment of a Chinese Department at Hong Kong Uni-versity (there had never been one previously since the university had been modelled on British universities) and a new government-run Chinese secondary school. Clementi's goal, then, was to counter the rising tide of Chinese nationalism by emphasizing traditional Chinese notions of hierarchy and loyalty. Thus, 'appeal was made to the cultural tradition of the native people to help safeguard foreign rule against the growth of nationalistic feel-ings among the younger generation' (Luk, 1991, p. 660).

Several years later, having transferred from Hong Kong to Malaya, Clementi was to try a different approach to limiting the growing influence of Chinese schools there. In this case, arguing against the promotion of English since it was expensive, threatened traditional ways of life and might lead to a class of discontented people who 'had acquired a distaste for their ancestral methods of earning a livelihood' (cited in *The Straits Times*, 13 February 1934), Clementi removed grants from the Chinese schools and urged them to teach Malay instead. With the Malay schools under clearer government supervision, this appeared an easier means of control than trying to regulate the Chinese curriculum, though ultimately it achieved little. His initiatives in Hong Kong, however, had lasting effects: according to Luk (1991), the report of the Committee on Chinese Studies in 1953, which has formed the basis of Chinese studies in the Hong Kong secondary school curriculum since the mid-1950s 'demonstrates considerable continuity with the cultural policy of Governor Clementi some 25 years before' (Luk, 1991, p. 667). The curriculum followed by students today, therefore, is closely linked to the curriculum formulated in the 1920s, a curriculum developed then to counter Chinese nationalism in the schools, redeveloped in the 1950s to counter communist influences and still held in place in the 1990s as part of British colonial rule.

The final stage in the process of control over and expansion of vernacular education came with the 1935 'Burney Report' (Burney, 1935). This report is generally seen as a watershed in Hong Kong education since it marked the crucial point when Hong Kong moved towards much greater public provi-sion of primary vernacular education. The report criticizes the government for its low expenditure on primary education, noting that 'primary education is all that the poorer Chinese can afford, and the Government is therefore giving least help to those who are least able to help themselves' (p. 7). It goes on: 'It is a serious weakness in Hong Kong's educational system, with results felt throughout the school careers of many of the children, that the schools in which the primary foundations are laid should be of so poor a quality.' (p. 9) The schools are also criticized for being too exam oriented, for giving students insufficient knowledge of Chinese, and for providing insufficient ability in English so that students need special help when they enter Hong Kong University and are unable to cope with the demands of spoken English in the business world (p. 11). The 'one-path system' is criticized for serving 'the needs of a minority . . . at the expense of the majority' (p. 12). Thus, children in rural schools return to the fields with a 'smattering of English' the acquisition of which has taken up most of their time in school.

Burney notes that there is a constant demand for English: '. . . there is a real and large demand for 'black-coated' labour in Hong Kong (nearly one quarter of the males are so employed) and also . . . there is an insistent demand on the part of Chinese parents for their children to be taught English' (p. 12). He suggests that the demand for English 'comes from parents and pupils, and the motive is utilitarian and vocational' while the demand from Chinese comes from 'educationists in the Colony, both English and Chinese, and is justified by the argument that any education is culturally inadequate which does not give the pupil a good knowledge of his native language and at least some acquaintance with its literature' (p. 24). His recommendations are that 'the teaching of English in the schools of Hong Kong should be reformed on a frankly utilitarian basis, i.e. that the pupils should be taught to understand, speak, read and write such and so much English as they are likely to need for their subsequent careers, and no more' (p. 24). The rest of the time should be devoted to more study of Chinese. This influential document, then, confirmed the orientation towards vernacular education and away from English. With its origins in a mixture of powerful Anglicist administrators – from Hennessy to Lugard – as well as the particular material contexts of Hong Kong, English had received more support than elsewhere. Gradually, however, with the need for greater control over Chinese education in the colony, and with the possibility of using this education to develop conservative moral authority, policies shifted towards Chinese education.

## Conclusions: language policies and colonial legacies

Beyond presenting an outline history of educational policies during Hong Kong's history, I have also been trying to read against the grain of many accounts of colonial history. Analyses that unquestioningly present this history as a glorious epoch for Britain and beneficial time for the colonies, or those that try to present a 'balanced' liberal evaluation, often end up doing little more than writing mere apologias for colonialism; those that present a view of colonialism as nothing but a simple-to-understand project of economic exploitation from which all cultural and educational ideas flowed, fail to capture the historical complexities and the current ramifications of colonial policies. In place of these views I have been trying to show the complexities and divergencies of colonial discourse, the possibility that different colonial administrators operating within different colonial discourses produced policies that may or may not have been the best for the economic exploitation of Hong Kong and China. As I have tried to show, we need to understand how Orientalist and Anglicist discourses, images of Self and Other, views on Chinese education or the need for muscular morality, intersect. And that policies favouring English and policies favouring Chinese frequently emerged from different approaches to using education for colonial purposes.

Although gaining a more complex grasp of the past is a sufficient goal in itself, there is another important purpose to pursuing these colonial histories. Colonialism has often been painted in simple terms, making it easy for a modern audience to laugh at the bigotries of the past. One of my goals in trying to shift the ways in which this is understood is not so much to exonerate the actions of our predecessors but to throw light on our own contemporary actions. It has been too easy to juxtapose a simple, bigoted colonial past with a complex, liberal present. I hope that this examination of the complexities of the past has started to raise questions about how education is understood in the colonial and neo-colonial present. The benefit of hindsight that a study of historical contexts allows has helped shed light on a key question in language education, namely that 'the belief that education can resolve inequality is based on the false assumption that the school system itself is not part of the institutional and historical patterns that sustain inequality. Schools are not extra-societal forces for cultural change; they are part of society' (Tollefson, 1991, p. 198). Thus, this historical perspective questions the common claim that the bestowal of education or access to literacy and languages are in some way inherently beneficial. The easy assumptions often made about a 'language of power', or of dominant and dominated languages, become more suspect in light of this historical analysis in which both English and vernacular languages were used to promote particular forms of colonial governance. As became clear here, language education policies were constantly designed to maintain the inequitable social conditions of Hong Kong.

One of the lessons we need to draw from this account of colonial language policy is that, in order to make sense of language policies we need to understand both their location historically and their location contextually. What I mean by this is that we cannot assume that promotion of local languages instead of a dominant language, or promotion of a dominant language at the expense of local languages, are in themselves good or bad. Too often we view such questions through the lenses of liberalism, pluralism or anti-imperialism, without understanding the actual location of such policies. As Crowley (1996) points out, although Gramsci and Bakhtin are often put together as part of the same canon of critical thought, they developed very different orientations towards language based in part on the different political contexts in which they worked. For Bakhtin, working in the Stalinist Soviet Union and its massive projects of centralization, including the standardization and spread of Russian throughout the empire, the necessary emphasis was on heteroglossia, on the diversity and differences within language being understood and promoted as a reaction against monoglossic centralization. For Gramsci, by contrast, working (and being imprisoned) in Mussolini's Italy, in which the emphasis was on the promotion of local Italian dialects as an expression of Italian identity (and a means to rule the country by maintaining diversity) the emphasis was far more on the need for a unified language to unite the peasantry.

According to Crowley:

> Gramsci's contention is that in the historical and political conjuncture in which he was located, rather than arguing for heteroglossia, what was required was precisely the organising force of a form of monoglossia. In particular what Gramsci argued for was the teaching of prescriptive grammar to the children of the working class and peasantry in order to empower them with literacy as part of a larger radical project.
>
> (1996, p. 43)

Thus, in the historical situation in which Gramsci was located 'a preference for heteroglossia over monoglossia would be a reactionary stance' (p. 45). If, then, an argument for monoglossia or heteroglossia is made in the abstract, without reference to the actual historical location of the languages and political struggles involved, the political outcomes of such an argument will be unclear. We need, therefore, clear, contextualized understandings of the political contexts of language policies, for 'although Bakhtin's preference for heteroglossia is correct in analysing particular historical examples (say, for instance, the formation of 'standard English' in the cultural hegemony of Britain), it is correct only with regard to this specific historical conjuncture' (p. 46). By contrast, 'the diffuse and politically disorganised situation of early twentieth century Italy, in which lack of common literacy amongst the national–popular mass served the interests of the governing class, requires a quite different analysis' (p. 46).

This understanding also has important implications for the present. Indeed the way in which both Anglicist and Orientalist discourses, support for both English and local languages, can be seen to have been complicit with the whole colonial project, raises some fundamental questions about current language policies. The promotion of both English and vernacular education policies in Malaya and Hong Kong were clearly in general in line with broader colonial policies of social stability and exploitation. This suggests that we need to investigate very carefully whose interests are served by different language policies. Thus, it is not enough to simply juxtapose a liberal multi-culturalism (possibly the descendant of Orientalism) with a rapacious, conservative pro-English stance (more obviously a descendant of Anglicism) in terms of the language ideologies that each seems to espouse. Rather, what such policies promote or deny must be looked at within the broader social, political and economic structures and ideologies that they support.

Finally, I have been trying to show how policies of language education both reflected and produced broader colonial discourses. By looking more contextually in this chapter at sites and causes of development of colonial discourses on language I have been trying to show not only that these developed in very clear response to material circumstances but also that they were more than mere justifications for material gain. In the constant negotiation of colonial language policy images of Self and Other, of English and of Chinese people, culture and language were always being produced, developed, redefined. Even if at times these discourses played a lesser role in the development of certain policies, it was the production of these discourses, I wish to argue, that was one of the major legacies of colonialism. These discourses, I have been suggesting, through the continued conjunction of their relationship to English, have come to adhere to the language. It is to such discourses of the Self (Chapter 5) and the Other (Chapter 6) that I now wish to turn.

# 5

# IMAGES OF THE SELF

## Our marvellous tongue

> Our infinitely adaptable mother tongue is now the world's lingua franca – and not before time.
>
> (Jenkins, 1995)

> More than 300 million people in the world speak English and the rest, it sometimes seems, try to.
>
> (Bryson, 1990, p. 1)

> Like the wandering minstrel in *The Mikado*, with songs for any and every occasion, English has the right word for it – whatever 'it' may be.
>
> (Claiborne, 1983, p. 4)

If one of the central aspects of colonial discourse has been to construct the native Other as backward, dirty, primitive, depraved, childlike, feminine, and so forth, the other side of this discourse has been the construction of the colonizers, their language, culture and political structures as advanced, superior, modern, civilized, masculine, mature and so on. Thus, as we saw in Chapter 2, for every construction of colonized people as indolent, native, feminized children, for example, there was a parallel construction of the colonizer as the severe schoolmaster, the knowledgeable and adult disciplinarian. As I argued in Chapter 1, this is part of the process of double reciprocation by which discourses construct each other and do so in relation to English. In this chapter I want to explore some of the implications of these cultural constructs of colonialism for how the English language has been understood and what sorts of implications this may have for language planning, language choice, and English language teaching.

In an earlier attempt to deal with this (Pennycook, 1994b), I argued that the expansionist rhetoric of writers on English in the nineteenth century was less significant in terms of reflecting a massive spread of English than in occasioning a huge increase in the extent to which English was studied. According to Crowley (1989, p. 71), 'the more the English nation extended the boundaries of empire, the more the English language was praised as a superior language and subjected to extensive study.' In trying to relate the expansionist rhetoric of the nineteenth century to the more subdued prose of what I termed the discourse of English as an International Language, I argued that these nineteenth-century discourses in a sense went underground, became submerged beneath the new scientific discourses of linguistics and applied linguistics. In retrospect, however, I think this argument was only partly right. First, as I argued in Chapters 3 and 4, the particular contingencies of colonial rule caused the rhetoric of Anglicism to play a lesser role in the formation of language policy. It did not, however, go away. Rather, the discourses of Anglicism spread through the discursive system of the empire and re-emerged in other contexts, particularly in Britain.

Second, rather than disappearing, such discourses have in fact stayed fairly constant and indeed are enjoying a period of rejuvenation in conjunction with the continued global expansion of English. As I suggested at the end of the last chapter, in order to understand the relationships between language policy and discourses on language, it is crucial to look in detail at the social, cultural, political and economic contexts from which such discourses and policies emerge, and in which they are then used. For complex contextual reasons, it was the discourses of Orientalism that prevailed as discourses informing British colonial language policy, while the discourses of Anglicism were in a sense redeployed as British constructions of language and identity within Britain itself. Towards the end of the twentieth century, however, in a wholly changed political context in which the global spread of English has become not so much part of colonial control but rather part of neocolonial exploitation (see Phillipson, 1992), English and Anglicism have re-emerged in a new light. The discourses of Anglicism still adhere to English, but now to a new English, a global English, and an English in popular demand. And, while the Empire formed an important discursive web for the spread of cultural constructions of colonialism, the new global empire in English forms an even more significant means for their promulgation.

An important point here, then, is that such discourses are far more prevalent (or at least more obvious) in various forms of popular culture – popular books on language, magazines, newspapers, and so on – than in more academic contexts. This, however, does not lessen in any way the possible effects of such discourses on the theories and practices of English language teaching, for I intend to argue in this and the next chapter that rather than identifying applied linguistics books, or books on language teaching, as the primary sources of influence on language teaching, it is more important to identify the broader context of popular culture as a major source of influence. As research into teacher reflection has started to show, teachers think and act in complex ways that may have little to do with the teacher training courses that supposedly formed them as teachers. Thus, I shall argue here that while the discourses of linguistics and applied linguistics are indeed influential in the making of English teachers (and indeed, as I shall also argue, similarly intertwined with the discourses of colonialism), what has often been overlooked is the point that those of us involved in language education are also inevitably surrounded by popular culture, by the everyday images of English. It may be these that are far more influential in the formulation of policies, curricula, practices, research agendas, and so on.

An important part of the argument I want to make here is that the origins of a great deal of thinking about English and English language teaching have their origins in the colonial context rather than in what is often assumed to be their provenance in Britain itself. This is part of my broader focus on colonialism as a site of cultural production, as the site from which images of Self and Other flowed, rather than as the site into which they were introduced. In his history of English language teaching (ELT), Howatt (1984, p. 71) comments that ELT forked into two streams at the end of the eighteenth century: one being the development of ELT within the Empire; the other being the influence of continental Europe on ELT. Although Howatt is no doubt right in suggesting that to study the development of ELT throughout the Empire would entail a vast and separate series of studies, it is a shame that he opts so completely for the European side of the fork, and even more so if one considers that it may indeed have been the imperial fork that was more significant. That is to say it was not so much that theories and practices of ELT were developed in Britain (with a strong European influence) and then exported to the Empire but rather that the Empire became the central testing site for the development of ELT, from where theories and practices were then imported into Britain. When Howatt opts for the European path of development – after mentioning the publication of John Miller's *The Tutor* in Bengal in 1797 – he lets a crucial path grow cold until it re-emerges with writers such as the extremely influential Michael West, the author of the *New Method Readers* (1927 onwards). The development of these readers was a result of an experiment conducted, not entirely coincidentally, in Bengal and reported in West's (1926) *Bilingualism (with Special Reference to Bengal)*. West (1888–1973), who worked in the Indian Education Service, and many other English language educators such as Thomas Prendergast (1806-1886) before him, who worked in the Indian Civil Service, were highly influential in the development of ELT.

A similar argument has been made with respect more particularly to the teaching of English literature by Gauri Viswanathan (1989). Taking issue with other studies of the development of English literature as a subject in Britain, even the better of which have done little more than acknowledge the relationship between the Indian Civil Service examinations (with their strong emphasis on English literature) and the expansion of English literature in schools and universities, she argues that although 'the amazingly young history of English literature as a subject of study (it is less than a hundred and fifty years old) is frequently noted,' far less appreciated is 'the irony that English literature appeared as a subject in the curriculum of the colonies long before it was institutionalized in the home country' (pp. 2–3). Viswanathan shows that because of the existence of an educated class of Indians who already exerted considerable control over their people and because of the policy of religious neutrality in education which prevented the British from promoting a firmer programme of moral discipline through the educational system, English literature was called into service 'to perform the functions of those social institutions (such as the church) that, in England, served as the chief disseminators of value, tradition, and authority' (p. 7). The development of English literature as a subject, then, was a response to the particular needs of the colonial administration in India. It was only later that this newly developed cultural curriculum of English literature, designed to develop moral and traditional views in a secular state, was imported into Britain and used to fulfill similar functions.

Theories and practices of ELT developed outside Britain, circulated around the Empire and often made their way back to Britain later. 'It is not just that the personnel who governed India were British,' remarks Cohn, 'but the projects of state building in both countries – documentation, legitimation, classification, and bounding, and the institutions therewith – often reflected theories, experiences, and practices worked out originally in India and then applied in Great Britain, as well as vice versa' (1996, pp. 3–4). As Cheng (1983) points out, for example, the Hong Kong primary school English syllabus developed in 1962–3 was based on the Makerere Conference Report, which Phillipson (1992) identifies as a crucial document in the development of neo-colonial policies in favour of more English being taught earlier and more often throughout the Commonwealth. It is not my intention here, however, to try to map out the development of language teaching methods in colonial contexts and their subsequent import to Britain (that would be another fascinating study in itself). Rather, I wish to focus here on one particular aspect of this colonial production of images: the construction of English. As Rajan (1993a) remarks, 'just as a British *national* identity was precisely formed – or assembled – under the pressures of British colonialism, so too it has a tendency to be reactivated as ethnocentrism' in the context of English language teaching (p. 152).

My argument here, then, is that the contexts of provision of education in English language teaching put back into play, in admittedly complex ways, parts of the colonial cultures produced by English language teaching. In this chapter, then, I shall develop the arguments of this book further by looking at the colonial origins and the colonial continuity of images of the Self, the colonizers and their language and culture. In order to show how these popular discourses on English appear in a fairly broad range of popular texts, I have used a selection of popular books on English, as well as newspaper and magazine articles. Towards the end of the chapter, I shall show how such discourses emerge in English language teaching materials, while also having broad currency among respected writers on language. In the next section I shall examine various discourses on English, pointing to some remarkable similarities between the rhetoric of nineteenth-century-writers on the English language and current writing on the global spread of English.

## Our marvellous tongue

### *The wondrous spread of English*

The nineteenth century was a time of immense British confidence in their own greatness, and writing on English abounded with glorifications of English and its global spread. Guest (1838/1882) argued that English was 'rapidly becoming the great medium of civilization, the language of law and literature to the Hindoo, of commerce to the African, of religion to the scattered islands of the Pacific' (p. 703). Trench (1881, p. 44) quotes Jacob Grimm, the German linguist, as stating in 1832 that 'the English language . . . may with all right be called a world-language; and, like the English people, appears destined hereafter to prevail with a sway more extensive even than its present over all the portions of the globe'. According to Read:

> Ours is the language of the arts and sciences, of trade and commerce, of civilization and religious liberty. . . . It is a store-house of the varied knowledge which brings a nation within the pale of civilization and Christianity. . . . Already it is the language of the Bible. . . . So prevalent is this language already become, as to betoken that it may soon become the language of international communication for the world.
>
> (1849, p. 48, cited in Bailey, 1991, p. 116)

Meiklejohn (1891, p. 6, cited in Crowley, 1989) stated the connection between Empire and the spread of English very explicitly: 'The sun never sets on the British dominions; the roll of the British drum encircles the globe with a belt of sound; and the familiar utterances of English speech are heard on every continent and island, in every sea and ocean, in the world' (cited in Crowley, 1989, p. 74). George suggested that:

> other languages will remain, but will remain only as the obscure Patois of the world, while English will become the grand medium for all the business of government, for commerce, for law, for science, for literature, for philosophy, and divinity. Thus it will really be a universal language for the great material and spiritual interests of mankind.
>
> (1867, p. 6)

For de Quincey, like George, it was a question not only of English spreading widely but also of replacing other languages: 'The English language is travelling fast towards the fulfilment of its destiny . . . , running forward towards its ultimate mission of eating up, like Aaron's rod, all other languages' (de Quincey, 1862, pp. 149–50). Finally, some writers, such as Axon (1888) boldly predicted the course of this spread over the next century: 'it is as likely as anything prospective can be in human affairs, that the Englishry of 1980 will amount to about 1,000,000,000 souls. . . . [A]ll these people will speak the same language, read the same books, and be influenced by the same leading ideas' (Axon, 1888, p. 204; cited in Bailey, 1991, p. 113).

A similar tenor to discussions of English and its global spread can frequently be found today, though with a number of interesting developments. Although the fervent triumphalism that appears so evident in these earlier descriptions of the spread of Empire and English is a less acceptable aspect of more recent discourses on the spread of English, I would like to suggest that the same celebratory tone seems to underlie recent, supposedly neutral, descriptions of English. Thus, it is interesting to compare Rolleston's (1911) description of the spread of English with Crystal's (1987) from *The Cambridge Encyclopedia of Language*:

> The British flag waves over more than one-fifth of the habitable globe, one-fourth of the human race acknowledge the sway of the British Monarch, more than one hundred princes render him allegiance. The English language is spoken by more people than that of any other race, it bids fair to become at some time the speech of the globe, and about one-half of the world's ocean shipping trade is yet in British hands.
>
> (1911, p. 75)

> English is used as an official or semi-official language in over 60 countries, and has a prominent place in a further 20. It is either dominant or well established in all six continents. It is the main language of books, newspapers, airports and air-traffic control, international business and academic conferences, science, technology, medicine, diplomacy, sports, international competitions, pop music, and advertising. Over two-thirds of the world's scientists write in English. Three quarters of the world's mail is written in English. Of all the information in the world's electronic retrieval systems, 80% is stored in English. English radio programmes are received by over 150 million in 120 countries.
>
> (Crystal, 1987, p. 358)

The similarities become more obvious when we turn to other books and articles on English. Bryson's (1990) book *Mother Tongue: The English Language* starts thus: 'More than 300 million people in the world speak English and the rest, it sometimes seems, try to' (p. 1). He goes on:

> For better or worse, English has become the most global of languages, the lingua franca of business, science, education, politics, and pop music. For the airlines of 157 nations (out of 168 in the world), it is the agreed international language of discourse. In India, there are more than 3,000 newspapers in English. The six member nations of the European Free Trade Association conduct all their business in English, even though not one of them is an English-speaking country.
>
> (p. 2)

and so on. 'For non-English speakers everywhere, English has become the common tongue' (p. 3). Claiborne (1983) opens his book *The life and times of the English language: The history of our marvellous tongue* with:

> By any standard, English is a remarkable language. It is, to begin with, the native tongue of some 300,000,000 people – the largest speech community in the world except for Mandarin Chinese. Even more remarkable is its geographic spread, in which it is second to none; its speakers range from Point Barrow, Alaska, to the Falkland Islands; from the Shetland Islands to Capetown at the Southern tip of Africa; from Hong Kong to Tasmania . . . English is also by far the most important 'second language' in the world. It is spoken by tens of millions of educated Europeans and Japanese, is the most widely studied foreign tongue in both the USSR and China, and serves as an 'official' language in more than a dozen other countries whose populations total more than a thousand million . . . English is the lingua franca of scientists, of air pilots and traffic controllers around the world, of students hitchhiking around Europe, and of dropouts meditating in India and Nepal.
>
> (pp. 1–2)

and so on and so on. Finally, in a newspaper article (from *The Times* of London) under the title 'The triumph of English' Jenkins (1995) reiterates much of the same list:

> When the Warsaw Pact was wound up it was wound up in English. When the G7 meets, it meets in English. . . . English is the global computer language. It is the language of news gathering and world entertainment. The only substantial world body that struggles to keep going in a 'foreign' tongue is the French-speaking European

Commission in Brussels. With luck, enlargement will put an end to that.

These seemingly celebratory descriptions of the global spread of English are tied to more explicit benefits in certain versions of this story. Burnett (1962), for example, draws the connection between the use of English and being 'civilized':

> Today English is written, spoken, broadcast, and understood on every continent, and it can claim a wider geographical range than any other tongue. There are few civilized areas where it has any competition as the lingua franca – the international language of commerce, diplomacy, science, and scholarship.
>
> (p. 12)

The connection to civilization is of course a common one (see many other quotes in this chapter), and gets replayed constantly. Here is Jespersen, who Randolph Quirk describes as 'the most distinguished scholar of the English language who has ever lived' (1982, p. iii), arguing that we may compare languages according to their logic: 'there is perhaps no language in the civilised world that stands so high as English' (1938/1982, p. 12). This argument takes on a slightly different tone in Robert Burchfield's (1985) *The English Language* when he argues that:

> English has also become a lingua franca to the point that any literate, educated person on the face of the globe is in a very real sense deprived if he does not know English. Poverty, famine, and disease are instantly recognized as the cruellest and least excusable forms of deprivation. Linguistic deprivation is a less easily noticed condition, but one nevertheless of great significance.
>
> (pp. 160–1)

According to Jenkins (1995), attempts to introduce artificial languages have failed because 'English has triumphed. Those who do not speak it are at a universal disadvantage against those who do. Those who deny this supremacy merely seek to keep the disadvantaged deprived.' As we shall see later, this notion of 'linguistic deprivation' for those who do not speak English and even for those who do not speak it as a native language starts to have very particular significance within this discourse.

At times, too, the descriptions of this global spread start to use terms even more reminiscent of the prose of George (1867) or de Quincey (1862) and their talk of 'destiny' and the inevitable spread of English being like a mighty river flowing towards the sea. An editorial in *The Sunday Times* (UK) (10 July 1994), responding to the attempts in France to limit the use of English in various public domains, thunders against the French for opposing the 'European lingua franca which will inevitably be English'. To oppose English is pointless, the editorial warns, since 'English fulfills its own destiny as Churchill's 'ever-conquering language'. With every shift in international politics, every turn of the world's economies, every media development and every technological revolution, English marches on'. The editorial then returns to slightly more sober language:

> No other country in Europe works itself into such a frenzy about the way English eases the paths of multi-national discussion and assumes an ever-growing role as the language of power and convenience. The Germans, Spanish and Italians have accepted the inevitable. So, further afield, have the Russians, Chinese and Japanese. If you want to get ahead, you have to speak English. Two billion people around the world are believed to have made it their second language. Add that to 350m native English speakers in the United States, Britain and the Commonwealth, and you have an unstoppable force.

After these remarkable claims for the global spread of English and its inevitable path towards ascendancy, the editorial goes on to reassert that France must acknowledge 'the dominance of Anglo-American English as the universal language in a shrinking world', and that 'no amount of protectionist legislation and subsidies can shut out the free market in the expression of ideas'. 'Britain,' it asserts, 'must press ahead with the propagation of English and the British values which stand behind it' with the British Council ('Once a target for those unable to see no further than the end of their nose, it now runs a successful global network with teaching as its core activity in 108 countries'), the BBC (which 'is told to exploit its reputation and products abroad as never before') helping with 'the onward march of the English language'. As we shall see, this juxtaposition of the spread of English with the protectionism of the *Académie Française* is a frequently repeated trope of these discourses.

An article in *U.S. News & World Report* (18 February 1985) called 'English: Out to conquer the world' starts with the usual cataloguing of the spread of English:

> When an Argentine pilot lands his airliner in Turkey, he and the ground controller talk in English. When German physicists want to alert the international scientific community to a new discovery, they publish their findings in English-language journals. When Japanese executives cut deals with Scandinavian entrepreneurs in Bangkok, they communicate in English.

(p. 49)

and so on and so on. The article also derides those who would oppose the 'inevitable' spread of English, for 'English marches on. "If you need it, you learn it," says one expert'. Despite various attempts to counter the spread of English, 'the world's latest lingua franca will keep spreading. "It's like the primordial ooze," contends James Alatis, . . . "its growth is ineluctable, inexorable and inevitable"' (p. 52). According to Burchfield (1985):

> The English language is like a fleet of juggernaut trucks that goes on regardless. No form of linguistic engineering and no amount of linguistic legislation will prevent the cycles of change that lie ahead. But English as it is spoken and written by native speakers looks like remaining a communicative force, however slightly or severely beyond the grasp of foreigners, and changed in whatever agreeable or disagreeable manner, for many centuries to come.
>
> (p. 173)

Finally, here is Claiborne (1983) again:

> From century to century the great river of English has flowed on, fed by all these streams [the languages of 'copper-hued Native Americans, blacks kidnapped into bondage, liquid-eyed Indian rajahs and craftsmen, narrow-eyed Malay pirates and merchants of Cathay'], and itself an inexhaustible source of song and story, of comedy and tragedy, of histories, sermons, orations and manifestos and of mere polite – or impolite – conversation. As it enriched the lives of past generations, so it will continue to enrich the lives of our children and their children's children – provided we take care that they learn how to understand and appreciate it.
>
> (p. 292)

Clearly, there is quite remarkable continuity in the writing on the global spread of English. Bailey (1991)[1] comments that 'the linguistic ideas that evolved at the acme of empires led by Britain and the United States have not changed as economic colonialism has replaced the direct, political management of third world nations. English is still believed to be the inevitable world language' (p. 121). Viswanathan (1989) observes that constructions of the inferior Other and the superior Self arose not so much out of a position of strength and confidence as from a position of vulnerability and beleaguerment. Such constructions produced rather than reflected a confidence in English and the continued use of such cultural images needs to be seen as having the same productive force. It is more important, then, to look beyond arguments about the descriptive adequacy of such statements – are these statements true or false? – and rather to look at their productive force and the conditions of possibility of their production. Thus my interest here is in exploring not so much whether such discourses are in some sense *true* but rather what such discourses *produce*, what, in a Foucauldian (e.g. 1980) sense, are their *truth effects*. And I want to argue that it is in the adherence of such discourses to English that we can see the continuing effects of the cultural constructs of colonialism.

### In praise of English

If there are many similarities in the ways the spread of English has been both exhorted and applauded over the last hundred years, there are also interesting similarities in the way the language itself has been praised as a great language. Nineteenth-century writing on English abounded with glorifications of the language, suggesting that on the one hand the undeniable excellence of British institutions, ideas and culture must be reflected in the language and, on the other, that the undeniably superior qualities of English must reflect a people and a culture of superior quality. Thus, the Reverend James George, for example, arguing that Britain had been 'commissioned to teach a noble language embodying the richest scientific and literary treasures,' asserted that 'As the mind grows, language grows, and adapts itself to the thinking of the people. Hence, a highly civilized race, will ever have, a highly accomplished language. The English tongue, is in all senses a very noble one. I apply the term noble with a rigorous exactness' (George, 1867, p. 4). And Archbishop Trench, discussing the ancestral legacy of English, asked:

> What can more clearly point out their native land and ours as having fulfilled a glorious past, as being destined for a glorious future, than that they should have acquired for themselves and for those who came after them a clear, a strong, a harmonious, a noble language? For all this bears witness to corresponding merits in those that speak it, to clearness of mental vision, to strength, to harmony, to noble-ness in them who have gradually shaped and fashioned it to be the utterance of their inmost life and being.
>
> (Trench, 1881, p. 3)

A key argument in the demonstration of the superior qualities of English was in the breadth of its vocabulary, an argument which, as we shall see, is still used widely today.

The article 'English out to conquer the world' asks how English differs from other languages: 'First, it is bigger. Its vocabulary numbers at least 750,000 words. Second-ranked French is only two thirds that size. . . . English has been growing fast for 1,000 years, promiscuously borrowing words from other lands' (1985, p. 53). According to Bryson (1990), the numbers of words listed in *Webster's Third New International Dictionary* (450,000) and the *Oxford English Dictionary* (615,000) are only part of the total number of English words since 'technical and scientific terms would add millions more'. Looking at which terms are actually commonly made use of, Bryson suggests that about '200,000 English words are in common use, more than in German (184,000) and far more than in French (a mere 100,000)' (p. 3). Claiborne (1983) asserts that 'For centuries, the English-speaking peoples have plundered the world for words, even as their military and industrial empire builders have plundered it for more tangible goods'. This plundering has given English:

> the largest, most variegated and most expressive vocabulary in the world. The total number of English words lies somewhere between 400,000 – the number of current entries in the largest English dictionaries – and 600,000 – the largest figure that any expert is willing to be quoted on. By comparison, the biggest French dictionaries have only about 150,000 entries, the biggest Russian ones a mere 130,000.
>
> (p. 3)

Jenkins (1995) explains that:

> English has not won the battle to be the world's language through a trial of imperial strength. As the American linguist Braj Kachru points out, English has achieved its hegemony through its inherent qualities, by 'its propensity for acquiring new identities . . . its range of varieties and above all its suitability as a flexible medium for literary and other types of creativity'.

The subtitle to Jenkins' article ('The triumph of English') is 'Our infinitely adaptable mother tongue is now the world's lingua franca – and not before time.'

Apart from clearly supporting a simple argument about the superiority of English, this view of the richness of English puts into play several other images of English that are extremely important: the notion of English as some pure, Anglo-Saxon language, the idea that English and English-speakers have always been open, flexible and integrationist, and the belief that because of their vast vocabulary, speakers of English are the ablest thinkers. The first of these emerges in 'English out to conquer the world' when the article suggests that 'All-told, 80 percent of the word stock is foreign-born' (p. 53). The implications of this statement seem to be that that 'English' refers to a language of Anglo-Saxon purity, a language that despite all its borrowings and enrichments is, at its heart, an Anglo-Saxon affair. This effort to construct some clear Anglo-Saxon lineage for English has a long history (see Bailey, 1991; Crowley, 1989). Writing in 1901, Earle argued that:

We do not want to discard the rich furniture of words which we have inherited from our French and classic eras; but we wish to wear them as trophies, as the historic blazon of a great career, for the demarcation and amplification of an imperial language whose thews and sinews and vital energies are essentially English.

(cited in Crowley, 1989, p. 74)

According to Burnett (1962), 'the long process of creating the historic seedbed of the English language actually began with the arrival of the first Indo-European elements from the continent' (p. 75). Claiborne (1983) goes further and claims that 'the story of the life and times of English' can be traced from 'eight thousand years ago to the present' (p. 5). Although both these claims – that 80 per cent of English could be foreign and that the language can be traced back over 8,000 years – seem perhaps most remarkable for the bizarreness of their views, they also need to be taken very seriously in terms of the cultural constructions they produce, namely a view of English as some ethnically pure Anglo-Saxon or Aryan language. Bailey (1991) comments that '"Restoring" a racially pure language to suit a racially "primitive" nation is an idea that reached its most extreme and dreadful consequence in Hitler's Reich, and its appearance in images of English has not been sufficiently acknowledged' (p. 270).

The second image that emerges here is that to this core of Anglo-Saxon has been added – like tributaries to the great river of English, as many writers like to describe this – words from languages around the world, suggesting that English and British people have always been flexible and keen to borrow from elsewhere to enrich the language. This image of English is then used to deride other languages for their lack of breadth and, especially when people have sought to safeguard languages from the incursions of English, to claim that English is democratic while other languages are not. Most commonly this argument is used against the French for their attempts to legislate against the use of English words. In the editorial 'Lingua Britannica' in *The Sunday Times* (10 July 1994), the French are attacked for their defensiveness and xenophobia: 'It is sad to see the French, with their great cultural heritage, being so defensive. . . . While France seeks to bring the shutters down against alien intrusions of its cultural heritage, the BBC is told to exploit its reputation and products abroad as never before. Who are the xenophobes here?' Who, indeed?

Thus, the image of English as a great borrowing language is used against any attempts to oppose the spread of English, the argument being that the diverse vocabulary of English is a reflection of the democratic and open nature of the British people, and that reactions against English are nothing but evidence that other people are less open and democratic. 'English need not be protected by French Academies, Canadian constitutions or Flemish language rioters,' Jenkins (1995) tells us. 'The world must just take a deep breath and admit that it has a universal language at last.' But Jenkins is of course merely repeating an old image of English, one that the linguist Jespersen was quite happy with: 'The English language would not have been what it is if the English had not been for centuries great respecters of the liberties of each individual and if everybody had not been free to strike out new paths for himself.' (Jespersen, 1938/1982, p. 14). And this linguistic democracy is, as ever, far superior to the narrow-minded protectionism of the French:

> the English have never suffered an Academy to be instituted among them like the French or Italian Academies . . . In England every writer is, and has always been, free to take his words where he chooses, whether from the ordinary stock of everyday words, from native dialects, from old authors, or from other languages, dead or living.
>
> (1938/1982, p. 15)

The notion of English as a great borrowing language also seems to suggest a view of colonial relations in which the British intermingled with colonized people, enriching English as they communed with the locals. Such a view, however, is hardly supported by colonial history. Kiernan (1969) mentions Macartney's observation of the British 'besetting sin of contempt for the rest of mankind' and that 'while other foreigners at Canton mingled socially with the Chinese, the British kept aloof' (p. 148). Kiernan goes on to suggest that 'the *apartheid* firmly established in India was transferred in a great measure to China. Everyone has heard of the "Dogs and Chinese not admitted" notice in the park' (p. 156). In Hong Kong, he points out, 'the position of the Chinese as subjects under British rule increased British haughtiness'. He quotes Bowring in 1858 as observing that 'the separation of the native population from the European is nearly absolute; social intercourse between the races wholly unknown' (p. 156). As Metcalf (1995) shows with respect to India, this apartheid policy extended to the division of cities, with railway lines often built to separate the 'native areas' from the white preserves, and houses built with extensive verandahs, gardens and gateways in order to keep the colonized at bay. These observations are backed up by Wesley-Smith's (1994) analysis of 'anti-Chinese legislation' in Hong Kong. Looking at the 'considerable body of race-based discriminatory legislation' in Hong Kong, Wesley-Smith points to one of the central aims of much of this legislation: the separation of Chinese and Europeans. In 1917, Governor May (who had replaced Lugard, see Chapter 4) wrote to the secretary of state about the importance of maintaining the Peak area as an all-European reserve: 'It would be little short of a calamity if an alien and, by European standards, semi-civilized race were allowed to drive the white man from the one area in Hong Kong, in which he can live with his wife and children in a white man's healthy surroundings' (cited in Wesley-Smith, p. 100).

If, then, the British tended to mingle with colonized or other people far less than did other Europeans, it is unlikely that the English language was in fact such an open, borrowing language as is claimed. Indeed, Bailey (1991) argues that the British 'sense of racial superiority made English voyagers less receptive to borrowings that had not already been, in part, authenticated by other European travelers' (p. 61). Thus, he goes on:

> Far from its conventional image as a language congenial to borrow- ings from remote languages, English displays a tendency to accept exotic loanwords mainly when they first have been adopted by other European languages or when presented with marginal social practices or trivial objects. Anglophones who have ventured abroad have done so confident of the superiority of their culture and per- suaded of their capacity for adaptation, usually without accepting the obligations of adapting. Extensive linguistic borrowing and language mixing arise only when there is some degree of equality between or among languages (and their speakers) in a multilingual setting. For the English abroad, this sense of equality was rare.
>
> (p. 91)

There are, therefore, serious questions to be asked about the image of democratic English put into play by the construction of English as a borrow- ing language. Indeed, the constant replaying of this image of English as an open and borrowing language, reflecting an open and borrowing people, is a cultural construct of colonialism that is in direct conflict with the colonial evidence.

The third, and probably most insidious, view produced by the insistence on English having a far larger vocabulary than other languages relates to thought. Having stated that English has more words than German or French, Bryson (1990) goes on to argue that:

> The richness of the English vocabulary, and the wealth of available synonyms, means that English speakers can often draw shades of distinction unavailable to non-English speakers. The French, for example, cannot distinguish between house and home, between mind and brain, between man and gentleman, between 'I wrote' and 'I have written'. The Spanish cannot differentiate a chairman from a president, and the Italians have no equivalent of wishful thinking. In Russia there are no native words for efficiency, chal- lenge, engagement ring, have fun, or take care.
>
> (pp. 3–4)

Now it is important to note here that this is not merely an argument that different languages cut the world up differently but rather that English, with its larger vocabulary, cuts the world up better. Claiborne (1983), having also claimed a larger vocabulary for English than for other languages, goes on to suggest that 'Like the wandering minstrel in *The Mikado*, with songs for any and every occasion, English has the right word for it – whatever 'it' may be' (p. 4). Thus:

> It is the enormous and variegated lexicon of English, far more than the mere numbers and geographical spread of its speakers, that truly makes our native tongue marvellous – makes it, in fact, a medium for the precise, vivid and subtle expression of thought and emotion that has no equal, past or present.
>
> (p. 4)

In case the implications of this are not clear, Claiborne goes on to claim that English is indeed 'not merely a great language but the greatest' (p. 4) and that 'Nearly all of us do our thinking in words, which symbolize objects and events (real or imagined) . . .' (p. 6). Clearly, then, in this view, if you are a speaker of English, you are better equipped than speakers of other languages to think about the world. In this view, English is a window on the world. According to Burnett (1962), 'not only in Asia and Africa, but in Europe, crisscrossed by linguistic frontiers and dissected by deep-rooted cultural loyalties, people of all classes now look to English as a window, a magic casement opening on every horizon of loquacious men' (pp. 20–1).

Such a view, as Cohn (1996) points out, has a long history. Looking at colonial views of language in India, Cohn suggest that 'Meaning for the English was something attributed to a word, a phrase, or an object, which could be determined and translated, at best with a synonym that had a direct referent to something in what the English thought of as a "natural" world' (pp. 18–19). There was, then, an abiding view that there was a natural world, with a natural system for naming it: English. Fernando (1986) has pointed to the dual fallacies contained in this view:

> one is the influential and peculiarly Western notion that 'Language' is capable of describing the whole of nature alone: nature can be put entirely and completely into words. The other submerged assumption is that English, particularly, is capable of doing this, that other languages – usually Asian ones – do not have the full range of concepts necessary for the purpose.
>
> (p. 108)

What is interesting here is the availability of this belief in contemporary books on English.

If writers on English are not praising its supposedly vast vocabulary, another direction in which they often turn is towards its supposedly simple grammar. This argument, too, is an old one:

> In its easiness of grammatical construction, in its paucity of inflection, in its almost total disregard of the distinctions of gender excepting those of nature, in the simplicity and precision of its terminations and auxiliary verbs, not less than in the majesty, vigour and copiousness of its expression, our mother-tongue seems well adapted by *organization* to become the language of the world.
> (Review of Bradshaw's *Scheme*, 1848; cited in Bailey, 1991, p. 108)

Jenkins (1995) argues that the global adoption of English is a result of the adaptability and simplicity of English: 'English has few inflections, endings or cases. Its grammar is based on simple word order. It has no clicks, tones or implosives.' After arguing that English has a greater vocabulary than other languages, and also that it is more flexible than other languages (another old favourite), Bryson (1990) goes on to argue for its simplicity. This takes a number of forms, such as simplicity of spelling and pronunciation: 'English is said to have fewer of the awkward consonant clusters and singsong tonal varieties that make other languages so difficult to master' (p. 6); uninflected pronouns: 'In German, if you wish to say *you*, you must choose between seven words: *du, dich, dir, Sie Ihnen, ihr,* and *euch.* This can cause immense social anxiety. . . . In English we avoid these problems by relying on just one form: *you*' (p. 8); gender and articles: 'English is mercifully free of gender. . . . In this regard English is a godsend to students everywhere. Not only have we discarded problems of gender with definite and indefinite articles, we have often discarded the articles themselves' (p. 8); and conciseness in words: 'German is full of jaw-crunching words like *Geisteswissenschaffeten (sic)*[2] (a social worker). . . . English, in happy contrast, favours crisp truncations: IBM, laser, NATO' (p. 9).

Such arguments recall the work of the linguist Jespersen (1938/1982), who asserts in the introduction to his book on *Growth and structure of the English language* that 'there is one expression that continually comes to mind whenever I think of the English language and compare it with others: it seems to me positively and expressly *masculine*, it is the language of a grown-up man and has very little childish and feminine about it' (p. 2). It is worth noting here, I think, how such constructions of English replicate the colonial constructions of the Other as childlike and feminine (see Chapter 2). Jespersen then goes on, at pains to show that he is engaged in the scientific study of language, to demonstrate his reasons for making such a claim. English has 'business-like, virile qualities,' he argues, which 'manifest themselves in such things as word-order' (p. 10). And such 'business-like shortness' (one of the masculine characteristics of English) can be found in such 'convenient abbreviations' of words and sentences that are so common in English (1938/ 1982, p. 7).

There are a number of points worth observing about these general arguments. The first question we might want to ask is why is it good on the one hand to have a supposedly vast and complex vocabulary and on the other a simple grammar? There would seem to be an equally valid argument (though equally problematic in other ways) that complex grammars are a sign of complex thinking. The point, of course, is that such apparent contradictions do not matter: there is no underlying rationale to the argument that English supposedly has more words than other languages or a less complex grammar; the issue is that English is better than other languages and that any evidence of difference can then be used to support that argument. It is also worth noting here that these arguments are not only ethnocentric in terms of their position relative to English and other languages, but also very Eurocentric: apart from the reference to the 'singsong tonal variations' of other languages, comparisons are almost always with European languages. Articles, grammatical gender, word classes, inflections, pronouns and so on are all played out in different combinations and varieties in other languages around the world.

But one significant implication of this supposed simplicity of English is that it makes it easy to learn: 'The current extraordinary spread of the English language around the world would never have begun, despite all the forces of history and all the facilities for its propagation, if English were a difficult language to learn' (Burnett, 1962, p. 27). For Burnett, this includes a general simplicity and elegance at all levels:

> It excels by reason of its basically simple rudiments – a hard core of perhaps one thousand energetic words which fill all the needs of ordinary communication, a few tolerant rules governing their use, and a logical underlying skeletal structure – which can be taught and learned more quickly than is possible in any other language spoken on earth today.
>
> (Burnett, 1962, p. 27)

But, whether the language supposedly has a vast vocabulary and simple grammar, or in the above example, 'one thousand energetic words' and 'a few tolerant rules' it is easy to learn. Indeed, beneath the centrepiece of Jenkins' article – a picture of two white men in the clothes of the church talking to a group of Africans (see figure 5) – is the explanation 'A missionary at work in Africa, circa 1800: more than a billion people are now thought to be English-speakers, so easy is the language to learn.' The spread of English, therefore, is not a result of politics or economics but of the simplicity of English. On the one hand, then, English is a language richer and more complex than any other, a language that allows for better and more precise

*Figure 5* Missionaries at work in Southern Africa

representations of the world. On the other hand, it is a simple and clear language that is easier to learn than any other. I am not as interested in pulling apart these arguments (to explain the extraordinary inaccuracies in these articles and books or to supply counterexamples, would fill dozens more pages) as I am in looking at their historical continuity and what they produce in terms of images of English.

### English and the great Eskimo snow myth

There is clearly a constant reciprocity between the construction of Self and Other, so that it is often difficult to discuss one without the other. In the constructions of English discussed above, it is evident that there are constant constructions of other languages as 'different': the clumsy spelling of Gaelic, the ugly word combinations of German, the illogical nature of gender, the difficulties of declensions, and then, as one moves out from the European heartland, the 'singsong tonal variations' of other languages, the strange 'exoticisms' of other languages. The great favourite of all these is of course the many words for 'snow' that 'Eskimos' supposedly have: 'The Eskimos, as is well known, have fifty words for types of snow – though curiously no word for just plain snow. To them there is crunchy snow, soft snow, fresh snow, and old snow, but no word that just means snow' (Bryson, 1990, pp. 4–5). Eskimos are not alone in this:

> The Italians, as we might expect, have over 500 names for different types of macaroni. . . . The residents of the Trobriand Islands of Papua New Guinea have 100 words for yams, while the Maoris of New Zealand have thirty-five words for dung (don't ask me why). Meanwhile, the Arabs are said (a little unbelievably, perhaps) to have 6,000 words for camels and camel equipment.
>
> (p. 5)

I would like to devote a bit of space here to this idea.

One of the things that is immediately striking about this tale of Eskimo words for snow (Trobriand Island words for yams, Maori words for dung, or Arab words for camels and camel equipment) is that there is no consistency to the number of supposed words. To give just one example, in a recent article on wine-tasting, Shield (1995) quotes 'Wine educator Alan Young' who argues that 'the average person has very limited abilities in describing colour. In contrast the Eskimos have more than 40 words to describe the color of snow.' Martin (1986) and Pullum (1989) give examples ranging from three to two hundred; 'But hey: nine, forty-eight, a hundred, two hundred, who cares? It's a bunch, right?' (Pullum, 1989, p. 278). Martin describes the development of the account of 'Eskimo words for snow' as 'a case study in the creation of an oral tradition and an object lesson on the hazards of superficial scholarship' (p. 418). One immediate problem, of course, is with the term 'Eskimo'; this term, seen now as an arctic version of other crude classifications such as 'Orientals', covers a wide range of languages and dialects, including Yupik and Inuit-Inupiaq.

The origins of this story can be found in Boas (1911), who presents four lexically unrelated words for snow: *aput* – snow on the ground, *qana* – falling snow, *piqsirpoq* – drifting snow, and *qimuqsuqi* – a snow drift. This was then taken up by Whorf, though even at this stage the number of words had already changed and, perhaps more importantly, the nature of the argument had shifted. Boas used the example to show that different language structures were not comparable: in the same way that English had many unrelated terms for different types of water (river, stream, lake, sea, liquid, rain, and so on), Eskimo has apparently different roots for types of snow. Boas was not saying more here than that different languages have different ways in which they have developed lexicon for different areas. Whorf, however, tried to make a much stronger argument concerning language, cognition and perception, suggesting that the different form of the lexicon was related to different ways of perceiving the world. This notion has been successively taken up by different writers (E.T. Hall and Roger Brown were two of the first to popularize the idea in the late 1950s), with varying numbers of words for snow but generally the same core argument that the existence of these words has some cognitive effect.

According to Martin one immediate error here is that the focus is on words rather than roots (thus overlooking the morphological variations in these languages). In West Greenlandic, for example, there are two roots for words that refer to snow: *qanik* – snow in the air, and *aput* – snow on the ground. Thus, she suggests, there is little difference here between these roots and the English words 'snow' and 'flake'. But more important than arguments over exactly how many words for snow there really are is the question as to why the example of 'Eskimo words for snow' has been trotted out so many times over the years. The constant use of this dubious example has tended to reduce a highly complex and interesting domain of inquiry concerning the relationship between language, culture and cognition to a trite statement: 'Thus is the complexity of the interrelations of linguistic structure, cultural behavior, and human cognition reduced to "Eskimo words for snow"' (Martin, 1986, p. 419). Furthermore, this example is always open to the question 'So what?' According to Martin, 'a self-evident observation – what is in our environment is likely to be reflected in our language – has become imbued with exaggerated meaning' (p. 420). Or as Pullum (1989) puts it, 'Among the many depressing things about this credulous transmission and elaboration of a false claim is that even if there *were* a large number of roots for different snow types in some Arctic language, this would *not*, objectively, be intellectually interesting; it would be a most mundane and unremarkable fact' (p. 278). Pullum goes on to argue that the idea of different people having different ranges of vocabulary is simply unremarkable. To transpose his argument, it would not be particularly interesting if someone argued that applied linguists have several different words for aspects of language learning or teaching where the general public may only have one. 'Only the link to those legendary, promiscuous blubber-gnawing hunters of the ice-packs could permit something this trite to be presented to us for contemplation' (p. 279).

What interests me here, however, is the relationship between Eskimo words for snow and images of English. Why is it that Bryson (1990) starts with the idea that English has more words than other languages, shows that other languages cannot make distinctions that English can make and then counterbalances this by observing that English cannot make all the distinctions made by other languages? If we follow Bryson's argument through, it becomes apparent that the issue here is not one of finding balance between languages but of once again promoting English at the expense of other languages. He starts his examples of distinctions that English cannot make with what seem to be important ideas in European languages; French and German, for example distinguish between types of knowledge (*connaître/ kennen* and *savoir/wissen*). The examples then become increasingly strange and exotic, however: the Italians have a word for the mark left on a table by a moist glass, while Gaelic speakers in Scotland have a word for the itchiness on the upper lip before sipping whisky. Some of these distinctions are not perhaps so valuable, he then suggests: 'The existence in German of a word like *Schadenfreude* (taking delight in the misfortune of others) perhaps tell us as much about Teutonic sensitivity as it does about their neologistic versatility' (p. 4).

It is then we encounter the 'fifty words for types of snow – though curiously no word for just plain snow' (p. 4) and '100 words for yams', 'thirty-five words for dung' etc. (p. 5). Whether or not Bryson is implying that there may in fact be such a thing as 'just plain snow' that is not recognized by the 'Eskimos' is not entirely clear. What does seem to be clear, however, is that as we move out across the world from the core language English, we find quaint and exotic uses of language, which suggest that various people are locked into their material circumstances. As Pinker (1994) explains, there is an ironic twist here: such arguments originally emerged 'as part of a campaign to show that nonliterate cultures were as complex and sophisticated as European ones. But the supposedly mind-broadening anecdotes owe their appeal to a patronizing willingness to treat other cultures' psychologies as weird and exotic compared to our own' (p. 64). Now Pinker, as we shall see, also suffers from a certain narrow-mindedness, and is picking up on this example in order to make an argument for universalism as opposed to relativism. This is not the argument I want to make here, though Pinker's observation that there is a patronizing exoticism here is well made. My interest, however, is how such exoticisms are made while at the same time praising English for its breadth of vocabulary. Thus, according to this argument, although English is not able to make every distinction that other languages make, most of these distinctions are merely exotic examples of peoples' location within a narrowly defined world.

A better understanding of the implications of the Eskimo snow myth can be found in the work of the great linguist Otto Jespersen. He explains that the more advanced a language, 'the more developed is its power of expressing abstract or general ideas. Everywhere language has first attained to expressions for the concrete and special' (1922, p. 429). He goes on to show that in 'the languages of barbarous races' there are often many words for one object. Thus, citing Sayce (1875) 'The aborigines of Tasmania had no words representing abstract ideas; for each variety of gum-tree and wattle-tree, etc. they had a name; but they had no equivalent for the expression "a tree" . . .' (p. 429). He goes on to list the many 'primitive' languages that cannot express such abstract notions: 'The Zulus have no word for "cow," but words for "red cow," "white cow," etc.'; 'The Lithuanians, like many primitive tribes, have many special, but no common names for various colours: one word for gray in speaking about wool and geese, one about horses, one about cattle, one about the hair of men and some animals, and in the same way for other colours' (p. 429). After a number of other examples,

Jespersen is able to conclude that 'Primitive man did not see the wood for the trees' (p. 430).

Thus the image Jespersen gives us is one in which the 'languages of wild tribes' reflect the ways in which the people are restricted to the minutiae of the everyday (p. 427). The savage has many words for particular things but cannot deal with abstract ideas, cannot 'see the wood for the trees'. And it is of course in the very English words 'tree' 'cow' grey' and so on that such abstractions can be revealed. Such a view of, say, the 'aborigines of Tasmania' should not, I believe, be seen in isolation from their extermination (see Chapter 1). This very construction of English and Aboriginal languages is part of the construction of such people as lesser beings. If the wholesale slaughter of people today along such lines seems less likely, it is worth considering that the issue may nevertheless be one of linguistic and cultural death by promoting English over other languages. Given that we have already been told that English has more words than any other language and had borrowed these from around the world, it is clear that English is a broad, international and diverse language, whose multiplicity of words reflects higher level concepts and distinctions compared to the small worlds represented in other languages. The example of the Eskimo words for snow, Trobriand Island words for yams, Maori words for dung, or Arab words for camels and camel equipment, therefore, is used to support the notion of the superiority of English.

This is not the only possible use to which one can put knowledge about such other languages, however. If the argument above tries to construct exotic Others locked into their worlds, as opposed to English with its broad, international vocabulary, Burnett (1962), as contrary as ever, continues to point to the simplicity of English in the face of other complex languages. The complexity of languages such as 'Eskimo' is evidence, he suggests, that they are primitive languages. In this view, it is the very simplicity of English which shows its superiority:

> The most spectacular advances made by English are in the so-called underdeveloped areas of the world. The polyglot populations of Asia and Africa find it much easier to learn English than to try to comprehend the speech of their nearest neighbours. For, contrary to popular supposition, languages evolve in the direction of simplicity. English, being a highly evolved, cosmopolitan, sophisticated language, has been refined and revised, planed down and polished through centuries of use, so that today it is far less complicated than any primitive tongue. Some of the most difficult languages in the world are spoken by some of the world's most backward people – e.g. the Australian aborigines, the Eskimos, the Hottentots, and the Yahgan Indians of Terra del Fuego.
>
> (p. 16)

Once again, of course, whichever way you cut it, English comes out on top.

### English under threat

The final aspect of the images of English that I want to discuss here is that English is threatened from various quarters. Such a notion, of course, is closely linked to ideas of purity in English, and in some ways appears to sit in a rather contradictory tension with the open and democratic version of English. Despite its apparent history of borrowing and openness, English becomes constructed as a language under threat from various sources. This image is of particular interest since it produces on the one hand a notion of a stable, pure and righteous version of the language and on the other hand images of the Other, as a threat to English. For Bryson (1990) and Claiborne (1983) the foe is generally an internal one: the tendency towards use of jargon in certain areas. For Claiborne, 'The unchecked flood of linguistic invention and borrowing that has made English what it has, like any flood, carried with it quantities of junk: clichés, ephemeral 'in' words, words that are self-consciously learned or self-consciously clever' (p. 5). Similarly, Bryson, having praised English for its succinctness compared with other languages, bemoans the 'occasional tendency in English, particularly in academic and political circles, to resort to waffle and jargon' (p. 9). Burnett (1962) also decries this threat: 'The war against the English language is thus a many-pronged offensive, waged amid the jungles of jargon, over oceans of Officialese, prairies of pedantry, and mountains of mish-mash, while the air oscillates with electronic frenzy' (p. 195). While these attacks on so-called jargon seem to do little more than put into place a view of a pure, unchanging and undefiled English under attack from popular and abstruse usage, other versions of this threat are more insidious in their implications.

Burchfield (1985) identifies a much more serious threat: Black English, which he describes as 'a separable, differentiated, fully structured spoken variety of English, not easily tied down to particular regions of the US, potently political in its animosity towards the structured patterns of Received American, colourful, animated, fancy, and subversive'. He lists a number of examples of Black English which make 'holes' 'in the standard American syntactical cobweb'. Significantly, all are examples of *absences* of standard forms: 'All my black brother' (uninflected plural), 'He a Black bitch' (absence of the verb 'to be'), and so on. Burchfield suggests that these are examples of a 'creolized form of English, shaped from a need to disdain the language of those to whom Blacks are opposed, and, at whatever distance, shaped by some undemonstrable ancestral memory of patterns of speech brought from Africa several generations earlier by African slaves.' Most importantly, however, it is a threat to standard English:

If it is possible to see a variety of English as a threat to the accept-
ability of the language handed down to white Americans from the
seventeenth century onward, this is it. Its dislocation of normal
syntax, its patterned formulas showing disregard for the traditional
shape of sentences make it at once deeply impressive and overtly
threatening to currently agreed standards.

(p. 164)

In this version of the threat to English, a pure, white, standard English is in
danger from a subversive, colourful, creolized Black English.

In a section of the *U.S. News & World Report* (18 February 1985) article
'English out to conquer the world', called 'It's at home where our language
is in distress' the dangers are seen as coming from a number of quarters: 'The
shortcomings of schools, waves of immigrants, TV addiction – all are taking
a toll on U.S. linguistic skills' (p. 54). The standard culprits for the supposed
decline in American standards of literacy are brought up once again, with
increased viewing of TV, the liberalism of schools in the 1970s and the rise
of 'bonehead English' courses at school and college villified for contributing
to the illiteracy of the American people. But the argument takes on a very
different twist when it turns to the effects of immigration to the US:

The increase in English-language illiteracy stems as well from the
swelling tide of immigrants entering the United States – 530,000 or
more legally and unknown number illegally each year. According to
the Census Bureau, about 11 percent of the population now reports
speaking a language other than English at home, with Spanish predominant by far.

(p. 55)

The article then goes on to quote Gerda Bikales, executive director of
US English, and his contention that 'the primacy of English is being challenged. . . . There is a general belief, nurtured to some extent by bilingual
education, that English is not all that necessary' (p. 55). It is important to
note the jumps that this argument makes. First, this article assumes that
apparent levels of literacy can be equated with threats to the language. Thus,
high levels of illiteracy among the unemployed become an unemployed,
working class threat to English. This argument is then taken further to suggest that the use of another language at home may also be a threat to English.
The general argument about the importance of literacy in general (literacy in
languages other than English by immigrant people is not discussed) has here
been replaced by an argument that suggests that English itself is threatened
by immigration. Somehow, then, the existence of people in America whose
first language is not English has become a threat to English. And, even the
sanctity of government in English is under threat.

153

## Teaching our marvellous tongue to speakers of other languages

In the sections above, I have been looking at constructions of English in various types of popular writing, from books on English to newspaper and magazine articles. I have tried to show how remarkably consistent discourses about the global spread of English, the superiority of the language, and the threats posed by other languages, have come to adhere to the language. I have also been suggesting that such images are present-day results of the cultural constructs of colonialism: while Anglicist discourse was downplayed in language policy in the colonial era, its constructions of English have re-emerged in a new era of neo-colonialism. A further argument here is that both the theories and practices of ELT take place in the context of these popular discourses on English. ELT does not occur in a social and cultural vacuum, influenced only by its own professed egalitarianism; rather the ideas and practices of ELT are constantly subject to the popular discourses that I have been analysing here. But, as I intend to argue in this section, these images of English do have more direct and immediate connections to domains such as English language teaching and language policy.

Two objections to my arguments might be that 1) Such praise is sung of any language, and particularly when that language becomes linked to a process of cultural domination; and 2) The coverage of books and articles here is highly selective and there is no clear link to English language teaching. In response I would say, first, that indeed many languages are praised by their users as superior to others, but it *does* matter that it is English that is being so elevated. English is widely used around the world, with often quite tragic consequences for other languages, children's education, and possibilities of future diversity. To the extent that such consequences derive from singing the praises of English, it matters a great deal that it is English that is under discussion here. Second, it is of course true that my analysis of these discourses on English cannot claim huge coverage across great numbers of texts, different media and so on. Nevertheless, I want to argue that these images are prevalent, and constantly reoccur, and it is the fact that they can be found in such diverse contexts that point to their wide use. I shall give some more examples below and show how these images start to get taken up in English language teaching materials.

As I have suggested, it is rare to find the stronger version of these images of English in more academic discourse. And yet, here is one of our recent specialists on language, writing in *Time* magazine: 'the breathtaking half-a-million-word vocabulary of English is built from the grass-roots contributions of countless slang slingers and jargon mongers' (Pinker, 1995, p. 29). And who does he then take aim at? Who else, of course, but the French? 'English has been estimated to contain three to six times as many words as French. Some might say centuries guarding the purity of the French language have left it with verbose expressions and a puny vocabulary. But then what can you expect from a bunch of suits?' (ibid). 'Other reiterations of these images occur in writing on ELT. In an article in *ELT Documents* on the possible cultural implications of teaching English, for example, Barrow (1990) discusses whether there is any reason to be wary of 'cultural imperialism'. He dismisses such concerns since English 'has an unsurpassed richness in terms of vocabulary, and hence in its scope for giving precise and detailed understanding of the world' (p. 3). Thus, while suggesting that teaching English does indeed have cultural implications, he argues that this should be welcomed by English teachers since 'some cultures are superior to others, at least in certain specific respects' (p. 8). Teachers, therefore, 'should have no qualms about the fact that they are directly introducing certain patterns of thought and values to students' since 'what is implicit in the English language may represent a better or truer way of understanding the world than is represented in certain other languages' (p. 9). While conceding for a moment that 'the reverse may of course also be true,' he goes on to explain that 'there are grounds for associating the richness and diversity of a language with superiority in terms of providing a true perspective, on the principle that the ability to make fine discriminations is part and parcel of subtle and realistic thinking and understanding. English, on these terms, is a relatively powerful language' (p. 9). This, then, is a clear example of the argument that the apparent richness and diversity of English can lead to better representations of the world.

Such images of English then reappear in materials directly targeted at language learners. *International English*, a glossy 'dossier' prepared by MacMillan publishers (1989) and available typically in libraries, language schools and British Council language centres, repeats many of the same themes: 'One billion people speak English. That's 20% of the world's population' (p. 2). It too goes on to list the domains in which English is used: politics ('many foreign leaders speak in English to international journalists' (p. 4)), pop music, computing, TV and film, science and medicine, business, air and sea travel, the Olympic Games, and Christianity ('There are millions of Christians on every continent. It's the world's most international religion. But when Christian leaders from different countries meet, the language they use is English' (p. 5)). And, of course, it cannot avoid the claim that 'There are more than 500,000 words in the Oxford English Dictionary. Compare that with the vocabulary of German (about 200,000) and French (100,000)' (p. 2). *International English* also repeats another of the images discussed earlier '80% of all English vocabulary comes from other languages' (p. 2), before going on to argue that the history of English apparently starts around 5,000 BC with 'a tribe called the Indo-Eoropeans': 'They were farmers and they had their own language. They discovered the wheel around 3,000 BC' (p. 6). I'm not sure whether the invention of the wheel and the development of English are supposed to be somehow interlinked, but why not?

Another ELT context of these images can be found in the opening pages of a popular current ESL textbook (*Headway Upper Intermediate*). Here many of the central images of English are reproduced: 'English has the largest vocabulary, with approximately 500,000 words and 300,000 technical terms.' 'Incredibly enough, 75% of the world's mail and 60% of the world's telephone calls are in English.' The three main characteristics of English are 'simplicity of form', 'flexibility' ('As a result of the loss of inflections, English has become, over the past five centuries, a very flexible language'), and 'openness of vocabulary' ('This involves the free admissions of words from other languages and the easy creation of compounds and derivatives.'). This last item then goes on to explain that while 'most world languages' have contributed words to English, language 'purists' in France, Japan and Russia are resisting the spread of English. As if to assure its readers, the section finishes by suggesting that although the global spread of English 'will no doubt continue,' the proposition 'that all other languages will die out is absurd' (p. 2). On the next page, students are asked to work out the questions to 'answers' such as 'Simplicity of form, flexibility, and openness of vocabulary'. They are then asked to say whether the text comes from a brochure for an English language school (discursively yes, linguistically no?), a preface to a book on modern language teaching (quite possibly), a dictionary (?) or an encyclopaedia (another possibility). The difficulties I had in answering this last question points, I think, to the ubiquity of these discourses.

The existence of these discourses in and around English has, I believe, a number of unfortunate consequences. One of the most insidious constructions that has emerged from the glorification of English and the denigrations of other languages is the relationship between native speakers and non-native speakers. This is, of course, one of the classic dichotomies that result from cultural constructs of colonialism, dividing the world into speakers of English (abbreviated most commonly merely to NS) and non-native speakers of English (NNS). The many problems with the NS-NNS dichotomy and the elevation of the former over the latter have been addressed by a number of writers (e.g. Auerbach, 1993; Oda, 1995; Phillipson, 1992; Rampton, 1990). The main points I wish to draw attention to here are, first, the way in which a construction of English as a superior language, when coupled to a belief that to know English is to have available a better way of describing the world, makes of the native speaker of English not merely a supposedly better teacher of English but also someone endowed with superior knowledge about the world. And second, I want to suggest that since this relationship is embedded in colonial constructions of Self and Other, to try to change the beliefs and practices around these constructs will require a major battle against deeply embedded cultural patterns.

Another product of the belief in the superiority of English emerges in the emphasis on English in anything from national language policies to classroom methodologies. Of course, one of the most obvious results of these discourses is to justify and promote the global spread of English. Thus, given the innate superiority of English, its spread can be explained in terms of the qualities of the language and people's demand for it: 'Of vastly greater import than the scale and momentum of the English irruption from its wellsprings in the West is the fact that it came in response to a worldwide and seemingly insatiable demand' (Burnett, 1962, p. 24). Burnett goes on to explain:

> How can this worldwide and apparently insatiable demand for English be explained? None of the external factors – business motivations, the extended military and economic influence of the English-speaking people, circumglobal pathways of communication and travel – can adequately account for the phenomenon. The essential catalyst lies in the internal anatomy of the language itself.
>
> (p. 26)

This colonial discourse, which makes the spread of English a property of the language itself, can be seen from the enthusiastic writers of the nineteenth century, through such writers as Burnett and down to the modern arguments for the importance of instruction in English in order to avoid 'linguistic deprivation'.

While other languages and cultures were constantly derogated (see Chapter 6), English was promoted as an essential language. As a primary school headmaster in a migrant holding centre in Australia remarked in 1951:

> The child must learn to think in English from the start . . . English is to be the base of all instruction. It is the avenue to mutual understanding. It is the key to the success of the whole immigration project . . . English must be spoken to the pupils and by them, all day and every day, in every activity, in school and out of it.
>
> (Cited in Collins, 1992, p. 111)

Here we can start to see the link between the promotion of English as a superior language and the promotion of English-only approaches to teaching. Howatt (1984) explains the growth of Direct Method approaches to English teaching in which teachers were expected to use English and only English in the classroom, as a product of European theories of language learning and teaching. Far more likely, however, is that such developments were a product of the colonial contexts of English teaching as well as a transference of European ideas themselves based on the colonial contexts of instruction of French, German and so on.

Although a great deal of teaching in and through English in the early colonial context had been done bilingually – either by teachers who were themselves bilingual or by the use of translators – around the turn of the century, fewer and fewer native speakers were capable of using local languages.

While local teachers still used both languages (and still in Hong Kong and many other parts of the world continue to do so), it was in the colonial context of British teachers and their local subjects that the highly influential ELT theories and practices were formed which stressed use of English and only English in the classroom. As Auerbach (1993) argues, the use of only English in ESL classes needs to be understood not so much in terms of its common pedagogical or psycholinguistic rationalizations but rather in terms of the ideological implications of an insistence on English. Drawing on Phillipson's (1992) analysis of underlying tenets of ELT theory that emerged as part of British neocolonial policy – English is best taught monolingually, by native speakers, as early as possible, as much as possible, and preferably to the exclusion of other languages – Auerbach argues that 'practices we take for granted as being pedagogically grounded have antecedents in overtly ideological tendencies' (p. 13).

What I want to argue is that such ideologies and practices have their origins deeply rooted in colonial constructions of English. Thus, although Auerbach is surely right in connecting the emphasis on monolingual English use in ESL classrooms to both the early twentieth century Americanization programs and to the more recent US English movement, the origins of these constructions of English and other languages (languages of the Other) lie in the cultural constructions of colonialism. Similarly, according to Wiley and Lukes (1996):

> Given the historical legacy of the ideologies of English only and standard English and their continuing differential impact across racial and ethnic groups, language professionals need to consider their implications for contemporary policy and practice and to contest policies and practices that perpetuate social inequities.
>
> (p. 530)

But, what I want to suggest is that unless we also see such ideologies in a broader context, as informed not merely by histories of American immigration and racial policy but also by broader discursive constructions that promote monolingualism in English as a superior condition to multilingualism across other languages, we will fail to see how these images of English have been constructed, and fail to see in what directions we need to work in order to oppose such ideologies.

As Viswanathan (1989) argues in the context of English studies, 'the role of empire in the history of English studies demonstrates conclusively that the main issues in curriculum will remain unaddressed as long as the debate continues to be engaged by appeals to either universalist or relativist value, religious identity or secular pluralism' (p. 167). Similarly, as long as we continue to discuss the global spread of English within a debate between a liberal tolerance of multiple standards and a conservative promotion of one or few standards, and thus fail to acknowledge the power of popular discourses on English, we shall remain isolated from the continuous history of colonial constructions of English. As I have been arguing, however, such constructions are only one side of the colonial coin: the 'TE' of TESOL. In the next chapter I shall turn to the 'SOL' side of the equation, the construction of the Other.

# 6

# IMAGES OF THE OTHER
## China and cultural fixity

The average resident went through his Far Eastern years con-
scious of the aliens around him only as beggars, or rioters, or
servants, and spent his lengthy leisure hours grumbling in his
club at everything Chinese because he was not getting rich fast
enough.

(Kiernan, 1969, p. 157)

In contemporary travel accounts, the monarch-of-all-I-survey
scene gets repeated, only now from the balconies of hotels in big
third-world cities.

(Pratt, 1992, p. 216)

In truth Chinese education is – *pace* the sinologues – no education at all. It is no 'leading out of' but a leading back to. Instead
of expanding the intelligence, it contracts it; instead of broadening sympathies, it narrows them; instead of making a man
honest, intelligent and brave, it has produced few who are not
cunning, narrow-minded and pusillanimous.

(Addis, 1889, p. 206)

Bateson Wright, a former headmaster of the Central School in Hong Kong,
commented around the turn of the century that the average Chinese student
was 'incapable of sustaining an argument, starting with false premises [*sic*] and
cheerfully pursuing a circuitous course to the point from which he started'.
In order to overcome such a lack of logic, Bateson Wright prescribed a 'rigid
course of geometrical study' (cited in Sweeting, 1990, p. 322). For anyone
involved in English language teaching, this comment may call forth uncomfortable associations. This construction of the illogical Other following
circuitous thought patterns that stand in such stark contrast to the linear logic
to which 'we' adhere, is a quite remarkable precursor to Kaplan's (1966) diagrams of different 'cultural thought patterns' (see figure 6), with 'Oriental'
students apparently pursuing a circuitous course in their writing and ESL
teachers giving their students a course of geometrical study in order to

English          Semitic          Oriental          Romance          Russian

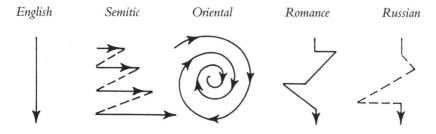

*Figure 6* Cultural thought patterns

remove those bends, curves and digressions that so bedevil the writing of the Other.

A number of years ago, when I was teaching in China, I was intrigued to see that one of the textbooks used for teaching writing at the senior levels of the undergraduate programme (a copied American undergraduate writing book) discussed in its introduction Kaplan's (1966) models of contrastive rhetoric. Shortly afterwards, I was listening to a student discussing some of her frustrations at trying to learn to write in English: why is it, she wanted to know, that English writing always went round and round and round, with its introductions, conclusions, topic sentences and the like, while Chinese was written in a straight, clear line? As she drew the patterns of text in the air, I saw Kaplan's diagrams being formed almost perfectly in reverse. More recently, I had an interesting conversation with an Anglo-Australian woman who used the family name of her Chinese husband. An assignment she had done for a lecturer in a distance learning programme (the lecturer knew only her name and had never met her) had been returned with a long explanation (including once again Kaplan's diagrams) of how Western writing was linear and clear and that she was still writing in the circular Chinese style. The Chinese name on the title page of the assignment had triggered a whole set of beliefs about culture, thought and learning. And when I discuss these constructs with my students, I find many of them, particularly those from East Asia, nod in recollection at textbook diagrams, circles drawn on blackboards, scribbles at the ends of essays, all repeating the same cultural construct of colonialism.

What such examples raise for me are a host of questions about how we construct the Others of ELT, our students. Why is it, for example, that Chinese students are so frequently and so consistently categorized as passive, rote-learners, whose logic follows a strange spiral pattern? One of the principal themes of this book has been the way in which particular cultural constructs of colonialism – producing images of the Other in juxtaposition to supposed norms of the Self – have deep roots in Western ways of thinking and occur and reoccur so often that we scarcely notice them. To take one recent and seemingly fairly trivial example, in a review of books on the history of fashion, the reviewer (Johnson, 1995) concludes that fashion is 'a Western phenomenon, in primitive societies styles in dress do not change' (p. 19). This brief statement draws on and recirculates a range of common assumptions: first, there is the dichotomy between 'the West' and 'primitive societies,' suggesting on the one hand a world of modernity and civilization and on the other a world out there of primitive societies. Second, Western society is given the characteristic of change, adaptability, progress. Third, by contrast, these so-called primitive societies are assumed to be static, unchanging, traditional. And finally, the author assumes – whether her information is based on the books she is reviewing or not – the right to speak about such primitive societies (the rest of the world) with easy authority.

This remains perhaps a trivial example, an everyday commonplace, but it is the very possibility of making such easy throw-away remarks that is a product of the discourses of Self and Other. This in turn reiterates a point worth re-emphasizing about some of the arguments underlying Chapters 5 and 6. As I suggested in the last chapter, we have been too often guilty in applied linguistics of assuming that what goes on in teaching, learning, testing, language policies and so forth is generally describable and understandable from within the rationalist domains of applied linguistic constructions of reality. My contention, by contrast, is that we need not only to look at how applied linguistics has been constructed in a very particular way and is therefore always bound by very partial descriptions of the world, but also at how language teaching happens in the public domain: teachers, students, parents, principles, applied linguists, government ministers, and others are all equally influenced by popular discourses on English, education and culture. When we teach, talk to our students, read their work, design a curriculum, promote a language policy, and so on, we do so not necessarily as the rational actors of applied linguistic discourses, but often as people influenced and swayed by many other discourses.

An argument I made in the last chapter, and which I intend to develop at greater length here, therefore, is that we need to see English language teaching as located in the domain of popular culture as much as in the domain of applied linguistics. To this end, I shall devote some space in this chapter to travel writing, not only as a genre that informs the understandings of the Other which English language teachers carry with them, but also as something written by English teachers. English teachers read books, have conversations and watch films which are not all models of applied linguistic cautious liberalism. Both Mark Salzman and Brian Johnson, whose books about China are discussed later in the chapter, worked as English teachers. Thus, it is crucial to look at how popular discourses on Self and Other, images of English and images of the Other, circulate and are recirculated through various media, in order to be better able to locate the attitudes, beliefs and activities that form much of ELT. What I am suggesting, then, is that not only do colonial constructs still circulate within ELT theories and practices but the domains in which much ELT occurs also make available many other colonial constructions.

In the last chapter I examined the effects on English and English language teaching of the construction of English as a superior language (Teaching English as a Superior Language – TESL?). In this chapter I shall focus on the other side of the equation, the discourse of the Other and how this has led to very particular views on the cultural others of TESOL (students and teachers on the peripheries of Euro-American life) and also particular views of culture and cultural difference. By looking at how China has been constructed in particular ways through the discourses of the West, I hope to show how such discourses operate. I have chosen China for a number of reasons: first, understanding China and representations of China has obviously been of particular importance to me as a teacher in both China and Hong Kong: and it is to some of the very examples that I shall be giving here that I myself turned in order to try to understand more about China; second, by looking at discourses on China, I am able to move one step away from the 'coal-face of colonialism,' those countries that were directly subjected to colonial rule for extensive periods of time; third, as mentioned in Chapter 2, after Japan, China was ranked fairly high on the European scale of racial quality. Looking at the discourses on China, then, is revealing since it shows more clearly how widespread the discourses of colonialism have been and that their production was not necessarily linked to the material conditions of colonialism.

## Orientalist discourses

Clearly, my interests here are akin in some ways to Said's (1978) larger discussion of Orientalism. Although I have already discussed a number of concerns to do with Orientalism in Chapters 3 and 4, it is worth making some further observations about the difficulties with dealing with this idea of Orientalist discourse. Said set out to show how the 'Orient' was systematically created by the discourses of writers, colonial authorities and scholars. Built around a distinction between 'East' and 'West', Orientalism constructed 'the Orient', determining largely what could be said about this constructed entity and acting as a basis for European justification of its imperialism. Dichotomizing the world into an East/West, We/They contrast, Orientalism then produced an essentialized, static Other, allowing Orientalist scholars to speak with paternalistic ease of 'The Arab', 'The Oriental Mind', or, as with the focus of this chapter, 'The Chinese'. Said describes Orientalism as 'a Western style for dominating, restructuring, and having authority over the Orient'. He suggests that:

> without examining Orientalism as a discourse, one cannot possibly understand the enormously systematic discipline by which European

culture was able to manage – and even produce – the Orient politically, sociologically, militarily, ideologically, scientifically, and imaginatively during the post-Enlightenment period. Moreover, so authoritative a position did Orientalism have that I believe no one writing, thinking, or acting on the Orient could do so without taking into account the limitations on thought and action imposed by Orientalism. . . . This is not to say that Orientalism unilaterally determines what can be said about the Orient, but that it is the whole network of interests inevitably brought to bear on (and there-fore always involved in) any occasion when that particular entity 'the Orient' is in question.

(p. 3)

Said's work has been immensely important and has given rise to a wealth of studies of how colonial discourse constructs the Other. And there remain close parallels with some of my arguments here about the continuity of the discourses of colonialism and arguments made by Said: 'The representations of Orientalism in European culture amount to what we can call a discursive consistency, one that has not only history but material (and institutional) presence to show for itself' (p. 273). Nevertheless, there are a number of problems with Said's work, or perhaps more importantly, problems that Said's work raises, that need to be discussed here before we continue. A cen-tral problem that has been raised by a number of writers (see Ahmad, 1994; Bhabha, 1983a; Clifford, 1988; Porter, 1994; Young, 1990) concerns Said's ambivalence about whether he is discussing Orientalism as a *misrepresentation* of 'reality' (i.e. Orientalism fails to describe accurately the reality of the Orient) or whether he is dealing only with Orientalism as system of *represen-tation* (i.e. the Orient is a construct of the discourse of Orientalism and thus there cannot be a question of *mis*representation). While Said often claims to be dealing with the latter, he is often tempted into talking in terms of the former and thus although (p. 273) he says that his whole point about Orient-alism is 'not that it is a misrepresentation of some Oriental essence', this fol-lows a statement (p. 272) that 'Islam *has* been fundamentally misrepresented in the West'. In the one view, then, there is a reality that is misrepresented and therefore a possibility that proper representation could indeed reveal the truth. In the other view, there is no reality outside the discourses that con-struct our realities, only the possibility of critically analysing the truth effects of those discourses. As Clifford puts it, Said's concept of discourse 'vacillates between, on the one hand, the status of an ideological distortion of lives and cultures that are never concretized and, on the other, the condition of a per-sistent structure of signifiers that . . . refers solely and endlessly to itself' (p. 260). While it is of course tempting to try to do both – to analyse dis-course as both representation and misrepresentation – such an analysis leaves ambiguous the key epistemological question as to whether one is dealing with a view of language and the world in which there is a reality that can be represented in language or whether one is working with a view that sees realities as produced through language. I shall endeavour in the following discussion to follow the second of these two options. As my discussion in the final chapter will reveal, this difference has crucial implications for how we construct a politics of opposition. Are we working towards uncovering the 'truth', the reality behind the words, or are we looking to construct counter-representations?

Said's work also raises other concerns. Although, as Clifford points out, Said's discussion of Orientalism raises highly significant points about how we understand culture, his own version of culture remains problematic. In both *Orientalism* and his more recent (1993) *Culture and Imperialism*, Said tries to show the 'worldliness' (1993, p. 13) of the texts he explores, how imperialism, colonialism, slavery, racial oppression, and so on can be, indeed must be, understood as crucial to the development of the poetry, philosophy and literature of the society that engages in those practices. And yet, while the attempt to draw such connections is a significant one, culture for Said 'always remains exclusively European high culture' (Young, 1990, p. 133). In *Culture and Imperialism*, Said explains his view of culture as referring to practices that are relatively autonomous from the economic, social and political realms, that 'often exist in aesthetic forms, one of whose principal aims is pleasure' (p. xii), and that include 'a refining and elevating element, each society's reservoir of the best that has been known and thought' (p. xiii). As far as the interests of this book are concerned, the issue is not one of looking for the connections between colonialism and 'culture' in this sense, of trying to see how colonialism is reflected in some version of culture-as-aesthetic-product, but rather of looking at how a broad range of texts reflect and produce cultural constructs. Culture in the following analysis, then, as in the previous chapters, is not taken to be some artistic domain but rather the much broader field of the ways in which we make sense of our lives.

Finally, Bhabha (1983a) points to the problem that Said works with a view of power in terms of binary opposition: the colonizers have power, the colonized do not. Furthermore, he tends to explain Orientalism or other imperialist discourses in terms of their single origins, namely in the imperializing practices of the European powers. As I have already argued (see Chapters 1 and 2), I have been trying to develop a slightly more subtle view of colonialism and culture here, whereby culture is not seen merely as a reflex of material conditions, and power operates in more complex ways than simply as something possessed by the 'powerful'. Thus I want to avoid a view in which cultural forms, ideologies or discourses are taken to have one social, political or economic origin. I am more interested here in tracing genealogically how various discourses on China have come into being, and continued and changed over time. It might seem, however, that my own discussion of Self and Other falls exactly into this kind of binarism. What I would emphasize, by contrast, is that these are not intended to represent a binary opposition of colonizing and colonized realities, but a colonizing strategy of representation. These cultural constructs, these discourses, are but two amongst many, but they are two that I see as highly significant for the ongoing representation of aspects of English language teaching.

There is a great deal more that could be written about colonial discourse, and a great number of arguments to be taken up and discussed (see, for example, Joshi, 1991; Singh, 1996; Spivak, 1987; Suleri, 1992; Thomas, 1994; Williams and Chrisman, 1994; Young, 1990, 1995). Given the extent of the debate on these topics, however, and despite my preference here largely to sidestep these debates and continue with my own concerns, a few final comments are in order. Although I have focused on the reciprocal construction of Self and Other in colonial discourse, I have not meant this to imply a simplistic construction of either. As I suggested in Chapter 1, one of my aims here has been to complexify the past and simplify the present, in an attempt to point to colonial continuities. In line with this thinking, and in light of my comments above, I intend to take up aspects of Homi Bhabha's (1983b) thinking on the notion of stereotypes, while rejecting other aspects of his work that depend on ambivalence and hybridity (for a criticism, see Jan Mohamed, 1985; and for problems with the notion of hybridity, see Young, 1995), or his problematically universalized use of psychoanalysis (see Young, 1990). What I am interested in is his discussion of the notion of *fixity*. Bhabha (1983b) argues that the stereotype is the 'major discursive strategy' of colonial discourse but that it is important that we go beyond the '*identification* of images as positive or negative to an understanding of the *process of subjectification* made possible (and plausible) through stereotypical discourse' (p. 18). In his critical discussion of Bhabha, Thomas (1994) points out that:

> it is generally presumed that colonial discourses depict colonized people pejoratively; yet, just as some sexist imagery can, at least superficially, exalt and celebrate women, attractive and even sympathetic constructions of colonized peoples may admire or uphold them in a narrow and restrictive way.
>
> (p. 54)

Drawing on these observations, then, I am interested not so much in how negative images of the Other are (re)produced, but how fixity is produced. To understand the productivity of colonial power, therefore, we need to go beyond subjecting its representations to normalizing judgements as to whether they are right or wrong, good or bad, and rather look at how images of the Other become *fixed*. This, I want to suggest has major implications for how the Other of TESOL comes to be represented.

166

Describing the image constructed of Malays by foreign writers during the colonial period, for example, Alatas (1977) describes this fixed colonial stereotype as having concluded:

> that the Malays are easy-going; that they are sensitive to insult; that they are prone to violent outbursts; that they are good imitators, lacking originality in thought and culture; that they are fond of idleness; but loyal to their chiefs and kings; that they are polite; that they are morally lax; but that they lack incentive or initiative for acquiring wealth; and that they are treacherous and wily.
>
> (p. 115)

Similarly, describing what he called 'Semitic consciousness' (referring mainly to Arabic peoples but also including Jews), T.E. Lawrence ('Lawrence of Arabia') was able to assert that:

> Semites had no half-tones in their register of vision. They were a people of primary colours, or rather of black or white, who saw the world always in contour. They were a dogmatic people, despising doubt, our modern crown of thorns. . . . They were a limited, narrow-minded people, whose inert intellects lay fallow in incurious resignation.
>
> (cited in Porter, 1994, p. 155)

My particular interest here will be of the fixity of representations of Chinese people, how cultural representations of 'the Chinese', 'they', become essentialized and fixed, how certain visions of China are put into play and then recirculate through different texts; how it is that the Brockhaus *Conversations-Lexicon* published in 1852 can say this about Chinese:

> Hard work, politeness, the love of peace and mildness are the hallmarks of the Chinese character. Nothing is more sacred to him than the love of a child or the fidelity of a subject. On the other hand, lust, gluttony, deceitful cunning in trade and traffic, cowardice and false flexibility, an intolerable national pride, rigid adherence to tradition, pitilessness, vindictiveness, and corruptibility form a strong dark side.
>
> (cited in Mackerras, 1989, p. 61)

and how it is that Bonavia (1982) in his book, *The Chinese*, can write 'They are admirable, infuriating, humorous, priggish, modest, overweaning, mendacious, loyal, mercenary, ethereal, sadistic, and tender. They are quite unlike anybody else. They are the Chinese.' (p. 16). And I am interested in seeing how discourses on China adhere to English (see Chapter 1), and how this relates to ELT both in terms of how representations of China put into play particular approaches to teaching and more generally in terms of how such fixed and essentialized notions of culture hold sway in many domains of language teaching.

### Images of China

Describing the development of Western images of China, Kiernan (1969) points out that it has been 'a very long process, quickening in its later stages, that turned the fabled Cathay of Europe's half-buried memories into a solid, humdrum China pervaded by an aroma of nightsoil' (p. 146). Generally, Mackerras (1989) suggests that:

> the dominant images of most periods have tended to accord with, rather than oppose, the interests of the main Western authorities or governments of the day. There has indeed been a 'regime of truth' concerning China, which has affected and raised 'the status of those who are charged with saying what counts as true' about that country.
>
> (p. 263)

The early period of writing on China (from Marco Polo to the sixteenth century) was predominantly positive: 'At the end of the sixteenth century, Europe may have believed it could teach the Chinese, but it was still prepared to admire them' (p. 27). This generally positive image continued through the seventeenth and eighteenth centuries as a vast body of writing about China was built up, the large part of it by Jesuit missionaries, who, while maintaining the wish to convert Chinese to Christianity, nevertheless did so from a position of admiration for Chinese culture and learning. It was not until the nineteenth century, Mackerras suggests, that the balance shifted from a predominantly positive to a predominantly negative view. The main reason for this was 'the rise of European, and especially British, imperialism from the time of the Industrial Revolution. For the first time Britain became a leader as a formulator of Western images of China' (p. 43). While contact with China during the preceding centuries had been limited to small-scale missionary activity and trading, from the middle of the nineteenth century until the fall of the Qing dynasty the main activities were 'imperialism, profit, and conversion to Christianity' (p. 264). This was the period in which China started to be seen as a country from which the West had nothing to learn, a country stuck far back on the inevitable upward march of progress, a country that could only start to move upwards on that long march if it adopted modern Western practices. This was the period 'when the 'Orientalist' approach to China reached its height, when Europe colonized not only parts of China, but also knowledge about it' (pp. 44–5). Crucial in this process was the arrival of British Protestant missionaries, with their condescending and negative views towards China, and the larger body of knowledge that was being established as part of the great colonial archive of knowledge about the other. 'The idea of China as a stagnant oriental despotism, which even a strong opponent of the capitalist system such as Karl Marx advocated, was used to justify Western intervention to force change upon a reluctant China' (p. 264).

It was during this period that some of the central and lasting images of China developed. Two crucial constructs were the passive Oriental and Oriental despotism. In the middle of the nineteenth century, Marx referred to China as 'a giant empire, containing about one-third of the human race, vegetating in the teeth of time' (1858a, p. 216). As John Stuart Mill argued (cited in Metcalf, 1995), 'Oriental' societies were 'brought to a permanent halt for want of mental liberty and individuality' (p. 32). This image of a stagnant China, peopled by passive subjects and despotic rulers has continued into the present. Perham suggests that 'The continuity of China's civilization and its extension over such a vast area and population through millennia of virtual isolation from the rest of the world, had bred in the people both conservativism and complacency' (1960, p. 291). She then goes on to argue that China's 'blind antagonism' in its dealings with the 'commercial powers' led it 'to strike out wildly like some large creature trapped in a net which only became more helplessly entangled with each movement' (p. 293). Spurr (1993) argues that this view of China as unchanging and conservative has continued to justify anything from imperial intervention to modern development policies: 'The argument that development – meaning economic and political modernization – is not compatible with Oriental passivity simply reformulates the Hegelian notion of the imperishability of the Oriental world, which can be conquered and subjugated, but never energized from within' (p. 73). As Blaut (1993) shows, such images of a static and unchanging China persist today in current textbooks on China (pp. 106–7). Indeed, so far has this view been carried in some quarters that it has even extended to the denial of Chinese inventions (paper, printing, gunpowder etc.): As Isaac Headland, an American missionary administrator in China wrote in 1912, 'reason and invention have remained dormant in the Chinese mind. They have never invented anything' (cited in Spurr, 1993, pp. 104–5). Another key early image was of the crowded and filthy conditions of Chinese life: in his book *Asia's Teeming Millions* (1931), Etienne Dennery dwelt at length on the notion of crowds: 'Crowds in the great Chinese cities, half sunk in dirt and mud, swarming like ants in dark, narrow winding alleys, in which the sickening stench of decaying meat or putrid flesh ever lingers' (cited in Spurr, 1993, p. 88). This view of the teeming hordes of China was to lead, as Kiernan (1969) points out, to the development of the concept of the 'Yellow Peril'.

Most obviously these images of China justified and even demanded as a moral imperative the conversion of the Chinese people to Christianity and enforced trading with European powers in order to expedite modernization and development. Two significant points worth noting here are that, first, these views were not limited to the personal arrogance of those directly involved in colonialism but rather became a central part of the general knowledge about countries such as China. The descriptions of China to be found in encyclopaedias such as *Encyclopaedia Britannica*, for example, Mackerras describes as 'extremely condescending, regarding China as an exotic, backward, only semi-civilized, and in some ways rather barbaric country' (p. 60). In *The Popular Encylopedia* (no date, circa 1891), Chinese people are described thus:

> In thickness of lips, flattened nose, and expanded nostril, they bear a considerable resemblance to the negro. In bodily strength they are far inferior to Europeans. . . . The Chinese are very deficient in courage. In their moral qualities there is much that is amiable. They are strongly attached to their homes, hold age in respect, toil hard for the support of their families, and in the interior, where the worst kind of foreign intercourse has not debased them, exhibit an un-sophisticated simplicity of manners which recalls the age of the patri-archs. In the great mass these qualities are counterbalanced or rather supplanted by numerous vices – treachery, lying, and numerous abominations.
>
> (p. 312)

And second, the development of such views was not dependent on the colonization of a country in a literal sense but rather on the broader process of colonization in the nineteenth and twentieth centuries. Thus, although China avoided some of the humiliations brought about by complete Western colonization (though it certainly suffered enough humiliations, leading to the return of Hong Kong being viewed as a major symbol of China regaining its pride), it was nevertheless the subject of the colonization of images produced about it. As the United States started to dominate world affairs in the twenti-eth century, so too did American missionaries and sinologists come to domi-nate the production of images of China. After the 1949 revolution, the general production of negative images of China was increased as part of the larger anti-communist ideology: 'For the United States, the leader of the 'free world' forces, a negative image of China was not only an ideological necessity but a weapon in international political rivalry, and thus the American government worked to reinforce these negative images of China' (Mackerras, p. 191). Despite some shifts in this discourse more recently, Mackerras suggests that 'commentaries and statements laden with Western values and regarding China as an inferior civilization which should expect only to learn from the West are still very easy to find' (p. 268).

In these cultural constructions of China, it has not only been the country and its people that have been fixed into a certain cultural stereotype, but also the language that has become an Other to European languages. As Tong (1993) argues, 'for centuries now, Western writers have had various misconceptions about the Chinese language; from Friedrich Schlegel to Jacques Derrida, these writers' treatment of Chinese falls back on a frame of reference that belongs to the Western tradition' (p. 46). Apart from perpetuating many myths and misunderstandings about Chinese, this tradition must also be seen as firmly located within the Western colonial tradition of constructing the Other. Chinese was seen as a contrast to Indo-European languages. For many writers, 'the Chinese language, monosyllabic, isolated, non-inflectional, incapable of generating prefixes and suffixes, and divided between speech and writing, was very much a primitive form of a linguistic system' (p. 29). Thus, Humboldt, contrasting Chinese with Sanskrit, was able to conclude that Chinese was necessarily inferior since it 'lacks imagination, is like mathematics in being purely designative and lexical' (cited in Tong, p. 38). While some encyclopaedias, such as *The Popular Encyclopedia* (no date; circa 1891) were prepared to acknowledge some qualities of Chinese literature – 'a literature of no mean description' – it nevertheless remained clear where such writing stood: '. . . though sometimes ludicrously overrated by being placed in competition with that of Europe' (p. 313). The prevailing view of Chinese language and literature is exemplified by an entry on Chinese Literature in the *New Standard Encyclopedia* of 1940:

> The Chinese language is monosyllabic and uninflectional . . . With a language so incapable of variation, a literature cannot be produced which possesses the qualities we look for and admire in literary works. Elegance, variety, beauty of imagery – these must all be lacking. A monotonous and wearisome language must give rise to a forced and formal literature lacking in originality and interesting in its subject matter only. Moreover, a conservative people . . . , profoundly reverencing all that is old and formal, and hating innovation, must leave the impress of its own character upon its literature.
>
> (Cited in Brown, 1980, p. 127)

### China writing, border-crossing and ELT

Just as Said (1978) identified a range of stereotypes dealing with the Arab world – the eternal and unchanging East, the sexually insatiable Arab, the 'feminine' exotic, the teeming marketplace, mystical religiosity, corrupt despotism, and so forth – it is possible to outline a similar series of stereotypes in writing on China: the exotic and eternal kingdom, the underdeveloped and backward, the paradoxically juxtaposed old and new, the crowded, dirty and poverty-stricken life, the smiling or inscrutable exterior hiding either bad intentions or misery, the passive Oriental and the despotic leader, the dullness of life under socialism, the uncaring nature of the Communist government, and so on. Such constructions occur across a broad range of writing, from textbooks to encyclopaedias. One domain in which they have a particular salience, and in which they have shown a remarkable resilience over time, is in travel writing.

Pratt (1992) illustrates at length how the discourses of travel writing have been interwoven with the discourses of colonialism, a key shift coming towards the end of the eighteenth century, when, 'as modern racist categories emerged,' and 'as European interventionism became increasingly militant,' the earlier humanist stance which allowed for far more appreciation of cultural differences 'disappeared as a discursive possibility' (p. 45). The new mode of writing becomes one in which local people are objectified as part of the landscape and 'naturalised' within the new scientific discourses of the nineteenth century. And thus a new colonial Other emerges as the 'standard apparatuses of travel writing produce non-European subjects for the domestic audience of imperialism' (p. 63). It also worth noting here, once again, how the construction of the Other occurs in the colonial context and then circulates through the discursive web of the empire.

While on some levels there may seem to be significant differences between nineteenth- and twentieth-century travel writing, there are also many continuities. In particular, Pratt points to the continuity in the way writers seek out some literal or metaphorical high ground and survey all that is beneath them with disarming authority: 'In contemporary travel accounts, the monarch-of-all-I-survey scene gets repeated, only now from the balconies of hotels in big third-world cities' (p. 216). Whereas the explorer Richard Burton found beauty, symmetry, order and the sublime in all he surveyed, more modern writers, such as the popular and prolific Paul Theroux, tend to find their opposites: ugliness, incongruity, disorder, and triviality. Whereas Burton saw beauty and hope from within the discourses of imperialism, Theroux sees dirt, confusion and triviality from within the discourses of 'underdevelopment.' Theroux, suggests Pratt, exemplifies 'a discourse of negation, domination, devaluation, and fear that remains in the late twentieth century a powerful ideological constituent of the west's consciousness of the people and places it strives to hold in subjugation' (p. 219). Such representations, as Pratt shows, are remarkably consistent across different times and places, so that 'the white man's lament seems to remain remarkably uniform across representations of different places, and by westerners of different nationalities. It is a monolith, like the official construct of the "third world" it encodes' (p. 220).

Such travel writing is significant to the picture I am trying to present here for several reasons. First, an investigation of this domain reveals the close interrelationships (intertextualities) between different domains of writing. In the same way that Threadgold (1997) shows how discourses of race and gender concerning murders committed by a 'half-caste Aboriginal' remain remarkably consistent over more than half a century, despite the fact that the texts she examined enter into critical dialogue with each other (see Chapter 1), I intend to show here that similar critical dialogue between texts on China also shows greater intertextual consistency than critical distance. The processes of dichotomizing between 'Us' and 'Them' and essentializing the resultant Other ('The Chinese'), and the characteristics of the stereotype and the paradox produce a discourse that constitutes China as dirty, backward, dull, ruled by a tyrannous Communist government, yet also exotic, mysterious and paradoxical. It is important to observe, therefore, that the stereotypes I am interested in here are not wholesale derogations of Chinese people but rather fixed images of paradox.

Such constructs of the paradoxical nature of China can frequently be found. Here is an English teacher in China dwelling on China as paradox. At one level China is seen as a paradox because new and old coexist: 'China is a paradox . . . They crowd around the stereo counter as loud Western style music pulses from the latest Japanese equipment' (Webb, 1986, p. 109); at another because it is seen as 'exotic' yet dirty and unpleasant; at another because it is eternal and unchanging (and backward) and also because it is changing too fast: 'If you want to see the real China – go now before the sauna baths and tennis courts take over . . . It is sad that with modernization those mysterious Oriental nights will be lost to us forever' (Webb, 1986, p. 110); at another because it is both different and the same, allowing the writer both to see the 'inscrutable' , the incomprehensible, and to condemn the familiar. As Said (1978, pp. 58–9) observes: 'What gives the immense number of encounters some unity, however, is the vacillation . . . Something patently foreign and distant acquires, for one reason or another, a status more rather than less familiar. One tends to stop judging things either as completely novel or as completely well-known'. The Other is both embraced and rejected, difference is both eternal and ephemeral. It is this paradox, or ambivalence, that gives the discourse its resilience. But it is also this constant stress on the apparently paradoxical nature of the Chinese – 'They are the most paradoxical of nations' announces Bonavia (1982, p. 16) in his book *The Chinese* – that refuses engagement with difference, that leaves the Chinese as an inscrutable Other.

Second, as a form of widely read popular culture, travel writing gives access to 'non-academic' discourses on China, which, as part of the popular cultural domain, may be at least as influential as the academic domain on the formation of language teachers. Third, I want to suggest much closer relationships between such travel writing and ELT, since two of the crucial texts that I will be looking at here were written by English language teachers in China (and note also Webb above). There is, therefore, a double form of border-crossing here: as the travel writers cross the borders that will define their next cultural entity, so travel writing crosses the borders between popular culture and ELT. And finally, this notion of the 'monarch-of-all-I-survey' is, I want to suggest, a central feature of applied linguistic discourse. As Singh (1996) points out, this view allows the colonial traveller to 'discover' empty lands and thus to deny the act of colonialism in the very moment of expressing European superiority and conquest. As I want to suggest in this chapter, it is the location of such discourses in relationship to English language teaching that allows the language teacher or applied linguist to take this same stance of master-of-all-I-survey and to construct the passive Other of TESOL as a tabula rasa, as a discovery to be enlightened, and thus to deny in the same instance the act of colonialism being performed.

To explore how China is represented in modern discourses of travel writing, I shall turn to three fairly recent instances by Paul Theroux, Mark Salzman, and Brian Johnston in an attempt to show how powerful such discourses can be in constructing stories about China. Through a close reading of the opening of Salzman's book, I shall suggest that in spite of his criticism of the naïve ethnocentrism of writers such as Theroux, he is nevertheless constrained by the same discourse. And by comparing these discourses with the opening of Johnston's more recent book, I shall try to demonstrate the consistency of these discursive constructions. It is important when examining the construction of such discourses to see them in terms of what they produce rather than what they reference, and thus while on the one hand they ultimately reveal more about the Self than any lived experiences of the Other, on the other hand they continue to (re)produce the same discursive constructs of the Other. Following this discussion of writing on China, I shall turn to look at its implications for ELT, both in terms of how specific constructions of China lead to specific pedagogical assumptions about teaching Chinese students, and more generally in terms of how the fixity of these essentialized cultural constructs is prevalent in applied linguistic versions of culture.

The two books that I want to start with here are important because of their popularity. *Iron and silk* by Mark Salzman (now also a film) and *Riding the Iron rooster* by Paul Theroux were both high in the *New York Times Book Review* best sellers list. Not only were they therefore widely read but they were also widely reviewed in popular magazines. Such reviews present a form of *distilled discourse*, plucking out the essential details for their audiences. These books are also interesting, as we shall see, because one was critically reviewed by the author of the other, and yet, as I shall argue, the reviewer, Mark Salzman, ended up reproducing more or less what he had criticized in his review. First, then, I would like to look at Paul Theroux's (1988) *Riding the iron rooster: By train through China.* Theroux is, of course, an old and respected hand at travel-writing: 'The world's pre-eminent travel-writer' (*Time*, 16 May 1988); one of 'the best of today's travel writers' (*The Economist*, 1988). And yet, as Salzman discusses in his review of the book, there are many problematic passages:

> [At the railway station at Baoji] everyone hawked, everyone spat, sometimes dribbling, sometimes in a trajectory that ran like candle-wax down the side of a spittoon . . . They walked scuffingly, sort of skating, with their arms flapping, with narrow jogging shoulders, or else hustling petlike, with their limbs jerking. They minced, they plodded, they pushed, keeping their hands out – straight-arming their way – and their heads down. They could look entirely grace-less – unexpected in Chinese.

> Mr Tian [his guide and translator for most of the trip] shrugged, shook my hand, and without another word walked off. It was the Chinese farewell: there was no lingering, no swapping of addresses, no reminiscence, nothing sentimental. At the moment of parting they turned their backs, because you ceased to matter and because they had so much else to worry about.

> It seemed to me that the Chinese . . . had no choice but to live the dullest lives and perform the most boring jobs imaginable – doing the same monotonous Chinese two-step from the cradle to the grave . . .

Such descriptions can be commonly found in writing on China. It is interesting to observe here how Theroux on the one hand dwells on practices such as spitting, and on the other, manages to make vast generalizations about Chinese life: 'the Chinese farewell', the 'monotonous Chinese two-step' and so on. Almost every review, however, was full of praise: 'not just an engrossing travel book but a brilliant piece of reporting' (Macleans, 1988). Macleans goes on to tell us that 'he sees everywhere signs of spiritual emptiness, a void that many have tried to fill with Western-style capitalism'. As suggested in the discussion earlier, this last emphasis on not only the dullness of Chinese life, but also on the West and especially capitalism as a savior, emerges as a common theme. Thus, in a review of Colin Thubron's book *Behind the Wall*, the book is described as a 'vivid and impressionistic picture of a modernizing China straining the bounds of Communist ideology in order to achieve capitalist dynamism' (*National Review*, 1988). Thubron's book and its reviews also dwell on the dirt: 'filthy hostels, spit-spattered floors, and food so bad he became too weak to feel upset by blank Chinese acceptance of dead bodies and regular executions' (Mirsky, 1987). Ultimately, in the distilled discourse of the review of *Riding the iron rooster*, we find China reduced to this: 'As Theroux makes excruciatingly clear, traveling alone in the Middle Kingdom is not for the faint of heart or stomach: the food is mostly vile, the toilets are filthy, and drafty coaches are invariably crowded with unbathed passengers who yammer and spit'. Fortunately, however, we are told there are some surprises, such as the 'fact' that '35 million Chinese still live in caves' (*sic*) (*Time*, 16 May 1988).

In his review of Theroux's book, however, in the *New York Times Books Review*, Salzman is strongly critical: 'most of the people Mr Theroux encountered looked upon him as either a rich tourist or a hostile foreign journalist, and treated him as such. Their behavior toward him cannot be assumed to be typically Chinese'; good descriptive passages 'get overshadowed . . . by the numerous conclusions Mr Theroux draws from his experiences that don't ring true'; ultimately, 'the result is an opinionated, petty and incomplete portrait of that country'. This review is of particular interest not so much because it goes against the grain of most reviews but because it is written by Mark Salzman, author of *Iron and silk*, the next book I intend to look at. The significance of this should not be overlooked: Salzman shows a sensitivity to the problems of travel-writing such as Theroux's, yet, as I hope to show, his own writing still takes up a subject position within the same discourse. Thus, we may see how a discourse may constitute knowledge and continue to construct cultural stereotypes even when the author appears aware of these dangers.

Based on Salzman's two years spent teaching English in Changsha, after Salzman had graduated from the Yale Chinese programme, *Iron and silk* was immensely popular when it came out in 1986: 'A book that describes the land and its people with such deftness and delight', says *Time*, 1987; 'if there was a prize for the most winning writer, Mark Salzman would cop it' (*New York Times Review of Books*). The book opens with the description of a half-day's delay at Canton (Guangzhou) railway station on his 'way out of China' (p. 13). Why does he start with this troublesome incident? (Given that he is carrying a bag containing five swords, four sabres, a staff, two hooked swords, some knives and a nine-section steel whip as he tries to get on the train, it is not surprising he has some trouble.) Why '*out of* China'? Would he say 'on my way out of France'? or 'on my way out of the USA'? This is a common phrase among travelers ('Beijing, Shanghai, Guangzhou, and then out'), suggesting that China is somehow prison-like and that it is generally desirable to get out rather than stay in. Salzman chooses to lay the blame on the station officials who, we are told in the last line of the first paragraph of the book, 'saw an opportunity to play their favorite game, Let's Make a Regulation' (p. 13). Then we are introduced to China Travel Service which 'specializes in imposing services on foreigners and then failing to carry them out properly' and an 'angry little woman in a blue uniform' who 'stalked in' and who, after he refused to move from an area reserved for those with tickets, 'turned maroon, glared at us and marched out, only to return after half an hour to repeat the interrogation' (p. 16). It is a common feature of the discourse on China to essentialize bureaucracy as the Other/foe and to represent it, as Salzman does, as mindless and inflexible, but also interesting is the continuing metaphor of the prison, with the stress on uniforms and inter-rogation. From the problems he encountered on his departure, Salzman switches to the problems he encountered on his arrival – 'getting in' and 'getting out' of China. The whole book, then, starts with the problems encountered with bureaucracy. Finally, he and his friends obtain their 'little permission slips' (p. 17) (pettiness of Chinese bureaucracy) and run across the 'monstrous platform, with the Chinese national anthem blaring over the loudspeakers' (p. 17) (inhuman, concrete architecture and constant political propaganda). On the train, we are told that he is woken by a loudspeaker with the song 'Without the Communist Party, There Would Be No New China' (p. 15); he goes to the restaurant car and orders a Western style breakfast, 'because I figured it might be the last Western food I would eat for some time' (p. 5). A list of some of the key words in these opening five pages gives us some idea of this representation of arrival and departure in China: insist, impose, need, have to, miserable, uniform, angry, frustration, glared, marched, interrogation, revenge, snapped, blaring, loudspeakers, and so on.

This, then, is Salzman's introduction to China. In the next few pages, he introduces us to the capital of Hunan province, Changsha, where he is to spend the next two years: the people 'are shoving to get off' (p. 8) the train, there is a 'growing crowd of peasants, mouths agape' (p. 10) (impolite/uncivilized), he is met at the station by 'somber men in Mao suits' (p. 10) (uniformity/dullness), who 'assumed postures and expressions that indicated warm, heartfelt greetings' (p. 10) (insincerity). Driving through the streets, we are told of buses driven 'as if by madmen' (p. 9) (uncivilized/unable to deal with modern technology). He continues:

> It was all a bit shocking, but the most shocking was how filthy everything looked. I had heard that China was spotlessly clean [!]. Instead, dishwater and refuse were thrown casually out of windows, rats the size of squirrels could be seen flattened out all over the roads, spittle and mucus everywhere, and the dust and ash from coal-burning stoves, heaters and factories mixed with dirt and rain to stain the entire city an unpleasant greyish-brown. The smell of nightsoil, left in shallow outhouse troughs for easy collection, wafted through the streets and competed with the unbelievable din of automobile horns to offend the senses. No one that I could see was smiling . . .
>
> (pp. 9–10)

Finally, they arrive at the campus: 'passing through an iron gate into a walled compound that contained more walls and gates. All the buildings were of gray concrete except for a few red brick ones, most of which were in the process of being either torn down or plastered with concrete so as to look "modern"' (walls, drabness, Western prerogative on modernization, Chinese superficial modernization). When he is shown to his room, we are told of the 'bars on my window' and the 'cement wall surrounding our house' (prison).

This, then, is the scene that Salzman sets. Easily identifiable are similar stereotypes and themes to those already mentioned, with the addition of a few new elements, particularly the 'China-as-prison' metaphor and the fight against bureaucracy. These appear to function as a particular way of constructing the Other as opponent. Interestingly too, Salzman's book centers around his learning Marshal Arts, a process which seems to describe not so much his learning self-control and self-discipline, but rather his learning how to beat the foe at their own game. It also touches on another common theme in the literature on travel – acquisition – that is, what can you get out of it? Salzman, leaving with a bag of weapons and skills in different arts is seen as not having wasted his time.

Turning briefly to the reviews of Salzman, there is a similar pattern to the reviews we looked at earlier: 'If there has ever been a better American ambassador to China, I don't know of him' (Selzer, 1987). Interestingly, both *Time* and Delia Davin in *The Times Literary Supplement* start their accounts with the notion of overcrowding: 'Mark Salzman was riding an overcrowded bus in Changsha . . .' and 'Travelling in an overcrowded local train . . .' Again, we may ask why do they start with these descriptions? And what exactly does overcrowded mean? *Time* goes on to relate Salzman's description of the dirt and unsmiling people in Changsha quoted above. Selzer (1987) has this to say: 'Well aware of the antipathetical philosophy of the society, irked by a crabbed bureaucracy whose instinct is to holler 'no' after any request and depressed by the lack of physical charms with which communism has cemented itself upon a charming people . . .'. I also wonder at the implications of describing Salzman's two-year stay as a 'two-year tour of duty'. Finally, the *National Review*, as expected, takes the opportunity to talk of the 'terribleness of twentieth-century China'. It seems pretty clear that whatever differences there may be between Salzman's and Theroux's empathy and understanding, both are constrained by the same discourse, and both books end up providing the reviewers with the same distilled discourse on China.

Turning briefly now to another book written by an English teacher in China, Brian Johnston's (1996) *Boxing with shadows*, I want to show once again the adherence of these discourses on China. Starting with page 1 ('arrival'), we find this:

The chartered plane from Hong Kong came down in darkness: no lights, just the black emptiness of a terrible void over China. Then suddenly, without warning, we hit a runway, and soon I was stumbling across the tarmac of Chengdu airport into a cavernous hall, as poorly lit as the set of some disaster movie. Customs officers sat in little wooden boxes with counters so low I had to crouch awkwardly for a glimpse of a hand, a green uniformed sleeve and a sullen face; a stamp in my passport and I was officially in the People's Republic.

Outside, a motley assortment of ill-dressed passengers was engaged in an unholy scrimmage for baggage, like a horde of rapacious scavengers squabbling over spoils on battlefields. I extracted my suitcase from the tumbled mound deposited unceremoniously in the middle of the hall, and shoved through the crowds to the exit. . . . I felt as if I had arrived at the ends of the earth: this cavernous and dusty, echoing airport perched in a black void was an antechamber to purgatory.

(p. 1)

From here we have similar descriptions of a ride in a taxi, driven by 'a shifty-looking character with a scar on his chin and a cigarette hanging limply from his lips', passing villagers who 'coughed and spluttered out of the darkness like disembodied souls' (p. 2). The next day, he goes on another car journey and looks out of the window at 'this vision of thousands cycling through the cold wilderness of depressing concrete buildings. It was the sort of thing one saw on television, these monotonous scenes of China, with all the people looking incredibly small, as if one were peering at them down the wrong end of a telescope. Here in real life they were not small. They seemed large and, in their sheer numbers, threatening' (p. 4). Eventually he reaches his university, past guards, walls and barriers, and recalls the warning that 'I, as a barbarian, would be living behind such a Great Wall; keeping foreigners and Chinese separate was a centuries-old custom' (p. 5). The intertextual echoes of these discourses on China need no further commentary.

Finally, it is worth noting that these common aspects of the discourses on China re-emerge not only in popular writing on China but also in the more 'serious' sinological work. To take one example, Anne Thurston (1993), a 'veteran China-watcher', in her article on recent changes in the special economic zones of China reproduces many of the same images. Using the powerful tool of many of the modern sinologists, an impressive command of economic, social and historical background information mixed with the on-the-ground local knowledge of a Chinese-speaking ethnographer, she nevertheless reproduces many of the standard tropes that have emerged in the discussion above. Here we have the 'the monarch-of-all-I-survey scene' (Pratt, 1992, p. 216) repeated from the balcony of the Holiday Inn in

Xiamen. We find the standard questioning of the 1949 revolution as a 'liberation' (p. 15), the claim that 'many Xiamenites' say that 'the wrong side won' in 1949 (p. 18), that "the rich (are) getting rich and the poor getting poorer,' as so many Chinese observe,' that 'to many Chinese . . . the growing economic disparities seem patently unfair' (p. 20), that 'everyone knows that nothing is fair, that things are bad and getting worse' (p. 26), that 'China is in a state of moral disarray' (p. 27) and finally that 'Everyone in China, including the highest leaders, recognizes that the country is suffering from a profound moral crisis' (p. 30). Meanwhile, this new China with its 'Deng-wrought contradictions' (p. 15) is clearly not a place she likes: 'My experience in China has taught me to err on the side of pessimism' (p. 34). She mocks the Taiwanese businessmen with whom she is flying to Xiamen as 'weathered, chain-smoking men in rumpled, ill-fitting suits and their loudly-attired female counterparts' (p. 15); the Taiwanese women's clothes were 'garish, their costume jewelry jangled ostentatiously, and when they walked, they wobbled uncertainly on their high-heeled shoes' (pp. 15–18). She cannot, of course, miss the opportunity to comment on spitting: the man next to her 'located the air-sickness bag and used it frequently as a makeshift spittoon' (p. 15). In the taxi taking her to the Holiday Inn in Xiamen, she talks to the driver about his hopes to make money but mocks his ignorance when he says he was unaware of the recent elections in the US and had never heard of Bill Clinton (I wonder if any Chinese have even considered that, say, a Cleveland cab driver would be conversant with Chinese politics). And of course, the buildings are 'gray-brown concrete-slab structures' (p. 19). And now that China is modernizing fast, the criticism of its dirtiness has shifted from a criticism of the dirt of backward countries to a criticism of pollution in modernizing countries: 'pollution-control devices are apparently unknown in China' and the 'symbols of China's modernization' are 'traffic jams, pollution and construction' (p. 19).

Chinua Achebe has remarked that 'travellers with closed minds can tell us little except about themselves' (1975, p. 40). I would suggest that he is right up to a point here. Travellers and travel writers may indeed tell us more about themselves than the place they are travelling in, but that telling about the Self is a telling that is discursively constructed. We do not, therefore, learn much about the lived realities of other contexts, but we do learn a great deal about how the Other is constructed in Western discourses. What I think by now must be manifestly clear – a point that I have perhaps belabored somewhat – is that there are a series of dominant discourses on China which, with a remarkable continuity with colonial discourses, constantly construct China in a very particular way, dichotomizing and essentializing to create a stereotyped vision denying any lived experience of Chinese people. The power of these discourses as they act both on and through people became evident as we saw even those such as Salzman, who showed some sensitivity toward China and distaste of the ethnocentric spite of writers like Theroux, nevertheless constrained to a subject position within the same discourse. It is, I would suggest, the power of such discourses as they construct China in a particular image that has also led to the popularity in the West of many recent books by Chinese writers on the terrors of China. From *Wild swans* (Chang, 1991) to *Falling leaves* (Mah, 1997) and *Life and death in Shanghai* (Cheng, 1986), Chinese writers have found ways of telling stories that the West is able to hear.

Now one might argue that the similarities in many of these discourses, particularly the similarities between say the opening of Salzman's and Johnston's books – and I haven't bothered to analyse them here or draw the obvious parallels between this and other texts in this chapter – are products of the similarity of experience, that is to say the similarities are based on the real world of China. Such a naïvely representational view of reality is surely inadequate, however. Far more convincing is the view that their experiences are similar because those experiences – or the subsequent writing of them – are constructed by similar discourses. What I have been trying to argue and demonstrate, then, is how these discourses on China construct the experience of China for travellers and readers. China becomes backward, dirty, crowded, ugly, and drab; life under communism is assumed to be a life of unremitting hardship; China is almost always inferior to the advanced, capitalist West; and yet there is also a mysterious, exotic, sometimes inscrutable, aspect to China, which is sometimes taken up as an aspect of dishonesty and at others as part of a vanishing exotic past. As I have been trying to emphasize, my point here is not to attempt some analysis of whether these descriptions are true or not. As it happens, I lived for three years in Xiangtan, a city not far from Changsha (where Salzman worked). I have often spent time in Changsha and could tell another story of what it is 'really like'. That, however, would miss the point: it is not the truth or falsity of discourse that is the interesting – or even the possible – question here, but rather the truth effects of these discourses. Such discourses work at multiple levels: as a mode of production of the symbolic (the texts and reviews), as a means of producing subject positions (the positions taken by Theroux, Salzman, Johnston, and readers), and as a means of knowing embedded in society's institutions (the publishing industry, schools, universities, and so on). Significant too has been the position of Salzman and Johnston as English teachers. It is such discourses, I have been suggesting, that construct part of the work and the knowledge of the Western English teacher overseas. Travel writers cross the national borders that they use to define each new cultural context (dwelling, as we saw, on the process), and at the same time this travel writing crosses the borders between popular culture and ELT.

## *The Chinese learner*

An interesting connection can be found between such discourses of travel writing and general textbook writing. A study by the Asia Society (1979) of how Asia is represented in 260 American textbooks found a number of similar themes, particularly a belief in the superiority of Western nations and concomitant belief in the inferiority of Asia. A predominant view was one that sees progress and modernization as a Western prerogative (the texts contained numerable terms such as 'underdeveloped', 'backward', 'primitive', 'tradition-bound', and so on), a linear progression from primitive conditions to televisions and toasters (modernization is often described solely in these terms of electronic gadgetry). Westernization and modernization are often conflated and always, it seems, seen as good and beneficial: 'In the twentieth century, the peoples of Asia and Africa have come alive. They have adopted the nationalistic creeds, the democratic ideals, and the modern science of the West . . .' (*Living World History*, 1974, p. 201). Asia is constantly described as 'catching up with the West'. This view of modernization as a Western prerogative then often comes into conflict with the assumed 'primitive' traditions and superstitions of the country. Commonly, this takes the form of dwelling on an apparent 'paradox' in the juxtaposition of old and new: 'Rocket experts ride buses alongside Indian mystics. Sacred cows share the streets with automobiles. Indian industries produce tractors, yet millions of peasants still use wooden plows. The contrasts are endless' (*India, Focus on Change*, 1975, p. 1); or 'All the Nakamuras sleep in one bedroom divided by a screen. The road to the house is not paved. There is a growing list of appliances in the Nakamura home, an electric refrigerator, stove, toaster and color television. Yet the bathroom is far from modern. The toilet is primitive, and there is no shower' (*China-Japan-Korea*, 1971, p. 196); or between harsh living conditions and many condescending descriptions of people, such as 'the friendly, fun-loving Filipinos' or 'the happy, gentle Thais'.

Throughout the books surveyed by the Asia Society (1979), negative constructions of the countries are highlighted, so that dirt, poverty, and crowded conditions are shown as the norm, and it is stressed that people do not have electricity or gas, and therefore no radios or televisions. Textbooks on China often dwelt on questions of poverty and disease and usually linked these to the evils of communism (many of these books have references to 'Red China', for they were written during the era of fierce anti-communism): 'The beggars . . . illustrate the hunger of China's people. Given all these conditions, disease spreads quickly. The Communist government has been unable to solve these problems that have plagued the nation' (*Eastern Lands*, 1968, p. 396). Once again we find the themes of dirt, backwardness, the miseries of socialism, and so on emerging. Sometimes it is tempting to sum up the discourse on China as expressing the view of 'getting out of China to the holy land where the toilets are clean'. Another article on travel in China in *Atlantic* (Fallows, 1988) repeats the same theme: 'If you reach Shanghai at the end of a journey through China, the clean bathrooms and functioning telephones of these hotels may have irresistible appeal'.

But I now wish to focus more specifically on ways in which the Chinese learner is constructed, and in particular in relationship to English language teaching. Having argued that the border-crossing of ELT and travel writing acts as an important site of the construction of the instructed Other, I also want to suggest more generally that we cannot divorce ELT from the discursive constructs of Self and Other, and thus the way ELT is understood and practiced frequently reflects and reproduces such discourses. This is not, of course, to suggest that all English language teaching is inevitably so defined but rather that there are inescapable connections here that need to be understood. Since this chapter has looked principally at constructions of China and Chinese, I shall look in this section at constructions of the Chinese learner, before moving on to suggest how the notion of cultural fixity operates more generally in ELT.

One thing I have tried to emphasize throughout this book is the remarkable continuities between past and present in the cultural constructions of colonialism. This is equally the case for views on Chinese language learners. Colonial documents reveal a number of common attitudes to Chinese education so that even educators with a generally liberal and progressive attitude to language education would share such views with their more conservative colleagues. Thus, Frederick Stewart, a highly influential figure in education during the second half of the nineteenth century in Hong Kong, who constantly argued for the importance of a balanced bilingual education for the students at the Central School (of which he was headmaster), nevertheless had little respect for Chinese educational practices: in his education report for 1865 he wrote, 'The Chinese have no *education* in the real sense of the word. No attempt is made at a simultaneous development of the mental powers. These are all sacrificed to the cultivation of memory.' (p. 138). Such views seem to have been commonly held by many colonizers who worked in Hong Kong or China. The Rev. S.R. Brown, Headmaster of the Morrison Education Society School, wrote in a report in 1844 that Chinese children are usually pervaded by 'a universal expression of passive inanity': 'The black but staring, glassy eye, and open mouth, bespeak little more than stupid wonder gazing out of emptiness'. This view is linked to Brown's view of Chinese schools, where a boy may learn 'the names of written characters, that in all probability never conveyed to him one new idea from first to last'. Despite this lack of education, the Chinese boy also comes 'with a mind to be emptied of a vast accumulation of false and superstitious notions that can never tenant an enlightened mind, for they cannot coexist with truth.' (cited in Sweeting, 1990, p. 21) The principal characteristics of Chinese boys are 'an utter disregard of truth, obscenity, and cowardliness' (p. 22).

Such views re-emerged in the 1882 Commission's (see Chapter 4) interview with the Bishop of Victoria: 'You know the way they learn; they memorate (*sic*), they hear the Chinese explanation, and this goes on from morning to night for years, and they get the classics into them' (1882, p. 6). And later:

> When a Chinaman goes to school he is given a little book, and he just simply sits and pores over it, not understanding the meaning of a character, and he goes on growing and getting other books which he does not understand at all, and at the end, when he is in his teens, he begins to have some explanation given to him.
>
> (p. 11)

This view can be found again in an article by Addis (1889) on education in China:

> In truth Chinese education is – *pace* the sinologues – no education at all. It is no 'leading out of' but a leading back to. Instead of expanding the intelligence, it contracts it; instead of broadening sympathies, it narrows them; instead of making a man honest, intelligent and brave, it has produced few who are not cunning, narrow-minded and pusillanimous.
>
> (p. 206)

He then goes on to discuss the 'sinologues' excuses for Chinese education:

> It is natural that those, who have devoted much time and labour to the study of a language and literature like Chinese, should be disposed to overrate the value of that which has cost them so much industry and effort to acquire, and occasional encomiums of the Chinese methods of instruction are only what we might expect. We are told, for instance, that it is eminently suited to the present system of government . . .
>
> (p. 206)

He goes on: 'The truth is that if the comparative test be applied, almost the only merit which can be claimed for Chinese education is that it strengthens the memory . . .' (p. 206). The poor state of Chinese education he compares with Hong Kong where 'half a century ago the island was peopled by a few half savage settlers steeped in ignorance and superstition' but where 'a foreign Government, by the impartial administration of wise and just laws, has made this dot on the ocean so attractive' (pp. 206–7).

These views on Chinese education and the Chinese learner both reflect the earlier discussion of images of Chinese and are almost remarkably consistent with more current stereotypes of Chinese students. It is also worth observing that this was a common view of the learning practices of other students in the Empire: as A. D. Campbell suggested in the Bellary district of India in 1823, the students had a 'parrot-like capacity to repeat, but not to understand what they had learned' (cited in Cohn, 1996, p. 52). This dismissal of local learning practices as nothing but 'parrot-like' memorization, however, seems to have been focused particularly on Chinese learners. Such views, with Chinese learners cast as passive, imitative memorizers, to be enlightened by the advent of the creative West, echo down to the present. Chinese learners are cast as passive/docile (cf. the passive unchanging Chinese), rote learners/memorizers (repetitive/unoriginal), illogical, and insincere. Reviewing stereotypes of Asian students both in Hong Kong and Australia, Biggs (1991) concludes that they 'are perceived by some as relentless rote learners, syllabus dependent, passive, and lacking in initiative' (p. 27). Biggs goes on to show that there is actually rather a strange paradox in the stereotypes of Asian students since there is also available an alternative view of 'The Brainy Asian'. In an attempt to resolve this paradox, Marton, Dall'Alba and Tse Lai Kun (1994) have shown that there are important distinctions to be drawn *within* forms of memorization rather than *between* memorization and understanding:

> the traditional Asian practice of repetition or memorization can have different purposes. On the one hand, repetition can be associated with mechanical rote learning. On the other hand, memorization through repetition can be used to deepen and develop understanding. If memorization is understood in this latter way, the paradox of the Chinese learner is solved.
>
> (p. 16)

My general concern here, however, as I have already argued, is not so much to refute constructions of the Chinese learner but rather to explore their problematic construction. I take it as a given that such constructions do not reference reality.

Discussions of Chinese students reproduce other common aspects of the discourses outlined above. Thus, when Murray (1982), for example, suggests that lecturers in China face 'a sea of glued-on smiles that do not even indicate whether the lecture is being understood' (p. 58), his representation of these students seems clearly related to the construction of Chinese people as inscrutable and/or insincere. Or when he claims that 'the wall between foreigners and natives is like the attitude of the ancient Chinese . . . back in the days of the Tang [dynasty: seventh to ninth centuries AD]' (p. 58), he is clearly representing China and its people as locked in an historical time-warp, as having failed to change and develop. Similarly, when Jochnowitz (1986) suggests that 'in order for the senior theses to be really good, China would have to be a different kind of society, one in which free classroom discussion and independent thinking were encouraged' (p. 526), his comments ultimately seem to have less to do with the social and political context of China and more to do with the long-lasting cultural construct of Chinese people as incapable of independent thought.

Within ELT, however, it is perhaps the construction of the Chinese learner as passive rote memorizer that echoes loudest. Maley (1983), for example, describes Chinese learning practices thus: 'The teacher, or the textbook, has the knowledge. In order to acquire it, it is sufficient for the student to commit it to memory' (p. 99). While it is of course the case that Chinese learning approaches often involve a great deal of memorization, the type of image produced by such statements is one of passive and pointless learning. By contrast, Sampson (1984) criticizes the way 'Western teachers respond to memorization with such derision and scorn' and points out that 'From the Chinese perspective, memorization is far from being an easy cop-out or a release from thinking. It is considered the initial step in assimilating a lesson' (p. 29). The central problem here is that different learning practices are not understood merely as different but are constructed within the larger framework of images of the Other, from which position it is all too easy to see Chinese students as static and deficient.

I have written at some length elsewhere (1996a) about the relationship between Western understandings of Chinese learning and problematically uncompromising accusations of plagiarism. From within such colonial constructs of our memorizing students, it is easy to see alternative learning practices and relationships to text as little more than backward, outmoded learning strategies. Once the students' authorial creativity is questioned and once they are positioned within these discourses of cultural derogation, students are treated as potential or actual criminals, with large warning signs posted around their assignments to make clear what the law is. 'If you copy other writers' words,' teaching materials for first year Arts Faculty students at Hong Kong University warn, 'pretending they are your own, you are engaging in what is known as plagiarism. **If you plagiarise in this way, you are guilty of intellectual dishonesty. You will be penalised heavily for this. Take care to avoid it, therefore.**'

Discussions of plagiarism among Chinese students frequently construct them in terms of their deficiencies in thought and honesty. Deckert (1992), for example, argues that Chinese suffer from an 'absence of individualism' and thus 'The institutions of China have opted for the transference of accumulated knowledge through the arduous routine of rote memorization' (p. 50). Some supposed cultural absence, therefore, leads to the negative and detrimental process of memorization. To take into account more modern Chinese cultural behaviour, Deckert also argues that much of modern Hong Kong life similarly lacks any ethical understanding of ownership and thus continues to lead students astray: 'Wherever students are found using illegal software, pirated and uncredited ESL materials, or entire books reproduced in local copy shops, they are left in the dark about some of the fundamentals of normal academic practice' (p. 52). Deckert (1993) goes on to argue that '. . . most Chinese students overuse source material through an innocent and ingrained habit of giving back information exactly as they find it. They are the proverbial rote memorizers or recyclers' (p. 133). It is, I would argue, not only this casting of Chinese students as 'proverbial rote memorizers or recyclers' but also the attribution of motive to 'an innocent and ingrained habit' that belittles not only these students and their learning practices but also the whole cultural background behind them, reducing their actions to a form of childlike innocence. It is also worth observing, in the larger context of the arguments of this book, that Deckert's research was done on Hong Kong Chinese students. Once again we can see how Hong Kong remains a key site of production of colonial discourse. And once again we may want to ask how much this is likely to change in a post-1997 Hong Kong.

## Conclusion: ELT and cultural fixity

What I think has become very clear from the examples discussed above is the continuity of views on China, Chinese people and Chinese education into the present day. From views on Chinese education as nothing but memorization to arguments that Chinese are circuitous thinkers, Chinese education is still often understood in the same terms. As I suggested earlier, I have focused on China both because this has been part of a personal project to understand how it is that the many Chinese students I have taught have been positioned in the ways that they have, and because China offers an example of how widespread the cultural constructs of colonialism have become. The connection to Hong Kong, furthermore, helps show how colonial constructions get recirculated and also how they are still in the process of being constructed. If, as I have suggested, however, images of Chinese have remained relatively benevolent when compared to colonial constructions of African and many Aboriginal peoples, it is important to consider (and indeed to investigate) how TESOL's Others are constructed.

To give but one example of this process of reciprocal construction, it might be useful to return to the Australian context once more. Visiting Groote Eylandt in Northern Australia to examine the English language and literacy in the workplace programmes, Bill Cope comes across a diagram in a book, which in the words of the manual, 'summarises some aspects of European and Aboriginal styles of learning':

| EUROPEAN SOCIETY | ABORIGINAL SOCIETY |
|---|---|
| Expected to learn by themselves | Learn from older wiser people |
| Learn by being told | Learn by doing |

| | |
|---|---|
| Learn in made-up situations | Learn in real-life activities |
| Learn for future | Learn for today's activity |
| Society in constant change | Traditionally stable society |

(Cope, 1995, p. 190)

As Cope laments, this diagram 'uses five cells to describe a history of two centuries' worth of differing' (1995, p. 189).

Finally, I want to conclude by returning to a theme raised earlier, namely that of cultural fixity. The importance of this notion is that it opens up a way of looking at cultural constructions not so much in terms of whether they are right or wrong but rather in terms of how they have become deterministically fixed. I have tried in the discussions above to maintain this rather Foucauldian stance by avoiding attempts to prove or disprove the truthfulness or falsehood of a particular issue and instead to focus on the ways in which representations of the Other are constructed and remain consistent. It has already become clear from the above examples that not only are Chinese learners constructed in particular ways but they are also fixed in these ways of behaving. They are seen as belonging to a 'traditional' and static culture which defines their thoughts and behaviours. What I want to suggest here is that such a view of culture is endemic to a great deal of TESOL theory. When students are considered to have cultures, these tend to be fixed and static and deterministic. Thus, it is common to talk in terms of Asian, or Japanese or Hispanic etc. students having certain characteristics as if these emerged from some preordained cultural order. This tendency to ascribe fixed (and often, though not always, negative) characteristics by dint of membership to a certain culture can be explained in terms of the colonial construction of the Other.

I started this chapter with a comparison between a comment made almost a hundred years ago by a British headmaster in Hong Kong and the diagrams of Robert Kaplan. Bateson Wright, it may be recalled, insisted that the average Chinese student was 'incapable of sustaining an argument, starting with false premises [sic] and cheerfully pursuing a circuitous course to the point from which he started' (cited in Sweeting, 1990, p. 322). Kaplan (1972) similarly argued that:

> The development of the paragraph may be said to be 'turning and turning in a widening gyre.' The circles or gyres turn around the subject and show it from a variety of tangential views, but the subject is never looked at directly. Things are developed in terms of what they are not, rather than in terms of what they are. Again, such a development in a modern English paragraph would strike the English reader as awkward and unnecessarily indirect.

(p. 46)

Such circuitous 'indirectness', Kaplan argues, is a result of the reliance on the classical literacy form of the 'Eight-legged essay' (*Ba-gu wen)*. What of course such arguments reproduce is both the view of the Other as deviant and the view of the Other as locked in ancient and unchanging modes of thought and action.

It is not my interest or intention here to vilify Robert Kaplan. What I am interested in, rather, is ways in which such cultural constructs of the Other as culturally fixed echo through the discourses of English language teaching. 'Culture' has become a category of fixity rather than an engagement with difference. According to Cope (1995), 'Liberal sensitivity to difference is a white lie' (p. 195). As Spack (1997) has recently shown, writing on cross-cultural rhetoric is still replete with 'static constructions of and generalizations about Chinese rhetoric and Chinese students' (p. 771), with many authors continually repeating these colonial tropes of Chinese learners, constructing Chinese students according to these static cultural categories, 'imposing an ethnocentric ideology and inadvertently supporting the essentializing discourse that represents cultural groups as stable or homogeneous entities' (p. 773). The 'SOLs' of TESOL are fixed and defined and determined by their cultures, whether this be in the way they write (cross-cultural rhetoric), the way they learn (learning strategies), or in the invitations for them to tell us about their own cultures. I have not filled this last section with another listing of examples of this. Rather, I would like to invite all of us involved in ELT to look at both the popular and academic discourses that inform our work and to consider how discourses of 'TE' and discourses of 'SOL' have been constructed.

# ENGLISH, CONTINUITY
# AND COUNTERDISCOURSE

Not so very long ago, the earth numbered two thousand million
inhabitants: five hundred million men, and one thousand five
hundred million natives. The former had the Word; the others
had the use of it.

>(J-P. Sartre, Preface to Fanon's *The Wretched of the Earth*,
1963, p. 7)

There are exclusive clubs in this city where maids are designated
certain areas and quite clear notices are put up to this effect.
Will the indignant do-gooders next suggest that the maids now
be allowed to sip Gins and Tonic in the Members' Bar? Experienced colonials, unlike the nouveau-expatriates, knew how to
employ staff and treat them well, without going overboard. . . .
(I)n the final analysis, it is a Chinese city and anyone who does
not respect the Chinese way, or understand a colonial lifestyle,
really ought to leave, without being told to do so.

>(Letter from Mina Kaye, *SCMP*, 14 December 1993)

Sometimes it comes to my mind that the compulsory learning of
English in schools is one of the British government's political
strategies. . . . In other words, the teaching of English is a kind
of cultural intrusion in Hong Kong and may be regarded as a
political weapon. . . . However, the above assumption does not
affect my decision about taking the degree course of English. I
love English simply because the language is fascinating. It is easy
to learn English but difficult to master it well. Moreover, English
is widely used in the world and because the territory is an international trade centre, many jobs require candidates possessing a
good command of English.

>(Eva Ma Wai Yin)

It is common in current liberal discourses on the role of English in the world
to pronounce that it is no longer tied to its insular origins, it is no longer
the property of Britain, or America, or Canada, or Australia; it is now the

property of the world, owned by whoever chooses to speak it, a language for all to use in global communication. But is it? Putting aside for a moment the crucial questions of access to English that such bland liberal pronouncements ignore, we are nevertheless confronted by a harder question, a question that I have tried to make central to this book: to what extent *is* English an un-encumbered medium of communication available to all its users, and to what extent is it, by contrast, a language that comes laden with meanings, a language still weighed down with colonial discourses that have come to adhere to the language? Before I go on to ask questions about how such adherences may be resisted and countered, it may be useful to restate some of the central arguments here.

I have taken as my central focus the English language, particularly in the context of English language teaching, arguing that the English language teaching enterprise has been important not so much because it led to the current massive spread of English around the world, but because on the one hand it was at the heart of colonialism and on the other because it is deeply interwoven with the discourses of colonialism. I have been trying, therefore, to locate English language teaching and policy within the broader context of colonialism, and to explore ways in which certain discourses become attached to a language. In making these arguments I have looked at colonialism particularly as a site of cultural production, as a context in which particular discourses about Self and Other, about the 'TE' and the 'SOL' of TESOL have been constructed.

My focus on language policy in India, Malaysia and Hong Kong was an attempt to show how, amid the often competing demands of colonial governance, various colonial language policies emerged that both reflected and produced colonial discourses. The need to provide education for Indian people was framed among sometimes competing and sometimes complementary discourses: the liberal discourse of the civilizing mission and the moral obligation to bring enlightenment to backward peoples; the need to provide a productive and docile workforce who would also become consumers within colonial capitalism; the various Orientalist positions, including an exoticisation and glorification of a distant Indian past and a belief that vernacular languages were the most efficient way to spread European knowledge in India; and the Anglicist insistence that English should be the language of education. And while these discourses had varying effects on colonial language policy, they also had important effects in terms of the production of the cultural constructs of colonialism. While the proper role for English was being debated, constructions of Self and Other were constantly produced, and as the debates wore on, such constructions came increasingly to adhere to English.

In my discussion of colonial language policy in Hong Kong, I tried to make the production of colonial discourse more concrete by showing how particular policies for English, and increasingly for Chinese, came in response to particular social and political circumstances. The arguments here suggested on the one hand that we need to look very carefully at current language policies within the broader social, political and economic structures and ideologies that they support, and on the other hand, that in the constant negotiation of colonial language policy, images of Self and Other, of English and of Chinese people, culture and language were always being produced, developed, redefined, recreated.

Moving, then, more closely to current contexts of English and English language teaching, I argued that the contexts of provision of education in English language teaching put back into play, in admittedly complex ways, parts of the colonial discourses that adhere to English. By looking at a broad range of texts, from popular books on English and newspaper articles to English teaching materials, I focused on the colonial origins and the colonial continuity of images of the Self, the colonizers and their language and culture. Such texts provided evidence of how remarkably consistent discourses about the global spread of English, the superiority of the language, and the threats posed by other languages, have come to adhere to the language. I suggested furthermore that theories and practices of ELT take place in the context of these popular discourses on English and that, as I showed, such images of English reoccur in teaching materials.

Turning to the other side of the colonial coin – the constructions of the Other – I showed how discourses on China and Chinese learners similarly constantly reproduced a series of images of the Other. These I then related more particularly to constructions of Chinese learners as passive, rote memorizers, a construction that once again shows remarkable consistency over time. Relating this more broadly to how TESOL's Others are constructed, I argued that students are frequently viewed as belonging to 'traditional' and static cultures which define their thoughts and behaviours. Such colonial constructions of the Other once again come to adhere to English, so that particularly in contexts of English language teaching they are reinvoked, put back into play in a way that constantly 'fixes' the Other.

If, as I suggested above, the adherence of such discourses makes English a language that cannot be seen so easily as the property of all, a language of neutrality and global communication, it might be argued that this is a highly deterministic position, implying that all contexts of English language use are bound by such discourses. It is not at all my intention, however, to construct such a narrow conception of possibility since, first, the discourses I have focused on here are clearly only a tiny set of discourses that occur in relationship to English. To claim to map out discourses that define the global use of English would be foolhardy indeed. And, second, I want to argue that this is not a closed and deterministic relationship but allows for resistance and change.

The central point I wish to make, however, is that such resistance and change is hard work, that the adherence of these discourses to English, and

192

their constant reinvocation in many contexts from travel writing to English language teaching, make attempts to change this relationship between language and discourse an uphill task. This is an important point to consider since, I would suggest, too much work that looks at postcolonialism suggests an easy appropriation of English, that turning English into a tool for one's own use is simply a matter of writing about the local context and sprinkling a few local words here and there. In this final chapter I intend to discuss some of the challenges, limitations and possibilities for change posed by the view of English and the discourses of colonialism that I have developed here.

## Colonial continuities

First of all I would like to return to some of my earlier discussion of Hong Kong. The theme I want to develop here is one of continuity. As I said in Chapter 1, the formal end of colonial rule in Hong Kong may signal far less of an end to colonialism than is thought, not only because of the continuing structures of neo-colonial capitalism and the continuing presence of a colonial culture, but also because of the continuing relationship between English and the discourses of colonialism. One of the most striking aspects of the colonial records that I dealt with in Chapter 4 is the similarities with current discourses in Hong Kong. Many comments that were made fifty or a hundred or more years ago have a remarkably similar ring to comments that can be read and heard in contemporary Hong Kong.

One example of this is the way the demand for English language teaching is discussed in terms of the supposedly pragmatic and mercantile orientation of the Hong Kong Chinese. In the 1882 Report of the Education Commission (see Chapter 4), the Bishop of Victoria argued that 'Their ambition is to get into a position to make money, and to make money at the open ports, and I don't think they would care much for any loss they might have as Chinese subjects in the country' (p. 8). This view of a solely pragmatic orientation to learning English is repeated frequently: '. . . the large attendance at Queen's College and the other Anglo-Chinese Boys Schools is due to a desire to acquire English for business purposes' (p. 503) (*Report of the Committee on Education, The Hong Kong Government Gazette*, 11 April 1902); in the same year, Frederick Stewart's comments from 1865 (see Chapter 4) are requoted: 'Nothing seems to find favour with the Chinese which does not bear a market value. Hence the comparative success of the Central School, English being convertible into dollars' (quoted in a petition for the establishment of a British school, *The Hong Kong Government Gazette*, 11 April 1902, p. 521); such sentiment can frequently be heard today. The significance of this continuity, I want to suggest, is not so much that Hong Kong Chinese have maintained a remarkably consistent mercantile and pragmatic attitude to English but rather that they have been constructed as such with remarkable consistency. Instead of explaining the repetition of various discourses by dint of some stable referent (the mercantile Chinese), I am suggesting, therefore, that the stability of these discourses is a product of the stability of colonial cultural constructions. To represent Hong Kong Chinese as demanding English solely for mercantile purposes seems to have been a similarly constant and long-lasting trope of Hong Kong colonial discourse, and has clearly been useful both in denigrating the Chinese as nothing but economic pragmatists and in explaining the promotion of English as a response to Chinese desires.

While such parallels (the derogation of Chinese learners as nothing but rote memorizers – discussed in Chapter 6 – is another good example of this) suggest striking continuities in the colonial constructs of Hong Kong, other parallels suggest similar continuities in Hong Kong education. It is, for example, a sobering lesson to see how little change there has been in many contexts between the hierarchies of staff in the nineteenth century, with Europeans at the top and Chinese at the bottom (see Sweeting, 1990, p. 257), and the way many current departments (especially English teaching centres) still function. Sweeting (1992, p. 44) discusses the way in which 'headmasters, senior teachers, and other important knowledge-brokers were non-Chinese, usually of British, other European, or American stock', and how these people 'planned, developed and implemented the curriculum' while the day-to-day teaching was done by '"Chinese assistants" who received far inferior employment terms' as if this were a practice only of the nineteenth century. One has only to look at the profoundly inequitable system of current employment terms that still exist, however, or the hierarchies of British (sometimes others) and Chinese teachers still in operation, especially in many English-teaching institutions, to see that little has changed. The example of English language education is, of course, both a continuation of the racist hierarchies of colonial rule and of the colonial construction of the inherent superiority of the native speaker (see Chapter 5).

Similarities between comments in the Burney Report (1935) and contemporary Hong Kong are quite striking. The criticisms of English ability have an uncanny ring with modern discourses:

> . . . not only do the pupils commonly speak English badly after their eight years' course, but even their understanding of the spoken language is often so poor that they have to be given further special training, on admission to the University, before they can listen to the lectures with profit. And the complaint is common with Hong Kong business men that recruits to their offices from the schools, though they will understand the written or printed word well enough, understand spoken English imperfectly and speak it badly.
>
> (p. 11)

This could have been written in the early 1990s when the English Centre at Hong Kong University was set up to remedy the 'problems' that students had when they arrived at the university and to try to deal with the concerns by the business community that students graduated with insufficient communicative skills. Another criticism from the Burney Report is that the teaching is driven by the exams: '. . . syllabuses are determined by speculation about questions likely to be set, and the curriculum is . . . very rigidly limited, in many instances, to examination requirements' (p. 11). These exams, furthermore, are criticized for their lack of relevance to the Hong Kong context. Again, little difference over sixty years. The schools are also criticized for giving students insufficient knowledge of Chinese. Another echo of modern times: one of the difficulties in recruiting staff from Britain: 'The cost of living is high in some respects, especially in rent, though senior teachers can usually secure Government houses at a rate of six per cent of their salaries, and service is cheap'. (p. 21)

Burney finds one reason for the lack of proficiency in English of some of the Chinese teachers is the 'racial segregation practised in the Government schools and sometimes in the Grant-in-Aid schools. European and Chinese teachers have separate common rooms, with the result that, although working daily in the same buildings, their social intercourse is very slight indeed.' (p. 22) This deep separation between Chinese and non-Chinese communities, which, as Wesley-Smith (1994) shows was encoded in a number of pieces of legislation, also continues to a large extent today. It was noted by Eitel (1895) a hundred years ago and still exists in Hong Kong. Luke and Richards (1982) suggest that the linguistic situation in Hong Kong is characterized by two monolingual communities coexisting in relative isolation from each other. Yee (1992) suggests that:

> through mutual xenophobic bias and colonial separation of peoples up to World War II and more, the bulk of the Hong Kong Chinese population developed a social accommodation which meant that they retained as much of their Chinese, primarily working-class Cantonese, customs and language patterns as possible and would pick up foreign patterns when essential to advancement.
>
> (pp. 299–300)

This division still has major implications for language learning and relationships between the expatriate and local communities today.

### English, expats, education and inequality

What then are the implications of such continuities? What I am suggesting is that continuities in various domains of life in Hong Kong are perpetuated by the reproduction of relationships through the discourses of colonialism that

195

adhere to English. Thus Hong Kong continues to be a site of production for colonial discourse. Such relationships are of course by no means limited to Hong Kong, but I intend to look briefly at education in this section to illustrate how I see such relationships operating. The central issue in discussions of Hong Kong education remains the 'medium of instruction'. Indeed, the conference that brought me to Hong Kong at the time of the Handback (see Chapter 1), although ostensibly about broader concerns, soon returned to the same reiterations of the same arguments. What was, in fact, quite remarkable about this event was how, on the eve of Hong Kong's return to China, yet another group of expatriate teachers sat around with their Chinese colleagues and reworked their way through these hundred-year-old debates.

I shall not reiterate these debates here (see the discussions in 1882, Chapter 4, for similar themes), but will point to a few significant concerns that touch on the themes of this book. First, it is worth noting that despite the eventual move to the vernacular we saw in Chapter 4, this process was reversed in the postwar period. As I suggested with respect to discourses on English in Chapter 5, such a move needs to be seen in the context of the re-emergence of Anglicism within a new global empire of communication. This move to greater English has, unfortunately, had serious effects on education. According to Yu and Atkinson (1988), 'English medium education in Hong Kong adversely affects many students' educational attainment' (p. 283). Similarly, So (1987) comments that 'there is much evidence indicating that EM instruction has created learning problems for many students' (p. 265). Quite simply, for large numbers of students in Hong Kong schools, an education through the medium of English is detrimental to their overall education: they learn little English (which is generally irrelevant to their daily lives) and inadequate subject matter.[1] Furthermore, with English filling such an inordinate amount of the school curriculum, students are often left with inadequate skills in Chinese. Thus, as Yee (1992) comments, 'the system is not just deficient in teaching English as a second language. Its policies and methods are so confused and contradictory that students do not even develop intellectual and creative depth in their own native tongue' (p. 302).

Unfortunately, the proposed solution to the problem of the education system is equally problematic. This proposal, based on the beliefs that only 30 per cent of secondary school students could benefit from an English medium education and that the mixed use of Cantonese and English in classrooms is necessarily detrimental, will assign students to English- or Chinese-medium streams at the beginning of secondary school on the basis of diagnostic exams in English at the end of elementary school. As a response to these proposals The Linguistic Society of Hong Kong (1992) suggests:

> streaming is on all accounts a regressive and socially divisive measure. It runs counter to the egalitarian spirit in education. If practised, what is bound to happen is that education through one's

mother tongue will be stigmatised. Those who learn through the Chinese medium will be those who cannot make it to English-medium classes. The damage that this will inflict on the self-esteem of the majority of learners is unthinkable.

(p. 161)

Postiglione (1992) remarks that the outcome of these proposals 'will be to further extend elitist elements in the educational system and further restrict access for those in the English streams to the University of Hong Kong and to government civil service positions' (p. 22). So (1992) also points out that this is not only a regressive move in general terms but also in more literal historical terms:

Having an English-medium cocoon at the top of the secondary sector with a large Cantonese segment at the bottom, which apparently is where the Streaming Proposal is leading us, is a form of ana-chronism that replicates the pre-1926 situation, and will not last for long even if the departing administration imposes it upon us.

(p. 88)

Once again, colonial echoes reverberate.

The products of such discourses must then be linked to broader issues of social inequity. One issue here is that on the one hand Hong Kong is a highly inegalitarian society and on the other hand English is perhaps the key determiner of whether one has access to positions of social and economic prestige. Leung's (1990) analysis of poverty and inequality in Hong Kong points to 'a picture of gross inequality in income distribution in the community' with the poorest ten per cent of households receiving 1.4 per cent of the population's total household income, and the richest ten per cent receiving 35.2 per cent of the income. The richest 20 per cent receive half of the total income (as much as the other 80 per cent), eleven times the income of the poorest 20 per cent (p. 71). Postiglione (1992) relates this 'staggering degree of income inequality in Hong Kong' (p. 23) to the school selection process, which he describes as 'brutal': 'Even though education is compulsory (and free) until age fifteen, less than 8 per cent survive to enter postsecondary, university-level education in Hong Kong' (p. 24). And intimately linked to this élitist education system is English since 'a successful English-medium secondary education has become the principal determinant of upward and outward mobility for the people of Hong Kong' (p. 78). Thus, with success in schooling closely linked to social class, and since 'Hong Kong students from lower social-class families are not receptive and prepared for English as a second language (ESL) as are students of a higher social background' (Yee, 1992, p. 302), parents are caught in an impossible situation: to provide their children with the possibility of a good education, they must opt for the better Anglo-Chinese schools, and yet in so doing, they often condemn their children to an educational dead end.

And yet, although it is parents who have constantly chosen English-medium schools for their children, they cannot be held responsible for the limited choice with which they are presented. That is a result of the micro-politics of colonial rule, such as 'the colonial support for elite schools and the preservation of the University of Hong Kong as a wholly English-medium institution' (Postiglione, 1992, p. 21). In fact, it is not only the maintenance of English as the medium of education at Hong Kong University that supports English-medium education in Hong Kong but also the narrow élitism of the system. Bray (1992) cites figures of 34,000 Hong Kong students in tertiary education overseas (compared to 19,000 in Hong Kong), of which 12,000 were studying in the United States, 10,000 in Canada, and 4,000 in the UK. He goes on to suggest that 'The chief reason why English-speaking countries receive so many more students than Chinese-speaking ones is that the Hong Kong government refuses to recognize degrees from the latter' (p. 90). Thus, an apparently small government policy has had major implications within Hong Kong for supporting the role of English in both secondary education and employment.

Another way in which English is constantly favoured not as overt government policy but rather in terms of lower-level decision-making has been in the constant favouring of expatriates for both work and advice (a process gradually being opposed through localization schemes). Thus, as Morris (1992) points out, the 'dependency on foreign curricula' in Hong Kong schools (most 'mainstream academic subjects' closely resemble British 'O' and 'A' level curricula) was:

> reinforced by the domination of expatriates at senior levels of the Education Department (ED) and the tertiary institutions; the use of overseas study visits by ED officials, especially to England to identify curricular trends and innovations for adoption in Hong Kong; and a reliance on visiting curriculum 'experts' from the United Kingdom.
>
> (p. 120)

Bray (1992) also points to the extent to which the education system has been 'heavily influenced by Western external advisers' (p. 86). Hong Kong University's policy of hiring the best 'international' candidate, as Bray points out, in practice means a high proportion (22 per cent) from the United Kingdom with most of the remainder from other Western countries (five per cent from the United States, 3.6 per cent from Canada, 5.4 per cent from Australia) (p. 88).

A typical example of this move to outside help was the controversial 'Expatriate English Teachers' Scheme' started in 1987. Funded by the government to the tune of US$6.8 million for the first two years, and run by the British Council, the scheme brought over 80 native speakers of English mainly from Britain and Australia to teach in local Hong Kong schools. Local teachers were also sent to Britain for language training. Although the Education Department could find no evidence that this scheme had produced any positive results after two years, the Government opted to continue for another two years until the programme eventually dissolved in disarray (Yee, 1992, pp. 301–2). Again it is often the small-scale connections between a colonial administration, an expatriate-dominated education department and an old handmaiden of the British Empire such as the British Council that lead to the instigation of such schemes. As Bickley's (1987) history of English language teacher education in Hong Kong reveals, the British Council was constantly called upon to provide support and 'expertise' in language education. Meanwhile, the field of English language teaching today in many ways still resembles a British Council Old Boys society. With the British Council's agenda for so many years having been the promotion of the global spread of English and the general interests of Britain (see Phillipson, 1992), it is surely problematic (though unsurprising) that so much of language educational policy in Hong Kong can be influenced by those who learned their trade in this great colonial institution (and see Rajan, 1993a).

The problem here, I want to suggest, is that 1) The discourses that adhere to English make certain views on English, English language teaching and Chinese available for these discussions; 2) Because of the role of English within the context of continuing colonialism (at least up to mid-1997), expatriate 'experts' have always had their Anglicist and Orientalist voices heard; and 3) The discourses of colonialism, particularly as they have developed in the later years of colonial rule, have constantly downplayed the role of colonialism. Thus, as we sat discussing once again the 'medium of education' on the eve of the Handback of Hong Kong, there was no space for discussing English as a colonial language. Challenges to the discourses of colonialism have been hard to make. Chan (1992), however, has delivered a fierce critique of the colonial education system, arguing that 'education in Hong Kong under British rule has been characterized by inequalities, privileges, patronage, discrimination as well as archaic hierarchies, inadequate planning and emphasis on quantity over quality' (p. xi). Chan goes on to explain the operation of this colonial education system in terms of five key elements:

1  policymaking in the hands of an unrepresentative elite operating an undemocratic structure of territory-wide educational governance;
2  over-bureaucratized and illiberal administration of educational institutions, from primary schools to universities;
3  systematic official discrimination against mother-tongue teaching and learning;

4   curriculum design that not only prevented the promotion of nationalistic sentiments but also independent thought and critical-analytical ability. This ensured schools would not become a healthy force in democraticizing Hong Kong, but rather a hindrance to this long-overdue process; and

5   legal and administrative patronage favoring 'British' (as against 'non-British') degrees and qualifications in academic recognition, professional accreditation, employment criteria, and scholarship awards regardless of merits.

(Chan 1992, p. xii)

Such comments on language, education and colonialism of course attract quick responses. Sweeting and Morris (1993), for example, argue that this understanding of colonialism is 'premised on the existence of a colonial conspiracy both to subjugate the natives and promote the interests of the colonial power' (p. 215). But in insisting that this supposed 'colonial conspiracy' is inconsistent with the complexities of educational planning in Hong Kong, they miss the point. As I have been arguing, the processes and effects of colonialism may indeed be varied and complex, but this should not be allowed to detract from the micropolitics of colonial rule, the constant and at times apparently trivial ways in which certain ideas are favoured over others, certain people are given jobs before others, certain decisions are made about the curriculum, certain images of the Self and Other are put into play.

What I have been trying to argue in this very brief look at recent issues in education in Hong Kong is that the adherence of discourses of colonialism to English reproduces not only those discourses of colonialism but also more material relations of colonialism. Although it cannot be said to have been government policy to promote English as widely as possible in Hong Kong and thus that the government has immediate responsibility for the current problems in the education system, it nevertheless seems to be the case that the sources of the problem can be found in the constant micropolitics of colonial governance, in the support for an élitist school system and an English-language university, in the refusal to acknowledge degrees from Chinese universities, in the constant use of English-speaking advisers and 'experts'. Coupled with the development of a highly inegalitarian society with English as the decisive distributor of possible social and economic advancement, the apparently laissez-faire policies of the colonial decision-makers in Hong Kong can be seen to have far more responsibility for the state of affairs than they admit. The dismantling of some of these colonial structures is under way, and yet the continuing reproduction of colonial discourses through English suggests these changes may not effect much change. What I want to suggest here, finally, is that in order to bring about change, discourse will have to change from constant cyclical discussion of the medium of education to an understanding of English and colonialism. This will require counterdiscourses to be developed that can start to challenge the adherence of colonial discourses to English.

## Available discourses and counterdiscourses

I have chosen in this book not to focus as much as one might expect on postcolonial writing, resistance, appropriation and so on. There have been a number of reasons for this. First, colonial and postcolonial resistance is being thoroughly well-documented elsewhere. Second, I am wary of this step, the move of the colonizer to recolonize the writings of the colonized. This is not to say that there should be no place here for looking at postcolonial writing; rather that the easy incorporation of 'Commonwealth Literature,' 'Third World Literature' or 'postcolonial literature' into the mainstream white academy has an uncomfortable ring of reappropriation to it (see, e.g. Ahmad, 1991). Postcolonial writers appropriate English and neocolonial literary critics reappropriate the postcolonial writers. Third, therefore, I have chosen to look inwards, to look at how the experiences of colonialism constructed Western discourses in relationship to English. This absence, however, may look too much like both an oversight and a deterministic view of the impossibilities of using English for counterdiscursive purposes. In order to counter such a view, I would like to discuss some of the issues that I think the development of counterdiscursive positions encounters.

First, I want to raise a further problem. Hanging on a wall in my parents' house in England is a document addressed to 'F. Hawkings Esq., Manager Lahai Estate', written on the 20 October 1936. 'Dear Sir,' it starts,

> We, the members of the staff and other employees of Lahai group beg leave to avail ourselves of this opportunity of testifying our sincere appreciation of your beneficent and able management and to bid farewell to your goodself and Mrs. Hawkings on the eve of your departure on transfer from this estate.

In between this eloquent opening and the conclusion, in which 'humble and fervent prayers for your long life, perfect health and uninterrupted happiness' are offered by 'Your most obedient servants, The employees of Lahai Group', the praises of F. Hawkings Esq. are loudly sung. 'During the six years of your regime, your behaviour towards those employed under you was always marked by extreme kindness and sympathy'; even though life on the estate is 'more or less an exile', 'kind treatment from our superiors' meant that 'we had no occasion to regret our sojourn to these hills'.

> Your courtesy, ardent desire to understand our wants and satisfy them as far as possible, your deep devotion to duty, your love of order and discipline and, above all, your ready forgiveness whenever

we committed mistakes, have put one and all of us under a deep debt of gratitude and obligation to you and we shall ever cherish happy memories of your various acts of goodness in our grateful minds.

Mrs Hawkings also comes in for a share of the praise for 'the ever-memorable deeds of charity and kindness' that she 'generously extended to those that have been sick and needy'; the employees pray that 'Almighty may vouchsafe to her a long life of ever more useful service to the suffering humanity'.

I have a similar document hanging on a wall in Melbourne, slightly larger and more ornate (see figure 7). This one is dated 23 October 1927, and is also addressed to 'Frank Hawkings Esq.', on his departure nine years earlier as manager from Peravanthanam Estate, Mundakayam. 'Dear Sir,' it opens, 'With painful feelings of deep and genuine regret, we, the Staff of the Peravanthanam Estate, Mundakayam, venture to avail ourselves of this opportunity, so kindly offered by you, to bid you farewell on the eve of your departure from our midst, to take up the Management of the Lahai Estate. While soliciting every good fortune for you, we still wish you had been longer spared to us. But rather than selfishly pine at our bad luck our hearts go with you, let us assure you Sir, at every tide of your fortune.' As in the later document, the manager's qualities are given extensive praise: 'Of broad views and large sympathies born of the noble heart, your uniform kindness, unruffled patience and amiable manners have left their indelible impression on our hearts and shall ever stand as examples for our future guidance.' Once again, thanks are also given to Mrs. Hawkings, 'who has always bestowed a mother's love and solicitude on us.' It closes by praying that 'you will pardon any wrongs that unknown to us and innocently we might have done to you'. 'Our sincerest prayers shall waft your footsteps to the goal you desire and help to crown all your efforts with the success that they richly deserve, making a long life happy and prosperous to you and useful to others.' It is signed by 'Your most obedient and loving boys, The staff of Peravanthanam Estate'.

Here, then, we have perhaps classic colonial documents written by the colonized. I know little of how they were produced – who put the texts together, what accounts for their similarities – and I have even less idea of how to read them. All I know with any assurity is that they were addressed to my grandparents. This allows me to tell some stories, to reflect on continuing familial connections to colonialism: my grandparents as managers of tea and rubber plantations in colonial India and my own work as an English teacher, particularly in Hong Kong. But how am I to read such documents? It is, in some ways, the very opacity of these documents that seems so interesting. What do we do with the words 'obedient servants' or 'your most obedient and loving boys'? Are these nothing but formulaic endings to

To

# FRANK HAWKINGS ESQ.,

## MANAGER,

### PERAVANTHANAM ESTATE, MUNDAKAYAM.

*Dear Sir,*

WITH painful feelings of deep and genuine regret, we, the Staff of the Peravanthanam Estate, Mundakayam, venture to avail ourselves of this opportunity, so kindly offered by you, to bid you farewell on the eve of your departure from our midst, to take up the Management of the Lahai Estate. While soliciting every good fortune for you, we still wish you had been longer spared to us. But rather than selfishly pine at our bad luck our hearts go with you, let us assure you Sir, at every tide of your fortune.

YOU have every reason for gratification, and even for self-congratulation, in the fact that within the short compass of the two years and a half of your tenure in this Estate, you have effected such vast improvements and such material developments on it, that the appreciative attention of your Principals thousands of miles away, has been drawn to your selfless work. Your untiring energy, your keen sense of duty and your unique administrative capacity have been rightly recognised and justly rewarded by your promotion to a more responsible post affording you still greater opportunities.

OF broad views and large sympathies born of a noble heart, your uniform kindness, unruffled patience and amiable manners have left their indelible impression on our hearts and shall ever stand as examples for our future guidance. Vain would be any attempt on our part to enumerate the invaluable services for which the Estate and ourselves are indebted to you; we would only pray

    "That in the chronicle of actions just and bright,

    May all your deeds, our faithful Sire, shine."

WE feel that we would be sadly failing in our duty if we missed this opportunity to express our heartfelt thanks to your beloved wife, Mrs. Hawkings, who has always bestowed a mother's love and solicitude on us and who has in a large measure helped to make your work on this Estate the success it is.

IN fine, we pray that you will pardon any wrongs that unknown to us and innocently we might have done to you. Our sincerest prayers shall waft your footsteps to the goal you desire and help to crown all your efforts with the success that they richly deserve, making a long life happy and prosperous to you and useful to others.

    *May we subscribe ourselves,*

    *Dear Sir,*

    *Your most obedient and loving boys,*

*Peravanthanam,*
*23rd October 1927.*

**THE STAFF OF THE PERAVANTHANAM ESTATE.**

V. G. PRESS, KOTTAYAM.

*Figure 7* To Frank Hawkings Esq.

letters, are they the echoes of Malayalam forms of courtesy, are they signify-ing colonial relations of power? Or all of the above? How do we read phrases such as 'your love of order and discipline', this 'regime', 'kind treatment from our superiors', 'your ready forgiveness whenever we committed mistakes' and 'we pray that you will pardon any wrongs that unknown to us and inno-cently we might have done to you'? Did the estate workers appreciate this love of order and discipline, as they seem to claim, or did they perhaps rather tolerate it, or resent it, or subvert it? Did my grandfather perhaps rather like to see himself as a man of discipline, an image that these workers chose to flatter? What colonial relations of power and what attitudes towards them are buried within and beneath this text?

Of course a colonial answer to these questions – a response that can still be readily heard in Hong Kong – would suggest that these 'natives' indeed appreciated the order, discipline, and superiority of their white masters (and indeed India would be far better off today if they were still able to benefit today from the order and discipline brought by the British). From this point of view, colonialism was indeed beneficial and benevolent, and these docu-ments are testimony to the appreciation (all too rare in many instances) of the local people. A more liberal approach to this question might acknowl-edge the problems of the broad exploitative framework of colonialism but would suggest that these documents are testimony to the good relationships that in fact existed in many instances between colonizers and colonized. A more critical reading would argue that the estate workers were the victims of colonial ideology, that they had internalized the colonial discourses of the White Man and thus erroneously believed in his superiority and their own inferiority. It is not my intention, however, to try to make further readings of this. That is not to say that there aren't things to be read out of (or into) this text. We might dwell further on the construction of my grandmother in her role of charity, on the exile to the hills of India that the Europeans favoured, or on the general construction of the White Man as bringer of prosperity.

But instead I want to leave these texts as warnings of opacity. We know almost nothing of their production and little of their reception (we do know they were kept). I am making this point for two reasons: first, as an adjunct to my statements above about the reading of postcolonial writing. As with this colonial writing, we need to tread warily with respect to its inter-pretation. Second, referring to Sartre's statement from his introduction to Fanon's *The Wretched of the Earth*, (1963, p. 7) that 'Not so very long ago, the earth numbered two thousand million inhabitants: five hundred million men, and one thousand five hundred million natives. The former had the Word; the others had the use of it'. In these documents, I think, the estate workers had the use of the Word, but they did not have the Word. And get-ting the Word entails a long struggle of appropriation. From these documents to the modern postcolonial writer in English has been a history of complex resistances.

### English and available discourses

I also want to point to the problem of availability. A central part of my argument here has been that the relationship between English and various discourses makes those discourses constantly available. The point, then, is not that English determines possible meanings, but that English renders certain discourses available or unavailable. I want to explore two aspects of this here. Returning to the context of Hong Kong, I want to look on the one hand at the availability of old colonial discourses in English, and on the other at the discursive possibilities that young students appear to have.

What better place to start than with the former Governor, Chris Patten, who in an article in *The Spectator*, reprinted in the *South China Morning Post* (14 January 1994) defended Britain's role in Hong Kong against attacks made by China, suggesting that their view of conspiratorial colonialism was bizarre: 'It's a bizarre view of our colonial history, a history in which we laid down the imperial burden with so little fuss, and such genial intentions to install and safeguard the institutions of a plural society' ('Braving the northerly winds', *SCMP*, 14 January 1994, p. 21). What I find remarkable about this passage is not so much that Patten defends the British colonial presence in Hong Kong – that was his job – but that he does so in terms so clearly echoing Kipling. My contention here is that it is the context of English in Hong Kong that makes such discourse particularly available to Patten, and it is the ways in which discourses of colonialism adhere to English that recreate these intertextual echoes.

Another context in which these colonial echoes can often be found is in the letters section of the *South China Morning Post*, As an example, here are various exchanges concerning the issue of the treatment of Filipina maids. In response to a letter by Elsa Katarungan (*SCMP*, 23 April 1993), which criticized the Ramos administration in the Philippines and ended 'We will continue to work like slaves all over the world because this administration is just as inept and corrupt as all the others before it', Sheila Grange took umbrage to this view of slavery:

> Does Ms Katarungan think that only the Filipino race are hard workers? Focusing primarily on Hongkong for the present, what about the expatriate manager who often leaves the house at 7:30 in the morning, returning often as late as 8 or 9 at night with a ton of paperwork to get through before the morning. What about the times he leaves on a business trip when officially his working day is over, or he travels to a destination on a Sunday?'
>
> (*SCMP*, 26 April 1993)

In December 1993 a heated debate started over whether a notice in a lift in a block of flats was discriminatory. The notice, positioned next to a sign saying 'No dogs allowed' (and therefore strangely echoing the famous signs of colonial Hong Kong and Shanghai that said 'No dogs or Chinese'), announced (in Tagalog and Chinese) that maids should use the service rather than the main lifts. Responding to the outcry over this sign, Robert Thio (*SCMP*, 3 December 1993) defended its use, arguing that 'I have observed that many Filipino maids speak loudly among themselves in the lifts of buildings and on public buses.' This, he argued, 'is a nuisance and generates resentment among other people.' He went on to argue that maids needed to be educated about how to behave in public. Not surprisingly, this letter produced a number of angry responses (e.g. M.C. Bose, *SCMP*, 16 December 1993; John W.L. Tse, *SCMP*, 27 December 1993), though there were others who could not see a problem here: 'In the name of common-sense and reason, what is wrong with requiring service staff – domestic servants – to use a service lift?' (R. T. B. Barrie, *SCMP*, 16 December 1993); and 'I am highly suspicious of the amount of publicity that has been given to it now at the end of 1993 in the twilight of British rule in Hong Kong' (Wendy Gilbert, *SCMP*, 27 December 1993).

The strongest response to the debate, however, came from Mina Kaye:

> Certain sectors of our community appear to have lost all semblance of rational thinking and objectivity. . . . There are exclusive clubs in this city where maids are designated certain areas and quite clear notices are put up to this effect. Will the indignant do-gooders next suggest that the maids now be allowed to sip Gins and Tonic in the Members' Bar? In Hong Kong, they are employed as maids and so, what is all this indignation about asking servants – yes, that's what they are and that does not make their contribution any less valuable in their own right – from being asked to use the service lift? The maids are not, and ought not to be, part of the employer's family. . . . It is a sad state of affairs that some employers choose to make their maids surrogate 'everything-else-except-maids'. Experienced colonials, unlike the nouveau-expatriates, knew how to employ staff and treat them well, without going overboard. . . . [I]n the final analysis, it is a Chinese city and anyone who does not respect the Chinese way, or understand a colonial lifestyle, really ought to leave, without being told to do so.
>
> (*SCMP*, 14 December 1993)

My point here is that in this replaying of colonial relationships and language, we can see the continuing availability of colonial discourse. It is this that links, say, the letter by Mina Kaye to the following:

In some parts of the world we have mixed bathing, and in others there are hours appointed for males, and hours appointed to females, but, in no other part of the world have we swimming baths erected by public consent, and with public money, where natives are allowed the use of the baths allotted to white people. . . . The white ladies objected to the white gentlemen bathing, but welcomed their black sisters in a 'true spirit of Christian charity'. This, in the presence of natives, was a direct blow to the prestige of the white race. It is in fact the placing of a black gin on a higher plane than a white man.

(*The Papuan Times*, 20 March 1912, cited in Nelson, 1982, p. 168)

The Australian occupation of Papua New Guinea; the British occupation of Hong Kong; the echoes of colonial discourse. But the significant point here is that with the availability of such colonial discourse in Hong Kong, and with its echoes in Australia at the end of the twentieth century, the possibilities of counter-discourse are always limited. It is with such considerations about colonial English in mind that I shall now turn to look at the question of students' relationships to English.

Resistance, as the literature on this notion suggests (see, for example, Giroux, 1983; Harlow, 1987), is not an easy and automatically beneficial space. In order to explore this more, I shall turn to some writing by students of mine in Hong Kong. This writing was in response to my request to various first year undergraduate students at the University of Hong Kong to reflect on their 'relationship to English'. What is interesting here is that while few students articulated a clear sense of English as a colonial language, their experiences with the language seemed to replay colonial relations in terms of the imposition of English, their rejection of it, and their unwilling accommodation to the language. What we see here, then, is an embodied relationship to English, a struggle and an accommodation with English, and yet little available discourse for articulating this relationship.

Probably the most striking aspect of this relationship is the deep-seated vehemence towards English that many of the students felt when they moved from elementary school (where English was a subject but not a medium) to secondary school, where suddenly they were confronted by classes taught in English. The force of some of this language shows how English is being written onto the bodies of these students:

When I finished my primary school, I entered an academic secondary school. I had to speak and listen to English in all subjects except Chinese and Chinese History. It was a hard time for me indeed. I could not understand what the teachers said for nearly one month since I was used to speaking and listening to Cantonese during the lesson in primary school. Besides, I found that the textbooks were all written in English. Whatever I tried my best to read the book, I could not grasp the meaning of many words. Every word looked like a monster, I wanted to kill them.

(Lilian Yeung)[2]

One obvious interpretation of this and some of the following statements is that since it is very hard to study through the medium of a second language, these students are recalling the difficulty of those early months. I want to suggest, however, that there is a slightly different way of reading these statements since it seems to me that these students are describing not merely a difficult period of learning but a process almost of brutalization. What I think emerges from a lot of these accounts is the start of a difficult and sometimes almost violent relationship to English:

From time to time, English, in my mind, has turned sour. It is tough and also dull. . . . I hate English. I know nothing about the meaning of some pattern of expression although I am familiar with them. Suddenly, my mind has been engulfed by those English words!

(Lawrence Ho)

At that time (secondary school) I met frustration after frustration because every subject other than Chinese and Chinese History were taught in English. Worse still, during assembly English was used instead of Cantonese. It was a real harsh time for me to adapt to the new environment. Although I hated English, I had to overcome it.

(Veronica Chow)

The first two years of my English studies were really a nightmare to me.

(Lucetta Kam)

I encountered many many difficulties in learning English. When I read English articles, I didn't understand because of the abundant vocabularies. When I wrote, I made many grammatical and spelling mistakes. When I listened, I couldn't hear a word. When I spoke, I hardly said a word. Therefore, at the beginning, attending English lessons was just like going to hell. But, when time goes by, I start realising the merits of learning English.

(Anita Tang Wing Kin)

As a secondary student in an English grammar school, I usually avoided reading English articles. Other than English newspapers and magazines, I hated reading the English version of notices or announcements, too.

(Wong Kam Hon)

There was a period when I hate English. Which is the first few months in my secondary school.

(Teresa Wan Hang Yee)

I hated English. It brought me a lot of troubles in my study.

(Priscilla Tang Man Ki)

If you want to enter a higher school or to get a higher position, a good command of English is a must. Therefore, parents and teachers put much pressure on the students. They force the students to do a lot of extra work. To these students, English is no longer an interesting language, but a nightmare.

(Amy Chan Fung)

The teachers also encouraged us to put up our hands in class to answer questions in English, in order to train our speaking skills. Punishment would also be given for those who spoke Cantonese in class. As a result, silence prevailed throughout all English lessons.

(Lily Tsang)

As I said, it might be possible to interpret these comments simply in terms of the educational difficulties faced by these students when they switched to English-medium secondary schools. Even from within this interpretation, however, it would have to be acknowledged that the students' remarks display a remarkable degree of vehemence towards English that would likely effect many of their learning experiences. But I want to suggest that this relationship of 'hatred' and of 'nightmares' is more profoundly linked to the colonial context of English, to the physical imposition of English on these students.

Another significant theme that arises from these essays is a questioning of the role of English in their lives. As many students suggest, it exists only as a language used for academic purposes and has little relevance to their daily lives. In this context, some students question the explanations given them by their teachers for learning English, since it seems perfectly possible to live one's life in Hong Kong with a knowledge only of Cantonese.

English rarely applies in our daily lives.

(Joanna Lui)

When I was born, I was a Chinese – a purely Chinese. Cantonese is my mother language. People I met are all Chinese – Hong Kong people. We communicate in Cantonese, but never English. Therefore, English, for myself, is only one academic subject which I must study well so as to pass the examinations and for further education.

(Joanne Ng Pui King)

The importance of English is even more obvious in the university. All the lectures and tutorials are taught in English. It is impossible for you to not understand English and survive in the university. I start doubting if Cantonese is our official language.

(Anita Tang Wing Kin)

It is rather ironic, students have to use double efforts for their studies since homeworks and tests are to be handed in English, but it is the idea in Cantonese that deep in their minds.

(Wan Wing Sze)

To me, English is mainly a tool for learning in school, not for communication in daily lives. As all my friends are Chinese, it is a general and straight thing for us to use Cantonese to communicate with others. Otherwise, one would think that you are quite arrogant as you speak lots of English which seems to be unnecessary.

(Wan Wing Sze)

I found English was meaningless to me and I didn't have good marks in this subject.

(Angela Chui Wing Yu)

It seemed that my relationship to English was confined to studies.

(Spencer Tse)

Why can my mother still fuse into the community without English?

(Wong Kam Hong)

What I mean is that English seems to be useless in our daily life. Outside the school, it is the world of Cantonese. When talking, Cantonese is the only language to communicate. When watching TV, most people would like to choose Chinese programmes. Even inside the school, I find that some teachers use Cantonese to teach English in English classes. Less practices and communication in English make me think that English is of no use. Why don't we cancel the subject? It's just a burden to me.

(Peg Lau Pui Man)

Once again, it might be possible to interpret such comments as expressing a lack of useful contexts in which to use English: English is not relevant to students' daily lives and therefore they lack both the incentive and the opportunity to develop English skills beyond the confines of the classroom. While this interpretation is no doubt useful, and indeed points to the important way in which students develop a split between English as academic language and Cantonese as everyday language, it does not seem to adequately address the ways in which these relationships between the everyday (private) and the academic, political and social domains (public) are also part of a colonial divide. This was more clearly articulated in the following comment:

> As I grew up, I began to question why every Chinese student in Hong Kong has to learn English and uses English in nearly all subjects. . . . Why did not the school teach us Putonghua, the official spoken language used by most Chinese? Although I and my classmates did not ask such questions directly to our teachers, they often told us that English is very important in Hong Kong and we should sharpen our language ability for our future career and studies. Hence, it is the reason why we are required to learn the language according to them. But we believed that the main reason of teaching English in school was that we were living in Hong Kong, a British colony. Our belief and the difficulty of English made me lose interest in this language so I always fell asleep in English lessons.
>
> (Brian Chui Shiu Bong)

Significantly, however, these comments have all been written by students for whom learning English has been a relatively successful exercise: they have not only done well enough in English to avoid the cut-off point at the end of form five (continuing into form six is dependent on passing an English exam) but they have also continued to the exclusive and English-only context of Hong Kong University. Thus, these students not only recall the pain of being forced to study in English and the general frustration at the strange role English comes to play in their lives, but they are also very acutely aware of the implications of their success in English. It is important to recall, therefore, that these statements are made by students who have 'made it' with English. Outside the walls of Hong Kong University there is a vast majority for whom there has been no easy accommodation with the language. For my students, however, there has quite often been a certain shift in affections:

> In short, my attitude towards English has changed a lot. Before, I treated her as an enemy but now she has become my intimate.
>
> (Mona Lee Siu Ling)

In my childhood it acted as my enemy. It was always my obstacle in my studies. . . . Gradually, now, English has become my lover.

(Stella Cheung Man Sze)

English in Hong Kong stands for authority and studying it will probably lead to a better prospect like better job opportunities, higher living standards etc.

(Simon Fu)

Learning in one language and talking in another is a common phenomenon for all non-English speaking countries. But we still have to learn English. After all, it is an influential language in the world.

(Anita Tang Wing Kin)

Even though English is not always being used in our daily life at this stage, we must face the reality that it is very useful in the outside world. Therefore, we should learn more about English to express ourselves for future use.

(Peg Lau Pui Man)

Most of the elder people of Hong Kong are not very familiar with English. They regard English as a conqueror. They think it attacks the Chinese culture. On the other hand, most youngsters consider English as God simply because having a good English foundation will guarantee a good job and a promising future.

(Stella Cheung Man Sze)

There is, then, a strange ambivalence towards English, even amongst these students for whom ability in English is almost certain to lead to future prosperity. This difficulty is perhaps best articulated in the following extract:

Sometimes it comes to my mind that the compulsory learning of English in schools is one of the British government's political strategies. When the number of natives in the colony far outnumbers the British rulers, policies like intermarriage are more efficient to control the colony. By enforcing the compulsory education, more people in Hong Kong are ready to accept the British culture, customs and of course, the government policy. And if the majority of the English speakers in Hong Kong regard the language as superior to Chinese, it is reasonable or rational for them to support the government policy. In other words, the teaching of English is a kind of cultural intrusion in Hong Kong and may be regarded as a political weapon. Whenever I think about this, I will be very upset because all of the students are under the control of the Education Department which put too much stress on English. Students are just like the slaves of the Department because they follow and obey exactly what the examination requirement said.

However, the above assumption does not affect my decision about taking the degree course of English. I love English simply because the language is fascinating. It is easy to learn English but difficult to master it well. Moreover, English is widely used in the world and because the territory is an international trade centre, many jobs require candidates possessing a good command of English. Therefore, I cannot deny that studying English can secure my future prospect.

(Eva Ma Wai Yin)

There are several implications I want to draw from these statements about English. First, they constitute a good example of what I (1994b) have called the 'worldliness' of English. They suggest an almost material nature to language as students struggle to deal with its presence in their lives and their bodies. Second, these statements raise interesting questions to do with resistance. Amongst most of these students there seems little available discursive possibility to articulate resistance to English in English. They tell of the pain of English, the nightmare of English, the usefulness of English, the love of English; but few seem to have available means of articulating a resistance to English. It is only in the words of this last student that we can see an understanding of English as 'cultural intrusion' and a 'political weapon'.

And finally, the patterns of colonialism are indeed replayed through relationships to English in Hong Kong. This ambivalent relationship, acknowledging on the one hand that English is a language of colonial authority and a cultural intrusion but on the other hand that it is the language of success and a language one may come to love, is one that can be found constantly in colonial contexts. From Chinua Achebe (1975) to C.L.R. James (1963), this is one of the fundamental dilemmas of colonialism and postcolonialism: how does one establish a relationship to the languages and cultures of the colonizers when they represent both colonial oppression and the possibilities for anti-colonial struggle? How does one work with a language that one may both hate as a language imposed in school and love as a language one has come to work with?

Thus, although these students generally have an unarticulated and ambivalent relationship to colonialism itself, the kind of ambivalences they seem to face with English echo many of the comments made about the postcolonial problematic of opposing the economies, political structures, cultures and languages of colonialism while at the same time doing so in and through a colonial language that has been part of one's social and educational life and which also allows access to a global audience. In his essay 'Biggles, Mau Mau

and I', for example, Ngũgĩ wa Thiong'o (1993) recalls the 'dance of contradictions' (p. 138) he faced when he read and enjoyed Biggles' exciting
escapades with the RAF, for it was this same RAF that was bombing the
Mau Mau independence fighters in Kenya for whom his brother was fight-
ing. Confronted for many years by the contradictions involved in writing in
the language that was also the language of neocolonial oppression in Kenya,
Ngũgĩ eventually vowed to give up writing in English and to write first in
Gikuyu. Other writers have not had, or have not chosen to adopt, such an
option and have continued to live with these contradictions. In his autobiographical work *Beyond a Boundary*, the Caribbean writer and political
tivist C.L.R. James (1963) recalls his love of the nineteenth-century British
novelist Thackeray and of cricket during his school years. Although he later
came to understand 'the limitation on spirit, vision and self-respect which
was imposed on us by the fact that our masters, our curriculum, our code of
morals, *everything* began from the basis that Britain was the source of all
light and leading, and our business was to admire, wonder, imitate, learn'
(pp. 38–9), he still acknowledges his 'inexhaustible passion' for cricket and
English literature (p. 43).

What I have been trying to show in this section is that before we start to
talk of resistance, opposition, counter-discourse, change, we need to consider
very carefully the limited possibilities. I do not wish this to sound defeatist,
but I do want to argue from my own experiences with colonialism in Hong
Kong and elsewhere that the power and the fixity of the discourses of
colonialism as they adhere to English are very great. From the farewell letter
to my grandparents, to the letters in the *South China Morning Post*, and the
writing of my students, we see English indelibly linked with the reproduction of colonial relations. But we need to find ways of changing these
relationships if the cultural constructs of colonialism are not to be constantly
replayed through English and English language teaching.

## Remaking English in Australia

Australia in 1997 has echoed with the profoundly racist discourses of Pauline
Hanson and her One Nation Party. In light of much of what I have written
about in this book, it may not be so surprising that even in 1997 an
Australian politician such as Hanson could reproduce such colonial tropes as
Aboriginal cannibalism, the denial of Aboriginal genocide, and the threat to
White Australia of the Asian hordes. I want to draw attention to two particular aspects of these discourses and the response to them. First of all, it is
evident that they draw on long-lasting and adherent discourses. The construction of the cannibalistic Other, as I discussed in Chapter 1, has a European history of some five hundred years. The warm response that Hanson's
speeches and writing received in many parts of Australia, furthermore,
showed that these discourses, which had been submerged beneath a veneer

of multicultural liberalism for a number of years, had nevertheless been lying dormant all that time. It did not take much to rekindle anti-Aboriginal and anti-Asian discourses, for these have long histories in Australia, from racist constructions of Aboriginal people from the time of the first invasion, through anti-Chinese discourse at the turn of the century, via the White Australia policy for the large part of this century, and up to the present day.

The second point deals with the inadequacy of the response to these discourses. Apart from the absence of critique from the political right (so-called Liberals), the problem has also been that critical response has, I think, failed to engage with the enormity of the task here. Various academics were wheeled out to dispute the veracity of Hanson's remarks about cannibalism and genocide. But, as I have been arguing here, the issue is not so much the truth and falsity of facts but the truth effects of discourse. The question is not simply one of presenting rectifying, 'good' images of Chinese, English, Aboriginal people and so on. This is why I did not attempt in Chapters 5 and 6 to show that the discourses on English and China were 'wrong'; rather I tried to shed critical light on what they produced. In the case of Hanson's revival of these discourses of colonialism, the point, therefore, is not to refute the facts (or certainly not only to refute the facts) but to point to how these constructions of Aboriginal and Asian Others are part of a long history of adherent discourses. The challenge, of course, is how to effectively deal with and oppose these discourses.

As I discussed in Chapter 1, the issue for Indigenous Australians cannot merely be through 'positive' representations of themselves. Such representations have already been reappropriated by an exoticizing, Orientalist discourse that turns Indigenous people into primitive beings in touch with the earth (Thomas, 1994; Jordan and Weedon, 1995), a sort of New Age nomad doing dreamtime and painting the desert. As Jordan and Weedon suggest, such an exoticized view of Aboriginal people already denies the history of colonialism that has inflicted such suffering, ignores those:

> who have faced genocide, who have been subjected to brutal attempts at assimilation, denial of civil rights, denial of basic human rights. These people, who constitute the overwhelming majority of the Australian Aboriginal population, are *not* the exotic natives of the White Western imagination. They are not a people who live 'in harmony with nature' but an uprooted, demoralized people living in the urban slums, shanty towns and remote reserves of contemporary Australia.
>
> (1995, p. 490)

As I pointed out on Chapter 1, both Mudrooroo (1995) and Nakata (1995) point to the crucial need for Aboriginal Australians to have access to the language and knowledge that constructs their Aboriginality, their race, their culture. Thus, while it is centrally through English that Indigenous people in Australia are racially defined, it is English that they need to know in order to understand those definitions, and to oppose them. One problem here is that language learning is so rarely discussed in these terms; generally, learning English (or other dominant languages) is seen as leading to social and economic advantage, while learning local languages is seen as an issue of linguistic and cultural maintenance. From the perspective I have been developing here, however, there are a number of different considerations: maintaining and using a local language becomes an issue of avoiding the reproduction of the English/discourse relationship I have discussed in this book. But important though this is, it fails to confront the relationships between English and defining discourses. It also leaves unexplored the discursive/linguistic relationships of the particular language being promoted and we should of course always be wary of assuming that linguistic/discursive connections in that language are not also in need of opposition. So we are presented with the double-edged sword of needing to learn English, not so much for social and economic advantage – as we know, such advantages will likely be denied anyway – but rather in order to understand better how one is being racially defined.

The liberal arguments for language rights, therefore, tend to miss the point since support and use of Indigenous languages, while important for cultural maintenance and development, does not confront the discourses that adhere to English (see Pennycook, 1998). They are particularly tied to English and must be confronted through English. This can be done in several ways. First, I hope a book such as this serves in part to pull apart the discourses that adhere to English. But it would be foolish to believe such a book will make much difference. As I argued in Chapters 5 and 6, it is as much in the domain of popular culture that these discourses circulate. Second, writing by Indigenous people, in English, may also break apart some of these discourses, dislodge them from their adherence to English. Thus the writing of Indigenous Australians (or many other postcolonial writers) can start to form a counter-discourse not of 'positive' images of Aboriginal people but rather of alternative stories, stories that tell of Indigenous lives torn apart by colonial brutality, of different lives, of different realities.

Third, we need concerted action on many fronts: we need to explore a range of postcolonial strategies, ways of teaching, learning, doing applied linguistics, and so on, that can be developed to oppose the cultural framings of self and other, of English and other cultures. What are the implications for English language teaching of trying to deconstruct, oppose and create counter-discourses to these dominant discourses? How can we move towards the decolonization of applied linguistics and the decolonization of English? How can we help our students develop cultural alternatives (cf. Pennycook, 1997)? And how prepared are those of us that work in English language teaching to confront the double-edged sword of English? Postcolonial English must include 'having the Word' not just the use of it.

I had hoped to end this book on a positive note, to talk more about resistance, opposition, change, postcolonialism. I had wanted to look at postcolonial writing as a way to narrate different realities in English about Australia. But now, in light of the resurgence of crass racism, the re-emergence of discourses that one might have hoped had started to be dismantled, I am less optimistic. I fear at present the writings of Mudrooroo, Kath Walker (Oodgeroo Noonuccal), Eve Fesl, and many others, important though they are, are not managing to shift the discourses that adhere to English in Australia. Or at least are only doing so very slowly. We should be wary too of the belief that this speaking from the margins somehow in itself inculcates power. As Luke (1996) has suggested, this particularly North American appropriation of postcolonial struggle, this view that to find a voice somehow brings empowerment is ultimately an individualist and romantic version of language and power. But neither have the liberal discourses of multiculturalism done much to shift the ways in which discourses adhere to English.

But perhaps such pessimism brings a salutary warning. The discourses I have mapped out in this book are powerful indeed, and replayed in many contexts. Perhaps it is good that before I went on to suggest with undue optimism that postcolonial writing is a powerful enough form of opposition, I needed to be rocked by the power of the problem I have been sketching here. Gazing across Hong Kong Harbour at this symbolic end to colonialism, wondering what the setting-sail of Governor Patten would mean for change in Hong Kong, I was concerned that the cultural constructs of colonialism were alive and well. And I believe now that I was more right than I had suspected. What we need, I believe, is action on many fronts. If postcolonial writing can break apart the discourses of colonialism, it needs to be postcolonialism in concert, not postcolonialism in fragmentation. Postcolonial writing, while at times seeming apparently condemned always to a position of defined locality, must also still be seen as anti-colonial writing, writing in opposition to the discourses of colonialism. Thus, given the well-being of such discourses, such writing needs to continue not only to narrate different worlds differently but to narrate against the colonial world. Such comments will be read, I hope, not as an injunction as to what postcolonialism needs to be, but as a warning as to what it is up against.

What I am suggesting, then, is that the power of English and the adherence of discourses render the task of postcolonial writing a difficult but a crucial one. Postcolonial writing needs to work in concert, in many different forms, to articulate both counterdiscursive arguments and alternative realities. We need alternative representations, alternative stories, alternative possibilities, and these need to be in our classes, our English classes, our linguistics and applied linguistics classes, our ESL classes, our teaching materials.

We need to work in and against English to find cultural alternatives to the cultural constructs of colonialism; we desperately need something different. But unless we can work alongside each other both to dislodge the discourses of colonialism from English and to generate counterdiscourses through English, colonialism will continue to repeat itself, in Australia, in English classes, in many contexts around the world.

# NOTES

## 1 ENGLISH AND THE CULTURAL CONSTRUCTS OF COLONIALISM

1 Despite the importance of Yee's statement here, there are problems: First, I think his numbers must surely be exaggerated if the issue is only deaths as a result of the opium trade. Second, the comparison with the Holocaust and its specifically targeted genocide, or with the slave trade and its brutal removal and treatment of Africans, needs to be made more circumspectly and cautiously than this.

2 I have borrowed this term from Clifford's (1988) discussion of Foucault: 'Foucault's overall undertaking has of course been scrupulously ethnocentric' (pp. 264–5). I am using it here, as I take Clifford to be, as a double-edged remark, acknowledging on the one hand the importance of Europeans of attempting to interpret systems of meaning only within a European framework, but suggesting on the other hand the limitations of this epistemological narrowness.

3 The term 'expatriate' itself is an interesting one, on the one hand distinguishing a certain group of people clearly from 'immigrants' and other darker-skinned arrivals, and on the other locating their identity not as 'foreigners' or 'outsiders' in a host community (as, to the annoyance of many 'expats,' do many local language descriptions: Japanese *Gaijin*, Chinese *Waiguoren*, Cantonese *Guailo*) but rather as people whose identity is defined by a decontextualized English/American etc. person overseas. Being an 'expatriate' locates one not as an outsider in a particular community but as a permanent insider who happens for the moment to be else-where. The very use of this term puts into play a host of significant discourses.

4 I am, of course, aware of the critique levelled at Said and others that this focus on the discourses of the colonizers once again ignores the discourses of the colonized. Nevertheless, given my project and the continued silence of the colonized in applied linguistics, I believe it also remains crucial to keep working on and against these colonial discourses.

## 2 THE CULTURAL CONSTRUCTS OF COLONIALISM

1 This book is also of great interest because it is seen as one of the key texts in the study of imperialism (see, for example, Curtin, 1971; Semmel, 1993; Thornton, 1965).

## 4 HONG KONG: OPIUM, RIOTS, ENGLISH AND CHINESE

1 It is worth noting, however, that Sweeting's meticulous documentation of education in Hong Kong does include pre-1842 education in Hong Kong.
2 As I suggested in Chapter 1, the comparisons with both the Holocaust and the slave trade are at times overblown and inappropriate. The slave trade destroyed the bodies, lives, cultures, languages and histories of countless Africans. Nevertheless, I think it is important to see the possibilities of making such comparisons.
3 Colonial Office documents.
4 Stewart urges Eitel to 'finish the quotation' from Macaulay and provides this ending, saying that he will show it to Eitel later. It is unclear what exactly Stewart is referring to here, though it does show that while Macaulay's views are seen as important, there was also considerable debate about what those views actually were.

## 5 IMAGES OF THE SELF: OUR MARVELLOUS TONGUE

1 I am much indebted generally to Richard Bailey's fascinating book *Images of English: A cultural history of the language* for a number of the ideas and sources in this chapter.
2 Bryson (1990) in particular is full of such inaccuracies – this word is misspelt and does not mean 'social worker'. Another example is his claim that 'In Japanese, the word for foreigner means "stinking of foreign hair"' (p. 7). The usual Japanese word for foreigner, *Gaijin*, means 'outside person'. The point of course is that vague 'facts' about other languages are just thrown in as exoticisms etc. – they are not of interest in themselves.

## 7 ENGLISH, CONTINUITY AND COUNTERDISCOURSE

1 It is worth noting that this supposedly 'English-medium' education is frequently in fact a mixture of English and Cantonese – these are after all Cantonese-speaking teachers teaching Cantonese-speaking students. While various purists have objected to this mixed-code classroom language, it may at least be more helpful to students than teaching purely in English. Nevertheless, the mixture of English textbooks and mixed English-Cantonese explanations clearly does not serve the school population well.
2 All these quotations from student essays were obtained with the permission of the students and their agreement that their real names should be used.

# BIBLIOGRAPHY

Achebe, C. (1975) 'An image of Africa', *Scrutiny*, 18 February, 31–43.

Addis, C. S. (1889) 'Education in China', *The China Review, XVIII*, 205–12.

Ahmad, A. (1991) 'Disciplinary English: Third-worldism and literature', in Svati Joshi (ed.), *Rethinking English: Essays in Literature, Language, History*, New Delhi: Trianka, (pp. 206–63).

Ahmad, A. (1994) '*Orientalism* and after', in P. Williams and L. Chrisman (eds), *Colonial Discourse and Postcolonial Theory: A Reader*, New York: Columbia University Press, (pp. 162–71).

Alatas, S. H. (1977) *The Myth of the Lazy Native*, London: Frank Cass.

Alston, L. (1907) *The White Man's Work in Africa and Asia: A Discussion of the Main Difficulties of the Colour Question*, London: Longmans, Green, and Co.

Annual Report (various years) 'The Annual Report on the State of The Government Schools for the Year. . . .' *Hong Kong Blue Book*, Government Printers.

Appiah, Kwame A. (1991) 'Is the post- in postmodernism the post- in postcolonial?' *Critical Inquiry*, 17 (Winter), pp. 336–57.

Arnold, T. (1815) *The Effects of Distant Colonisation on the Parent State*. A prize essay recited in the Theatre at Oxford, 7 June 1815.

Asia Society, The (1979) 'Asia in American textbooks', in E. Smith and L. F. Luce (eds), *Toward Internationalism: Readings in Cross-cultural Communication*, Rowley, MA: Newbury House.

Auerbach, E. (1993) 'Reexamining English Only in the ESL classroom', *TESOL Quarterly*, 27(1), 9-32.

Avineri, S. (ed.) (1968) *Karl Marx on Colonialism and Modernization, his Despatches and other Writings on China, India, Mexico, the Middle East and North Africa*, New York: Doubleday.

Axon, W. (1888) 'English the Dominant Language of the Future', *Stray Chapters in Literature, Folk-lore, and Archaeology*, London: John Heywood.

Bailey, R. (1991) *Images of English: A Cultural History of the Language*, Ann Arbor, MI: The University of Michigan Press.

Bakhtin, M. (1986) *Speech Genres and Other Late Essays*. Austin, TX: University of Texas Press.

Barrow, R. (1990) 'Culture, values and the language classroom', in B. Harrison (ed.), *Culture and the Language Classroom: ELT Documents*, London: British Council.

Bhabha, H. K. (1983a) 'Difference, discrimination and the discourse of colonialism', in F. Barker, *et al.* (ed.), *The Politics of Theory*, Colchester: University of Essex.

Bhabha, H. K. (1983b) 'The other question', *Screen*, 24(6), 18–35.

Bickley, V. (1987) 'Developments in English language teacher education', in R. Lord and H. N. L. Cheng (eds), *Language Education in Hong Kong*, Hong Kong: Chinese University Press, (pp. 187–218).

Biggs, J. (1991) 'Approaches to learning in secondary and tertiary students in Hong Kong: Some comparative studies', *Educational Research Journal*, 6, 27–39.

Blaut, J. M. (1993) *The Colonizer's Model of the World: Geographical diffusionism and eurocentric history*, New York: The Guilford Press.

Boas, F. (1911) 'Introduction', *The Handbook of North American Indians, Vol. I, Bureau of American Ethnology Bulletin*, 40 (1), Washington, DC: Smithsonian Institute.

Bonavia, D. (1982) *The Chinese*, Harmondsworth: Penguin.

Brantlinger, P. (1990) *Crusoe's Footprints: Cultural Studies in Britain and America*, New York: Routledge.

Bray, M. (1992) 'Hong Kong education in an international context: The impact of external forces', in G.A. Postiglione (ed.), *Education and Society in Hong Kong: Toward One Country and Two Systems*, Hong Kong: Hong Kong University Press, (pp. 83–94).

Brown, H. D. (1980) *Principles of Language Learning and Teaching*, Englewood Cliffs, NJ: Prentice Hall.

Bryson, B. (1990) *Mother Tongue: The English language*, London: Hamish Hamilton.

Burchfield, R. (1985) *The English Language*, Oxford: Oxford University Press.

Bureau of Education (H. Sharp, ed.) (1920) *Selections from Educational Records, Part I, 1781–1839*, Calcutta: Superintendent of Government Printing.

Bureau of Education (J.A. Ritchie, ed.) (1922) *Selections from Educational Records, Part II: 1840–1859*, Calcutta: Superintendent of Government Printing.

Burnett, L. (1962) *The Treasure of our Tongue*, London: Secker and Warburg.

Burney, R. (1935) *Report on Education in Hong Kong*, Hong Kong: Government of Hong Kong.

Caldecott, A. (1901) *English Colonisation and Empire*, London: John Murray.

Cantlie, J. (1906) Hong Kong, *India, Ceylon, Straits Settlements, British North Borneo, Hong-Kong*, London: Kegan Paul, Trench, Trabner and Co., (pp. 498–531).

Césaire, A. (1972) *Discourse on Colonialism*, New York: Monthly Review Press (Joan Pinkham trans.).

Chai Hon-Chan (1964) *The Development of British Malaya 1896–1909*, Kuala Lumpur: Oxford University Press.

Chakravarty, S. (1989) *The Raj Syndrome: A Study in Imperial Perceptions*, Delhi: Chanakya Publications.

Chan, Ming K. (1992) 'Foreword', in G. A. Postiglione (ed.), *Education and Society in Hong Kong: Toward One Country and Two Systems*, Hong Kong: Hong Kong University Press.

Chan, Ming K. (1994) 'Hong Kong in Sino-British Conflict: Mass mobilization and the crisis of legitimacy', in M. K. Chan (ed.), *Precarious Balance: Hong Kong between China and Britain, 1842–1992*, Hong Kong: Hong Kong University Press.

Chang, Jung (1991) *Wild Swans: Three Daughters of China*, New York and London: Simon and Schuster.

Cheng, Nien (1986) *Life and Death in Shanghai*, London: Grafton.

Cheng, W. (1983) 'The changing patterns of English language teaching in Hong Kong', *The Chinese University Education Journal*, 11(1).

Chirol, V. (1910) *Indian Unrest*, London: Macmillan.

Chrisman, L. and Williams, P. (1994) 'Colonial discourse and post-colonial theory: An introduction', in P. Williams and L. Chrisman (eds), *Colonial Discourse and Postcolonial Theory: A Reader*, New York: Columbia University Press.

Claiborne, R. (1983) *The Life and Times of the English Language: The History of our Marvellous Tongue*, London: Bloomsbury.

Clark, M. (1962) *A History of Australia*, Carlton, VI: University of Melbourne Press.

Clifford, H. (1927) *In Court and Kampong*, London: The Richards Press.

Clifford, J. (1988) *The Predicament of Culture: Twentieth-century Ethnography, Literature and Art*, Cambridge, MA: Harvard University Press.

Cohn, B. (1996) *Colonialism and its Forms of Knowledge*, Princeton, NJ: Princeton University Press.

Collins, J. (1992) 'Migrant hands in a distant land', in G. Whitlock and D. Carter (eds), *Images of Australia*, St Lucia: University of Queensland Press.

Cope, B. (1995) 'The language of forgetting: A short history of the word', *RePublica*, 2, 182–206.

Crowley, T. (1989) *The Politics of Discourse: The Standard Language Question in British Cultural Debates*, London: Macmillan.

Crowley, T. (1996) *Language in History: Theories and Texts*, London: Routledge.

Crystal, D. (1987) *The Cambridge Encyclopedia of Language*, New York: Cambridge University Press.

Curtin, P. (ed.) (1971) *Imperialism*, London: Macmillan.

Davin, D. (1987) 'Eating Bitterness', Review of *Iron and silk*, *Times Literary Supplement*, 711, 3 July.

de Quincey, T. (1862) *Recollections of the Lakes and the Lake Poets*, Edinburgh: Adam and Charles Black.

Dean, M. (1994) *Critical and Effective Histories: Foucault's Methods and Historical Sociology*, London: Routledge.

Deckert, G. (1993) 'Perspectives on plagiarism from ESL students in Hong Kong', *Journal of Second Language Writing*, 2 (2), 131–48.

Deckert, G. (1992) 'A pedagogical response to learned plagiarism among tertiary-level ESL students', *Occasional Papers in Applied Language Studies* (Baptist College, Hong Kong) November, 49–56.

Deedes, W. (1994) 'Churchill: Bigot only of the time', *Eastern Express* (Hong Kong), 12 April 1994.

Defoe, D. (1910) *The life and adventures of Robinson Crusoe*, Oxford: Clarendon Press.

Dirks, N. (1996) 'Foreword', in B. Cohn (ed.), *Colonialism and its Forms of Knowledge*, Princeton, NJ: Princeton University Press.

Dreyfus, H. and Rabinow, P. (1983) *Michel Foucault: Beyond Structuralism and Hermeneutics*, Brighton: Harvester.

*Economist, The* (1988) Review of *Riding the Iron Rooster* and *Behind the Wall*, 308, 23 July, 77–8.

Eitel, E. J. (1895) *Europe in China*: Kelly & Walsh/Luzac & Company, reprinted in 1983 by Oxford University Press, Hong Kong.

English out to conquer the world (1985) *U.S. News and World Report*, 18 February.

Eyre, A. G. (1971) *An Outline History of England*, London: Longman.

Fallows, J. (1988) 'Shanghai surprise', *Atlantic*, 262, July, 78.

Fanon, F. (1963) *The Wretched of the Earth* (Constance Farrington, trans.) Harmondsworth: Penguin.

Fanon, F. (1967) *Black Skin, White Masks*, New York: Grove Press.

Fernando, L. (1986) *Cultures in Conflict: Essays on Literature and the English Language in South East Asia*, Singapore: Graham Brash.

Foucault, M. (1979) *Discipline and Punish: The Birth of the Prison*, New York: Vintage Books.

Foucault, M. (1980) *Power/Knowledge: Selected Interviews and Other Writings, 1972–1977*, New York: Pantheon.

Foucault, M. (1984a) 'On the genealogy of ethics: An overview of work in progress', in P. Rabinow (ed.), *The Foucault Reader*, New York: Pantheon.

Foucault, M. (1984b) 'Nietzsche, history, genealogy', in P. Rabinow (ed.), *The Foucault Reader*, New York: Pantheon.

Frykenburg, R. (1988) 'The myth of English as a "colonialist" imposition upon India: A reappraisal with special reference to South India', *Journal of the Royal Asiatic Society*, 2, 305–15.

Fulton, G. D. (1994) 'Dialogue with the other as potential and peril in *Robinson Crusoe*', *Language and Literature*, 3(1), 1–20.

George, J. (1867) *The Mission of Great Britain to the World, or Some of the Lessons which she is now Teaching*, Toronto: Dudley and Burns.

Giroux, H. A. (1983) *Theory and Resistance in Education: A Pedagogy for the Opposition*, South Hadley, MA: Bergin & Garvey.

Government of India (1960) *Selections from Educational Records of the Government of India, Volume 1, Educational Reports, 1859–1871*, Delhi: National Archives of India.

Government of India (1963) *Selections from Educational Records of the Government of India, Volume II: Development of University Education, 1860–1887*, Delhi: National Archives of India.

Guest, E. (1838/1882) *A History of English Rhythms*, London: George Bell and Sons.

Harlow, B. (1987) *Resistance Literature*, New York: Methuen.

Hobson, J. A. (1902) *Imperialism: A study*, London: James Nisbet & Co.

Holland, S. (1977) 'Australia, Rhodesia and South Africa: A comparison', in F. S. Stevens and E. P. Wolfers (eds), *Racism: The Australian Experience. A Study of Race Prejudice in Australia. Volume 3: Colonialism and After*, Sydney: Australia and New Zealand Book Company (2nd edn, pp. 187–212).

*Hong Kong Government Gazette* (various years), Hong Kong: Government Printers.

Howatt, A. P. R. (1984) *A History of English Language Teaching*, Oxford: Oxford University Press.

Howell, A. P. (1872) *Education in British India, 1870–71*, Reprinted in Government of India (1960), pp. 301–573.

Hoyles, M. (1977) 'The history and politics of literacy', in M. Hoyles (ed.), *The Politics of Literacy*, London: Writers and Readers Cooperative.

Hulme, P. (1986) *Colonial Encounters: Europe and the Native Caribbean, 1492–1797*, London: Routledge.

Hyam, R. (1990) *Empire and Sexuality: The British experience*, Manchester: Manchester University Press.

James, C. L. R. (1963) *Beyond a Boundary*, New York: Pantheon Books.

Jan Mohammed, A. R. (1985) 'The economy of manichean allegory: the function of racial difference in colonist literature', *Critical Inquiry*, 12 (1), 59–82.

Jenkins, S. (1995) 'The Triumph of English', *The Times*, 25 February.

Jespersen, O. (1922) *Language: Its Nature, Development and Origin*, London: George Allen & Unwin Ltd.

Jespersen, O. (1938/1982) *Growth and Structure of the English Language*, Oxford: Basil Blackwell.

Jochnowitz, G. (1986) 'Teaching at a provincial Chinese university', *American Scholar*, 55 (4), 521–7.

Johnson, D. (1995) 'Rags!' *New York Review of Books*, 42, 16 February, 19–21.

Johnston, B. (1996) *Boxing with Shadows: Travels in China*, Melbourne: Melbourne University Press.

Jordan, G. and Weedon, C. (1995) *Cultural Politics: Class, Gender, Race and the Modern World*, Oxford: Blackwell.

Joshi, Svati (ed.) (1991) *Rethinking English: Essays in Literature, Language, History*, New Delhi: Trianka.

Jupp, T. C., Roberts, C. and Cook-Gumperz, J. (1982) 'Language and disadvantage: the hidden process', in J. Gumperz (ed.), *Social Identity*, Cambridge: Cambridge University Press.

Kachru, B. J. (1986) *The Alchemy of English: The Spread, Functions and Models of Non-native Englishes*, Oxford: Pergamon.

Kaplan, R. (1966) 'Cultural thought patterns in intercultural education', *Language Learning*, 16, 1–20.

Kaplan, R. (1972) *The Anatomy of Rhetoric: Prologemena to a Functional Theory of Rhetoric*, Concord, MA: Heinle and Heinle.

Kelly, L. G. (1969) *Twenty-five Centuries of Language Teaching*, Rowley, MA: Newbury House.

Kiernan, V. G. (1969) *The Lords of Human Kind: European Attitudes Towards the Outside World in the Imperial Age*, London: Weidenfeld & Nicolson.

Lang, J. (no date) *Outposts of Empire*, London: T.C. & E.C. Jack.

Lang, W. H. (no date) *Australia*, London: The Caxton Publishing Company.

Lethbridge, H. J. (1895/1983) 'Introduction' to E. J. Eitel (ed.), *Europe in China*, Hong Kong: Oxford University Press, p. vii.

Leung, B. K. P. (1990) 'Poverty and inequality', in B. K. P. Leung (ed.), *Social Issues in Hong Kong*, Hong Kong: Oxford University Press.

Liddell, A. C. (1910) 'Introduction', to Daniel Defoe, *The Life and Adventures of Robinson Crusoe*, Oxford: Clarendon Press.

Linguistic Society of Hong Kong (1992) 'A blueprint for linguistic chaos: A critique of the Report of the Working Group Set up to Review Language Improvement Measures', in Luke Kang Kwong (ed.), *Into the Twenty First Century: Issues of Language in Education in Hong Kong*, Hong Kong: Linguistic Society of Hong Kong, pp. 157–65 (Appendix 1).

Loh Fook Seng, P. (1970) 'The nineteenth century British approach to Malay education', *Jurnal Pendidekan*, 1 (1), 105–15.

Loh Fook Seng, P. (1975) *Seeds of Separatism: Educational Policy in Malaya 1874–1940*, Kuala Lumpur: Oxford University Press.

Lugard, F. D. (1910) *Hong Kong University: Objects, History, Present Position and Prospects*, Hong Kong: Noronha.

Lugard, F. D. (1926) *The Dual Mandate in British Tropical Africa*, (3rd edn), Edinburgh: William Blackwood and Sons.

Luk Hung-Kay, B. (1991) 'Chinese culture in the Hong Kong curriculum: Heritage and colonialism', *Comparative Education Review*, 35 (4), 650–68.

Luke, A. (1996) 'Genres of power? Literacy education and the production of capital', in R. H. A. G. Williams (ed.), *Literacy in Society*, London: Longman, (pp. 308–38).

Luke, K.K. and Richards, J. (1982) 'English In Hong Kong: Functions and status', *English World Wide*, 3, 47–64.

Lyon, D. (1994) *Postmodernity*, Minneapolis: University of Minnesota Press.

Macaulay, T. B. (1835/1972) 'Minute on Indian Education', in J. Clive and T. Pinney (eds), *Thomas Babington Macaulay: Selected Writings*, Chicago: University of Chicago Press.

Mackerras, C. (1989) *Western Images of China*, Hong Kong: Oxford University Press.

Macleans (1988) Review of *Riding the Iron Rooster*, 101, 15 August, p. 51.

Mah, Adeline Yen (1997) *Falling Leaves: The True Story of an Unwanted Chinese Daughter*, London: Penguin.

Maley, A. (1983) 'Xanadu – "A miracle of rare device": The teaching of English in China', *Language Learning and Communication*, 2 (1), 97–104.

Mangan, J. A. (1985) *The Games Ethic and Imperialism: Aspects of the Diffusion of an Ideal*, Harmondsworth: Viking.

Mani, L. (1989) 'Contentious traditions: The debate on sati in colonial India', in K. Sangari and S. Vaid (eds), *Recasting Women*, New Delhi.

Martin, L. (1986) '"Eskimo words for snow": A case study in the genesis and decay of an anthropological example', *American Anthropologist*, 88 (2), 418–23.

Marton, F., Dall'Alba, G. and Tse Lai Kun (1994) 'The paradox of the Chinese learner', in D. A. Watkins and J. A. Biggs (eds), *The Asian Learner Research and Practice*, Hong Kong: Hong Kong University Press.

Marx, K. (1853) 'The British rule in India', *New York Daily Tribune*, 3804, 25 June, New York: International Publishers, (pp. 35–41).

Marx, K. (1857) 'English ferocity in China', *New York Daily Tribune,* 4984, 10 April, New York: International Publishers, (pp. 112–15).

Marx, K. (1858a) 'The opium trade', *New York Daily Tribune,* 5433, 20 September, New York: International Publishers, (pp. 213–16).

Marx, K. (1858b) 'The opium trade', *New York Daily Tribune,* 5438, 25 September, New York: International Publishers, (pp. 217–20).

Maxwell, G. (1927) 'Some problems of education and public health in Malaya' in P. H. Kratoska (ed.) *Honourable Intentions: Talks on the British Empire in South-East Asia delivered at the Royal Colonial Institute, 1874–1928*, Singapore: Oxford University Press (1983).

Maykutenner (Vicki Matson-Green) (1995) 'Tasmania: 2', in A. McGrath (ed.), *Contested Ground: Australian Aborigines under the British Crown*, St Leonards, NSW: Allen & Unwin.

226

McGrath, A. (1995a) 'A national story', in A. McGrath (ed.), *Contested Ground: Australian Aborigines under the British Crown*, St Leonards, NSW: Allen and Unwin, (pp. 1–54).

McGrath, A. (1995b) 'Tasmania: 1', in A. McGrath (ed.), *Contested Ground: Australian Aborigines under the British Crown*, St Leonards, NSW: Allen and Unwin, (pp. 306–37).

McGrath, A. (ed.) (1995c) *Contested Ground: Australian Aborigines under the British Crown*, St Leonards, NSW: Allen and Unwin.

Mellor, B. (1992) *Lugard in Hong Kong: Empires, Education and a Governor at Work, 1907–1912*, Hong Kong: Hong Kong University Press.

Memmi, A. (1965) *The Colonizer and the Colonized*, (Howard Greenfield, trans.), New York: Orion Press.

Metcalf, T. (1995) *Ideologies of the Raj*, Cambridge: Cambridge University Press (Indian edition: New Delhi: Foundation Books).

Miners, N. (1981) *The Government and Politics of Hong Kong* (3rd edn), Hong Kong: Oxford University Press.

Mirsky, J. (1987) 'Serious complaints: Review of *Behind the Wall* and *Chinese Characters*', *Times Literary Supplement*, 11 September, p. 973.

Morris, P. (1992) 'Preparing pupils as citizens of the Special Administrative region of Hong Kong: An analysis of curriculum change and control during the transition period', in G.A. Postiglione (ed.), *Education and Society in Hong Kong: Toward one country and two systems*, Hong Kong: Hong Kong University Press, (pp. 149–66).

Mudrooroo (1995) *Us Mob: History, Culture, Struggle: An Introduction to Indigenous Australia*. Sydney: Angus and Robertson.

Mühlhäusler, P. (1996) *Linguistic Ecology: Language Change and Linguistic Imperialism in the Pacific Region*, London: Routledge.

Mulvaney, J. and Harcourt, R. (1988) *Cricket Walkabout: The Australian Aborigines in England*, Melbourne: Macmillan.

Murray, D. M. (1982) 'The great walls of China', *Today's Education*, 71 (pp. 55–8).

Nakata, M. (1995) 'Better', *Republica*, 2, 62–74.

Nandy, A. (1983) *The Intimate Enemy: Loss and Recovery of Self under Colonialism*, Delhi: Oxford University Press.

*National Review* (1987) 'Review of *Iron and Silk*', 39, 25 September, p. 62.

*National Review* (1988) Review of *Behind the Wall*, 40, 16 September, p. 48.

Ndebele, N. (1987) 'The English language and social change in South Africa', *The English Academy Review*, 4, 1–16.

Nelson, H. (1982) *Taim Bilong Masta*, Sydney, NSW: ABC Books.

Ng Lun Ngai-ha (1984) *Interactions of East and West: Development of Public Education in Early Hong Kong*, Hong Kong: Chinese University Press.

Ngũgĩ wa Thiong'o (1986) *Decolonizing the Mind: The Politics of Language in African Literature*, London: James Currey.

Ngũgĩ wa Thiong'o (1993) *Moving the Centre: The Struggle for Cultural Freedom*, London: James Currey.

Niranjana, T. (1992) *Siting Translation: History, Post-structuralism and the Colonial Context*, Berkeley, CA: University of California Press.

Niranjana, T. (1993) '"History, really beginning": The compulsions of post-colonial pedagogy', in R. S. Rajan (ed.), *The Lie of the Land: English Literary Studies in India*, Delhi: Oxford University Press, (pp. 246–59).

Oda Masaki (1995) *Native and Nonnative EFL Teachers: Building the Profession Together*, Paper presented at the 29th annual TESOL convention, 28 March–1 April, Long Beach, California.

Outlaw, L. (1990) 'Toward a critical theory of "race"', in D. Goldberg (ed.), *Anatomy of Racism*, Minneapolis: University of Minnesota Press, pp. 58–82.

Pennycook, A. D. (1994a) 'Anglicism and Orientalism', *Trans/forms*, 1 (1), 49–72.

Pennycook, A. D. (1994b) *The Cultural Politics of English as an International Language*, London: Longman.

Pennycook, A. (1996a) 'Borrowing others' words: Text, ownership, memory and plagiarism', *TESOL Quarterly*, 30(2), 201–30.

Pennycook, A. (1996b) 'Language policy as cultural politics: The double-edged sword of language education in colonial Malaya and Hong Kong', *Discourse: Studies in the Cultural Politics of Education*, 17(2), 133–52.

Pennycook, A. (1997) 'Cultural alternatives and autonomy', in P. Benson and P. Voller (eds), *Autonomy and Independence in Language Learning*, London: Longman, (pp. 35–53).

Pennycook, A. (1998) 'The right to language: Towards a situated ethics of language possibilities', *Language Sciences*, 20(1), 73–87.

Perham, M. (1960) *Lugard: The Years of Authority 1898–1945*, (Vol. 2) London: Collins.

Phillipson, R. (1992) *Linguistic Imperialism*, Oxford: Oxford University Press.

Piaget, J. (1971) *Psychology and Epistemology*, New York: Grossman Publishers.

Pinker, S. (1994) *The Language Instinct*, London: Penguin.

Pinker, S. (1995) 'Chasing the jargon', *Time*, 45 (13 November), TD (Time Digital), 28–9.

Platt, J., Weber, H., and Ho, M. L. (1984) *The New Englishes*, London: Routledge and Kegan Paul.

Poliakov, L. (1982) 'Racism from the Enlightenment to the age of Imperialism', in R. Ross (ed.), *Racism and Colonialism*, The Hague: Martinus Nijhoff, pp. 55-64.

Porter, D. (1994) '*Orientalism* and its problems', in P. Williams and L. Chrisman (eds), *Colonial Discourse and Postcolonial Theory: A Reader*, New York: Columbia University Press, (pp. 150–61).

Postiglione, G. A. (1992) 'The decolonization of Hong Kong education', in G. A. Postiglione (ed.), *Education and Society in Hong Kong: Toward One Country and Two Systems*, Hong Kong: Hong Kong University Press, (pp. 3–38).

Pratt, M. L. (1992) *Imperial Eyes: Travel Writing and Transculturation*, London: Routledge.

Pullum, G. K. (1989) 'The great Eskimo vocabulary hoax', *Natural Language and Linguistic Theory*, 7, 275–81.

Quirk, R. (1982) 'Introduction', in O. Jespersen (ed.), *Growth and Structure of the English Language*, Oxford: Basil Blackwell.

Rahim, S. A. (1986) 'Language as power apparatus: Observation on English and cultural policy in nineteenth-century India', *World Englishes*, 5 (2/3), 231–9.

Rajan, R. S. (1993a) 'Brokering English studies: The British Council in India', in R. S. Rajan (ed.), *The Lie of the Land: English Literary Studies in India*, Delhi: Oxford University Press, (pp. 130–55).

Rajan, R. S. (1993b) 'Fixing English: Nation, language, subject', in R. S. Rajan (ed.), *The Lie of the Land: English Literary Studies in India*, Delhi: Oxford University Press, (pp. 7–28).

Rajan, R. S. (ed.) (1993c) *The Lie of the Land: English Literary Studies in India*, Delhi: Oxford University Press.

Rampton, M. B. H. (1990) 'Displacing the "native speaker": expertise, affiliation and inheritance', *ELT Journal*, 44(2), 97–101.

Read, H. (1849) *The Hand of God in History; or, Divine Providence Historically Illustrated in the Extension and Establishment of Christianity*, Hartford: H. Huntington.

Report (1883a) *Report of the Indian Education Commission, 3 February 1882*, Calcutta: Superintendent of Government Printing.

Report (1883b) *Report of the Education Commission appointed by His Excellency Sir John Pope Hennessy, K.C.M.G. . . . to consider certain questions connected with Education in Hong Kong, 1882*, Hong Kong Government (1883).

Robson, M. (1992) *The Potent Poppy*, Hong Kong: FormAsia.

Rolleston, C. J. (1911) *The Age of Folly: A Study of Imperial Needs, Duties, and Warning*, London: John Milne.

Said, E. W. (1978) *Orientalism*, London: Routledge and Kegan Paul.

Said, E. W. (1993) *Culture and Imperialism*, London: Vintage.

Salzman, M. (1986) *Iron and Silk*, New York: Random House.

Salzman, M. (1988) 'He hated sightseeing: Review of *Riding the Iron Rooster*', *New York Times Book Review*, 93, 19 June, p. 17.

Sampson, G. P. (1984) 'Exporting language teaching methods from Canada to China', *TESL Canada Journal*, 1(1), 19–31.

Sartre, J.-P. (1957) 'Introduction' to Albert Memmi (1965) *The Colonizer and the Colonized*, (Howard Greenfield, trans.), New York: Orion Press.

Sartre, J.-P. (1963) 'Preface' to F. Fanon, *The Wretched of the Earth* (Constance Farrington, trans.) Harmondsworth: Penguin.

Savage, V. (1984) *Western Impressions of Nature and Landscape in Southeast Asia*, Singapore: Singapore University Press.

Sayce, A. H. (1875) *Principles of Comparative Philology*, 2nd edn, London, (no publisher given).

Searle, C. (1983) 'A common language', *Race and Class*, 34 (3), 45–54.

Selzer, R. (1987, Feb 1) 'From China with love: Review of *Iron and Silk*', *New York Times Review of Books*, 92, 1 February, p. 9.

Semmel, B. (1993) *The Liberal Ideal and the Demons of Empire*, Baltimore: Johns Hopkins University Press.

Shapiro, M. (1989) 'A political approach to language purism', in B. Jernudd and M. Shapiro (eds), *The Politics of Language Purism*, Berlin: Mouton de Gruyter.

Shield, M. (1995) 'Quality on the nose', *The Sunday Age*, 12 February, p. 6.

Showalter, E. (1981) 'Feminist criticism in the wilderness', *Critical Inquiry*, Winter, 179–205.

Singh, J. (1996) *Colonial Narratives/Cultural Dialogues: 'Discoveries' of India in the Language of Colonialism*, London: Routledge.

229

Smith, C. T. (1985) *Chinese Christians: Elites, middlemen, and the church in Hong Kong*, Hong Kong: Oxford University Press.

So, D. W. C. (1987) 'Searching for a bilingual exit', in R. Lord and H. N. L. Cheng (eds), *Language Education in Hong Kong*, Hong Kong: Chinese University Press, (pp. 249–68).

So, D. W. C. (1992) 'Language-based bifurcation of secondary schools in Hong Kong: Past, present and future', in Luke Kang Kwong (ed.), *Into the Twenty First Century: Issues of Language in Education in Hong Kong*, Hong Kong: Linguistic Society of Hong Kong, (pp. 69–96).

Spack, R. (1997) 'The rhetorical construction of multilingual students', *TESOL Quarterly*, 31 (4), 765–74.

Spivak, G. C. (1987) *In Other Worlds: Essays in Cultural Politics*, New York: Routledge.

Spivak, G. C. (1993) 'The burden of English studies', in R. S. Rajan (ed.), *The Lie of the Land: English Literary Studies in India*, Delhi: Oxford University Press, (pp. 275–99).

Spolsky, B. (1995) *Measured Words*, Oxford: Oxford University Press.

Spurr, D. (1993) *The Rhetoric of Empire: Colonial Discourse in Journalism, Travel Writing, and Imperial Administration*, Durham: Duke University Press.

Steiner, G. (1959) 'The hollow miracle', *Language and Silence*, reprinted in Steiner, G. (1984) *A Reader*, Harmondsworth: Penguin, (pp. 207–20).

Straits Settlements (various years) *Straits Settlements Annual Departmental Reports*, Singapore: Government Printing Office.

Suleri, S. (1992) *The Rhetoric of English in India*, Chicago: University of Chicago Press.

Sweeting, A. E. (1990) *Education in Hong Kong, pre-1841 to 1941: Fact and opinion*, Hong Kong: Hong Kong University Press.

Sweeting, A. E. (1992) 'Hong Kong education within historical processes', in G. A. Postiglione (ed.), *Education and Society in Hong Kong: Toward One Country and Two Systems*, Hong Kong: Hong Kong University Press, (pp. 39–81).

Sweeting, A. E. and Morris, P. (1993) 'Educational reform in post-war Hong Kong: Planning and crisis intervention', *International Journal of Educational Development*, 13 (3), 201–16.

Swettenham, F. (1907/1955) *British Malaya*, London: Allen & Unwin.

Tatlow, A. (1993) *'Those savages – that's us': Textual anthropology*, inaugural lecture from the Chair of Comparative Literature, University of Hong Kong, 22 October, University of Hong Kong. Published in *Supplement to the Gazette* (Hong Kong University), Vol. XXXX, p. 1.

*The Popular Encylopedia* (no date, circa 1891). London: Blackie and Son Ltd.

Theroux, P. (1988) *Riding the Iron Rooster: By Train through China*, New York: Putnam.

Thomas, N. (1994) *Colonialism's Culture: Anthropology, Travel and Government*, Oxford: Polity Press.

Thornton, A. P. (1965) *Doctrines of Imperialism*, New York: John Wiley and Sons.

Threadgold, T. (1997) *Feminist Poetics: Poeisis, Performance, Histories*, London: Routledge.

Thubron, C. (1987) *Behind the Wall*, London: Heinemann.

Thurston, A. (1993) 'The dragon stirs', *The Wilson Quarterly*, Spring, 10-34.

*Time* (1987) 'Gong Fu. Review of *Iron and Silk*', 129, 2 March, p. 26.

Tollefson, J. (1991) *Planning Language, Planning Inequality: Language Policy in the Community*, London: Longman.

Tong, Q.S. (1993) 'Myths about the Chinese language', *Canadian Review of Comparative Literature*, March–June, 29–47.

Trench, R. C. (1881) *English Past and Present*. London: Macmillan and Co.

Trocki, C. A. (1990) *Opium and Empire: Chinese Society in Colonial Singapore, 1800–1910*, Ithaca, NY: Cornell University Press.

Tsai Jung-fang (1994) 'From antiforeignism to popular nationalism: Hong Kong between China and Britain, 1839–1911', in M. K. Chan (ed.), *Precarious Balance: Hong Kong between China and Britain, 1842–1992*, Hong Kong: Hong Kong University Press, (pp. 9–25).

Van Arkel, D. (1982) 'Racism in Europe', in R. Ross (ed.), *Racism and Colonialism*, The Hague: Martinus Nijihoff, (pp. 55–64).

Viswanathan, G. (1989) *Masks of Conquest: Literary study and British rule in India*, London: Faber and Faber.

Webb, A. C. (1986) 'China as a travelling English teacher saw it', *English Journal*, 75 (3), 109–10.

Wesley-Smith, P. (1994) 'Anti-Chinese legislation in Hong Kong', in M. K. Chan (ed.), *Precarious Balance: Hong Kong between China and Britain, 1842–1992*, Hong Kong: Hong Kong University Press, (pp. 91–105).

West, M. (1926) *Bilingualism (with special reference to Bengal)*, Calcutta: Bureau of Education, India.

West, R. (1906) 'Introduction', *India, Ceylon, Straits Settlements, British North Borneo, Hong-Kong*, London: Kegan Paul, Trench, Trabner and Co., (pp. ix–xxvii).

Wiley, T. and Lukes, M. (1996) 'English-only and standard English ideologies in the US', *TESOL Quarterly*, 30 (3), 511–35.

Williams, A. (1995) 'TESOL and cultural incorporation: Are we doing the devil's work?' *TESOL in Context*, 5 (1), 21–4.

Williams, P. and Chrisman, L. (eds) (1994) *Colonial Discourse and Postcolonial Theory: A reader*, New York: Columbia University Press.

Williams, R. (1983) *Keywords: A vocabulary of culture and society*, (2nd edn), London: Fontana.

Winstedt, R. O. (1956) *The Malays: A cultural history*, London: Routledge and Kegan Paul.

Yee, A. H. (1992) *A People Misruled: The Chinese stepping-stone syndrome*. Singapore: Heinemann Asia.

Young, J. D. (1994) 'The building years: Maintaining a China–Hong Kong–Britain equilibrium 1950–71', in M. K. Chan (ed.), *Precarious Balance: Hong Kong between China and Britain, 1842–1992*, Hong Kong: Hong Kong University Press, (pp. 131–47).

Young, R. (1990) *White Mythologies: Writing history and the West*, London: Routledge.

Young, R. (1995) *Colonial Desire: Hybridity in theory, culture and race*, London: Routledge.

Yu, V. W. S. and Atkinson, P. A. (1988) 'An investigation of the language difficulties experienced by Hong Kong secondary school students in English-medium schools: 1, The problems', *Journal of Multilingual and Multicultural Development*, 9 (3), 267–83.

# INDEX

233